SQL for Data Scientists

SQL for Data Scientists

A Beginner's Guide for Building Datasets for Analysis

Renée M. P. Teate

WILEY

In my data science career talks, I warn about tech industry gatekeepers.
This book is dedicated to the gate-openers.

About the Author

Renée M. P. Teate is the Director of Data Science at HelioCampus, leading a team that builds predictive models for colleges and universities. She has worked with data professionally since 2004, in roles including relational database design, data-driven website development, data analysis and reporting, and data science. With degrees in Integrated Science and Technology from James Madison University and Systems Engineering from the University of Virginia, along with a varied career working with data at every stage in a number of systems, she considers herself to be a "data generalist."

Renée regularly speaks at technology and higher ed conferences and meetups, and writes in industry publications about her data science work and about navigating data science career paths. She also created the "Becoming a Data Scientist" podcast and @BecomingDataSci Twitter account, where she's known to her over 60k followers as "Data Science Renee." She always tells aspiring data scientists to learn SQL, since it has been one of the most valuable and enduring skills needed throughout her career.

About the Technical Editor

Vicki Boykis is a machine learning engineer, currently working with recommendation systems. She has over a decade of experience in analytics and databases across numerous industries including social media, telecom, and healthcare, and has worked with Postgres, SQL Server, Oracle, and MySQL. She has previously taught courses in object-oriented programming (OOP) for Python and MySQL for massive open online courses (MOOCs). She has a BS in Economics with Honors from Penn State University and an MBA from Temple University in Philadelphia.

Acknowledgments

When I first started this book in Fall 2019, I was new to the book authoring and publication process, and I couldn't have anticipated how everything around us would change due to a deadly pandemic and political upheaval. I want to first acknowledge the healthcare and other essential workers who risked their lives during this era of COVID-19. Nothing any of us have accomplished throughout this time would have been possible without your selfless efforts saving lives and allowing some of us to work safely from home. I also want to thank those who continue fighting for equality in the face of injustice. You inspire me and give me hope.

As a first-time book author, the process of transferring my knowledge and experience to the page, and bringing this book to completion, has been a major learning experience. I would like to thank the team at Wiley for taking the chance on me and for all of your work, especially project editor Kelly Talbot for guiding me through this process, improving my content, and eventually getting me across the finish line!

I was so excited when I found out that Vicki Boykis, whose writing about our industry is fascinating and insightful, would be my technical editor. Her thoughtful feedback was invaluable. I truly appreciate her sticking with me throughout this extended process.

I would also like to thank my family and teachers, who encouraged my interest in computers and technology from a young age and fostered my love of reading, and my friends and mentors who have helped me continue to progress in my education and my career since. Those who have had an impact on me are too numerous to list, but know that I acknowledge your role in helping me get to where I am today. My parents and sister, my husband and step-children, my teachers and managers, my colleagues and friends, your time and energy and patience is so appreciated.

And I want to give heartfelt thanks to my husband and my step-son, Tony and Anthony Teate, for always believing in me, giving invaluable feedback, and bearing with me during this extended project. Tony has been a vital part of my "data science journey" from the very beginning, and I'm fittingly wrapping up this long phase of it on his birthday (Happy Birthday, Sweetheart!). The love and support the two of you have shown me is beyond measure. I love you.

Before I close, I want to give shout-outs to two special communities. First, one that might be a bit unexpected: the vegetable gardening community on Instagram. Growing a garden in my backyard while enjoying your company online honestly helped me get through some of the difficult aspects of writing this book, especially during a pandemic. The fictional Farmer's Market database used in every example was inspired by you.

And last but not least, to the data science communities in my local area (Harrisonburg and Charlottesville, Virginia—data science isn't only done in big cities!) and online, plus those of you reading this book. I feel blessed to be a part of such a vibrant professional community, and honored that you value my experience and advice. Thank you to everyone who has been a part of my data career to date, and who has let me know I have been a part of yours.

— Renée M. P. Teate

Contents at a Glance

Contents

Introduction

Who I Am and Why I'm Writing About This Topic

When I was first brainstorming topics for this book, I used two questions to narrow down my list: "Who is my audience?" and "What topic do I know well enough to write a book that would be worth publishing for that audience?"

The first question had an easy initial answer: I already have an audience of data-science-learning Twitter followers with whom I share resources and advice on "Becoming a Data Scientist" that I could keep in mind while narrowing down the topics.

So then I was left to figure out what I know that I could teach to people who want to become data scientists.

I have been designing and querying relational databases professionally for about 17 years: first as a database and web developer, then as a data analyst, and for the last 5 years, as a data scientist. SQL (Structured Query Language) has been a key tool for me throughout—whether I was working with MS Access, MS SQL Server, MySQL, Oracle, or Redshift databases, and whether I was summarizing data into reporting views in a data mart, extracting data to use in a data visualization tool like Tableau, or preparing a dataset for a machine learning project.

Since SQL is a tool I have used throughout my career, and because creating and retrieving datasets for analysis has been such an integral part of my job as a data scientist, I was surprised to learn that some data scientists don't know SQL or don't regularly write SQL code. But in an informal Twitter poll I conducted, which received responses from 979 data scientists, 19% of them reported wanting to learn, or learn more, SQL (74% reported already using SQL professionally). Additionally, 55% of 713 respondents who were working toward becoming data scientists said they wanted to learn, or learn more, SQL. So, my target audience had an interest in this topic.

According to an analysis of online job postings conducted by Jeff Hale of Towards Data Science, SQL is in the top three technology skills that data scientist jobs require. (See `towardsdatascience.com/the-most-in-demand-skills-for-data-scientists-4a4a8db896db`.) In an Indeed BeSeen article, Joy Garza lists SQL as one of the top-five in-demand tech skills for data scientists. (See `https://web.archive.org/web/20200624031802/https://www.beseen.com/blog/talent/data-scientist-skills/`.)

After learning how many working and prospective data scientists wanted to learn SQL, and how much of a need there is in the industry for people who know how to use it, SQL dataset development started to move to the top of the list of topics I could share my knowledge of with others.

There are many SQL books on the market that can be used to learn query syntax and advanced SQL functions—after all, the language has been around for 45 years and has been standardized since the late 1980s—but I hadn't found any definitive resources to refer people to when they asked me if I knew of any books that taught how to use SQL to construct datasets for machine learning, so I decided to write this book to cover SQL from a data scientist's point of view.

So, my goal in writing this book is not only to teach you how to write SQL code but to teach you how to think about summarizing data into analytical datasets that can be used for reports and machine learning: to use SQL like a data scientist does. Like I do.

Who This Book Is For

SQL for Data Scientists is designed to be a learning resource for anyone who wants to become (or who already is) a data analyst or data scientist, and wants to be able to pull data from databases to build their own datasets without having to rely on others in the organization to query the source system and transform it into flat files (or spreadsheets) for them.

There are plenty of SQL books out there, but many are either written as syntax references or written for people in other roles that create, query from, and maintain databases. However, this book is written from the perspective of a data scientist and is aimed at those who will primarily be extracting data from existing databases in order to generate datasets for analysis.

I won't assume that you've ever written SQL queries before, and we'll start with the basics, but I do assume that you have some basic understanding of what databases are and a general idea of how data might be used in reports, analyses, and machine learning algorithms. This book is meant to fill in the steps between finding a database that contains the data you need and starting the analysis. I aim to teach you how to think about structuring datasets for analysis and how to use SQL to extract the data from the database and get it into that form.

Why You Should Learn SQL if You Want to Be a Data Scientist

If you can use SQL to pull your own datasets, you don't have to rely on others in your organization to pull it for you, enabling you to work more efficiently. Requesting datasets usually involves a process of filling out a form or ticket describing in detail what data you need, waiting for your request to be fulfilled, then often clarifying your request after seeing the initial results, and then waiting again for modifications. If you can edit your own queries, you can not only design and retrieve your own datasets but then also adjust calculations or add fields as needed.

Additionally, running a SQL query that writes to a database table or exports to a file—effectively snapshotting the data in the form you need it in for your analysis—means you don't have to retrieve and reprocess the data in your machine learning script every time you run your code, speeding up the usually iterative model development process.

Some summaries and calculations can be done more efficiently in SQL than in other types of code, as well, so even if you are running the queries "live" each time you run your script, you may be able to lower the computational cost of your code by doing some of the transformations in SQL.

Finally, because it is a high-demand tech skill in data scientist job postings, learning SQL will increase your marketability and value to employers.

What I Hope You Gain from This Book

My goal is that by the time you finish reading this book and practicing the queries within (ideally both on the provided example database and on another database of your choosing, so you have to modify the example queries and apply them in another context), you will be able to think through the process of creating an analytical dataset and develop the SQL code necessary to generate your intended output.

I hope that even if you end up needing to use a SQL function that's not covered in this book, you will have gained enough baseline knowledge from the book to go look it up online and determine how to best use it in the query you are developing.

I also hope that this book will help you feel confident that you can pull your own data at work and get it into the form you need it in for your report or model without having to wait on others to do it for you.

Conventions

This book uses MySQL version 8.0–style SQL. No matter what type of database system you use (MS SQL Server, Redshift, PostgreSQL, Oracle, etc.), the query design concepts and syntax are very similar, when not identical across platforms. So, if you work with a database system other than MySQL, you might have to search for the equivalent code syntax for a few functions in the book, but the overall dataset design concepts are platform-independent, and the SQL keywords are cross-platform standards.

When you see code displayed in the following style:

```
SELECT * FROM Product
```

that means it is a complete SQL query that you can use to select data from the Farmer's Market database described in Chapter 1, "Data Sources." If you're reading the printed version of this book, you can go to the book's website to get digital versions of the queries that you can copy and paste to try them out yourself.

Reserved SQL keywords like SELECT will appear in all-uppercase throughout the book, and column names will appear in all-lowercase. This isn't a requirement of SQL syntax (neither are line breaks), but is a convention used for readability.

Be aware that the Farmer's Market database will continue to evolve, and I will likely continue adding rows to its tables after this book goes to print, so the data values you see in the output when you run the queries yourself may not exactly match the screenshots included in the printed book.

Reader Support for This Book

Companion Download Files

As you work through the examples in this book, you may choose either to type in all the code manually or to use the source code files that accompany the book. All the source code used in this book, along with the Farmer's Market database, is available for download from both sqlfordatascientists.com and www.wiley.com/go/sqlfordatascientists.

How to Contact the Publisher

If you believe you've found a mistake in this book, please bring it to our attention. At John Wiley & Sons, we understand how important it is to provide our customers with accurate content, but even with our best efforts an error may occur.

In order to submit your possible errata, please email it to our Customer Service Team at wileysupport@wiley.com with the subject line "Possible Book Errata Submission".

How to Contact the Author

I'm known as "Data Science Renee" on Twitter, and my username is @becomingdatasci. I'm happy to interact with readers via social media, so feel free to tweet me your questions and suggestions.

Thank you for giving me the chance to help guide you through the topic of *SQL for Data Scientists*. Let's dive in!

Data Sources

As a data analyst or data scientist, you will encounter data from many sources—from databases to spreadsheets to Application Programming Interfaces (APIs)—which you are expected to use for predictive modeling. Understanding the source system your data comes from, how it was initially gathered and stored, and how frequently it is updated, will take you a long way toward an effective analysis. In my experience, issues with a predictive model can often be traced back all the way to the source data or the query that first pulls the data from the source. Exploring the data available for your analysis starts with exploring the structure of the source database.

Data Sources

Data can be stored in many forms and structures. Examples of *unstructured* data include text documents or images stored as individual files in a computer's file system. In this book, we'll be focusing on *structured* data, which is typically organized into a tabular format, like a spreadsheet or database table containing limited-length text or numeric values.

Many software applications enable the organization of data into structured forms. One example you are likely familiar with is Microsoft Excel, for creating and maintaining spreadsheets. Excel also includes some analysis capabilities, such as pivot tables for summarizing spreadsheets and data visualization tools for plotting data points from a spreadsheet. Some functions in Excel allow you to connect data in one spreadsheet to another, but in order to create a true relational database model and define rules for how the data tables are interconnected, Microsoft offers a relational database application called Access.

My first experiences with relational database design were in MS Access, and the basic Structured Query Language (SQL) concepts I learned in order to query data from an Access database are the same concepts I have used throughout my career—in increasingly complex ways. I have since extracted data from other Relational Database Management Systems (RDBMSs) such as MS SQL Server, Oracle Database, MySQL, and Amazon Redshift. Though the syntax for each can differ slightly, the general concepts, many of which you will learn in this book, are consistent across products.

SQL-style RDBMSs were first developed in the 1970s, and the basic database design concepts have stood the test of time; many of the database systems that originated then are still in use today. The longevity of these tools is another reason that SQL is so ubiquitous and so valuable to learn.

As a professional who works with data, you will likely encounter several of the following popular Relational Database Management Systems:

- Oracle
- MySQL
- MS SQL Server
- PostgreSQL
- Amazon Redshift
- IBM DB2
- MS Access
- SQLite
- Snowflake

You will also likely work with data retrieved from other types of files at some point, such as CSV text files, JSON retrieved via API, XML in a NoSQL database, Graph databases with special query languages, key-value stores, and so on. However, relational SQL databases still dominate the industry for structured data storage and are the most likely database systems you will encounter on the job.

Tools for Connecting to Data Sources and Editing SQL

When you start an analysis project, the first step is often connecting to a database on a server. This is generally done through a SQL Integrated Development Environment (IDE) or with code that connects to the database without a graphical user interface (GUI) to run queries that extract the data and store it in a structure that you can work with downstream in your analysis, such as a dataframe.

The IDE referenced for demonstration purposes throughout this book is MySQL Workbench Community Edition, which was chosen because we'll be querying a MySQL database in the examples. MySQL is open source under the GPL license, and MySQL Workbench CE is free to download.

Many other IDEs will allow you to connect to databases and will perform syntax-highlighting of SQL (highlighting keywords to make it easier to read and to spot errors). All major database systems support Open Database Connectivity (ODBC), which uses drivers to standardize the interfaces between software applications and databases. Whoever has granted you permission to access a database should give you documentation on how to securely connect to it via your selected IDE.

You can also connect to a database directly from code such as Python or R. Search for your preferred language and the type of database (for example, "R SQL Server" or "Python Redshift") and you will find packages or add-ons that enable you to embed SQL queries in your code and return results in the form of a dataframe or other data structure. The database system's official documentation will also provide information about connecting to it from other software and from within your code. Searching "MySQL connector" brings up a list of drivers for use with different languages, for example.

If you are writing code in a language like Python and will be passing a SQL statement to a function as a string, where it won't be syntax highlighted, you can write SQL in a free text tool that performs SQL syntax highlighting, such as Notepad++, or in a SQL IDE, and then paste the final result into your code.

Relational Databases

If you have never explored a database, you can think of a database table like a well-defined spreadsheet, with row identifiers and named column headers. Each table may store different subsets and types of data at different levels of detail.

An *entity* is the "thing" (object or concept) that the table represents and captures data for. If there is a table that contains data about books, the entity is "Books," and the "Book table" is the data structure that contains information about the Book entity. Some people use the terms *entity* and *table* interchangeably.

You may see me using the terms *row* and *record* interchangeably in this book: a record in a database is like a row in a table and displayed the same way. Some people call a database row a *tuple*.

You may also see me using the terms *column*, *field*, and *attribute* as synonyms. A column header in a spreadsheet is the equivalent of an attribute name in a table. Each column in a database table stores data about an attribute of the entity.

For example, as illustrated in Figure 1.1, in a table of Books there would be a row for each book, with an ISBN number column to identify each book. The ISBN is an *attribute* of the book entity. The Author column in the row in the Books table representing this book would have my name in it, so you could say that "the **value** in the Author **field** in the *SQL for Data Scientists* **record** in the Books **table** is 'Renée M. P. Teate'." Or, "In the Books **table**, the **row** representing the book *SQL for Data Scientists* contains the **value** 'Renée M. P. Teate' in the Author **column**."

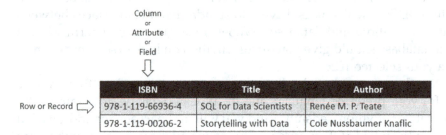

Column
or
Attribute
or
Field

ISBN	Title	Author
978-1-119-66936-4	SQL for Data Scientists	Renée M. P. Teate
978-1-119-00206-2	Storytelling with Data	Cole Nussbaumer Knaflic

Row or Record ⇨

Figure 1.1

A database is a collection of related tables, and a database schema stores information about the tables (and other database objects), as well as the relationships between them, defining the structure of the database.

To illustrate an example of a relationship between database tables, imagine that one table in a database contains a record (row) for every patient that's ever scheduled an appointment at a doctor's office, with each patient's name, birthdate, and phone number, like a directory. Another table contains a record of every appointment, with the patient's name, appointment time, reason for the visit, and the name of the doctor the patient has an appointment with. The connection between these two tables could be the patient's name. (In reality, a unique identifier would be assigned to each patient, since two people can have the same name, but for this illustration, the name will suffice.) In order to create a report of every patient who has an appointment scheduled in the next week along with their contact information, there would have to be an established connection between the patient directory table and the appointment table, enabling someone to pull data from both tables simultaneously. See Figure 1.2.

Patients

Patient Name	Patient Birthdate	Patient Phone Number
Diane Hyson	3/4/1970	(540) 555-1212
Leon Stevens	11/10/1952	(703) 555-1234

Appointments

Patient Name	Appointment Time	Appointment Reason	Doctor Name
Diane Hyson	2/28/2020 2:30pm	Annual Check-Up	Dr. Urena
Leon Stevens	3/2/2020 10:00am	Treatment	Dr. Hammad
Leon Stevens	3/9/2020 10:00am	Follow-Up	Dr. Hammad

Figure 1.2

The relationship between the entities just described is called a *one-to-many relationship*. Each patient only appears in the patient directory table one time but can have many appointments in the related appointment-tracking table. Each appointment only has one patient's name associated with it.

Database relationships like this one are depicted in what's called an *entity-relationship diagram (ERD)*. The ERD for these two tables is shown in Figure 1.3.

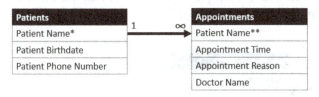

Figure 1.3

NOTE In an ERD, an infinity symbol, "N", or "crow's feet" on the end of a line connecting two tables indicates that it is the "many" side of a one-to-many relationship. You can see the infinity symbol next to the Appointments table in Figure 1.3.

The *primary key* in a table is a column or combination of columns that uniquely identifies a row. The combination of values in the primary key columns must be unique per record, and cannot all be NULL (empty). The primary key can be made of values that occur in the data that are unique per record—such as a Student ID Card number in a table of students at a university—or it can be generated by the database and not carry meaning elsewhere "in real life," like an integer value that increments automatically every time a new record is created. The primary key in a table can be used to identify the records in other tables that relate to each of its records. When a table's primary key is referenced in another table, it is called a *foreign key*.

NOTE Notice that the NULL value is described in this section as "empty" and not as "blank." In database terms, NULL and "blank" aren't necessarily the same thing. For example, a single space " " can be considered a "blank" value in a string field, but is not NULL, because there is a space character stored there. A NULL is the absence of any value, a totally empty field. NULLs are treated differently than blanks in SQL.

As mentioned, using the Patient Name in the previous example is a poor selection of primary key, because two patients can have the same name, so your primary key won't necessarily end up uniquely identifying patients. One option that is common practice in the industry is to create a field that generates an auto-incrementing integer to serve as a unique identifier for each new row, so as not to rely on other values unique to a record that may be a privacy concern or unavailable at the time the record is created, such as Social Security numbers.

So, let's say that instead, the doctor's office database assigned an auto-incrementing integer value to serve as the primary key for each patient record in the Patients table and for each appointment record in the Appointments table. Then, the appointment-tracking table can use that generated Patient ID value to link each appointment to each patient, and the patient's name doesn't even need to be stored in the Appointments table. In Figure 1.4, you can see a database design where the Patient ID is serving as a primary key in the Patients table, and as a foreign key in the Appointments table.

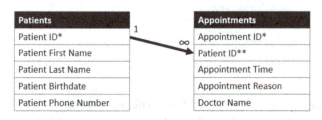

Patients

Patient ID	Patient First Name	Patient Last Name	Patient Birthdate	Patient Phone Number
1	Diane	Hyson	3/4/1970	(540) 555-1212
2	Leon	Stevens	11/10/1952	(703) 555-1234

Appointments

Appointment ID	Patient ID	Appointment Time	Appointment Reason	Doctor Name
100	1	2/28/2020 2:30pm	Annual Check-Up	Dr. Urena
101	2	3/2/2020 10:00am	Treatment	Dr. Hammad
102	2	3/9/2020 10:00am	Follow-Up	Dr. Hammad

Figure 1.4

Another type of relationship found in RDBMSs is called *many-to-many*. As you might guess, it's a connection between entities where the records on each side of the relationship can connect to multiple records on the other side. Using our Books example, if we had a table of Authors, there would be a many-to-many relationship between books and authors, because each author can write multiple books, and each book can have multiple authors. In order to create this relationship in the database, a junction or associative table will be needed to capture the pairs of related rows. See Figure 1.5.

Figure 1.5

In the ERD shown in Figure 1.5 you can see that the ISBN, which is the primary key in the Books table, and the Author ID, which is the primary key in the Authors table (denoted by asterisks) are both foreign keys in the Books-Authors Junction table (denoted by double asterisks). Each pairing of ISBN and Author ID in the junction table would be unique, so the pair of fields can be considered a multi-column primary key in the Books-Authors Junction table.

By setting up this database relationship so that we don't end up with multiple rows per book in the Books table or multiple authors listed per book in the Authors column of the Books table and have a junction table that only contains the identifiers matching up the related tables, we are reducing the amount of redundant data stored in the database and clarifying how the entities are related in real life.

The idea of not storing redundant data in a database unnecessarily is known as database *normalization*. In the book database example, we only have to store each author's full name once, no matter how many books they have written. In the doctor's office example, there's no need to store a patient's phone number repeatedly in the Appointments table, because it's already stored in the related "patient directory" table, and can be found by connecting the two tables via the Patient ID (we will cover SQL JOINs, which are used to merge data from multiple tables, in Chapter 5, "SQL JOINs"). Normalization can reduce the amount of storage space a database requires and also reduce the complexity of updating data, since each value is stored a minimal number of times. We won't go into all of the details of normalization here, but if you are interested in learning more about it, research "relational database design."

Dimensional Data Warehouses

Data warehouses often contain data from multiple underlying data sources. They can be designed in a normalized relational database form, as described in the previous section, or using other design standards. They may contain both "raw data" extracted from other databases directly, and "summary" tables that are combined or transformed versions of that raw data (for example, the analytical datasets you will learn to build in this book could be permanently stored as tables in a data warehouse, to be referenced by multiple reports). Data warehouses can contain historical data logs with past and current records, tables that are updated in real time as the source systems are updated, or snapshots of data to preserve it as it existed at a past moment in time.

Often, data warehouses are designed using dimensional modeling techniques. We won't go in-depth into the details of dimensional modeling here, but one concept you are likely to come across when querying tables in data warehouses is a "star schema" design that divides the data into facts and dimensions.

The way I think of facts and dimensions is that a record in a *fact table* contains the "metadata" of an entity, as well as any *measures* (which are usually numeric values) you want to track and later summarize. A *dimension* is property of that entity you can group or "slice and dice" the fact records by, and a *dimension table* will contain further information of that property.

So, for example, a transactional record of an item purchased at a retail store is a *fact*, containing the timestamp of the purchase, the store number, order number, customer number, and the amount paid. The store the purchase was made at is a *dimension* of the item purchase *fact*, and the associated store *dimension table* would contain additional information about the store, such as its name. You could then query both the fact and the dimension tables to get a summary of purchases by store.

If we transformed our doctor's office database into a star schema, we might have an appointments fact table capturing the occurrence of every appointment, which patient it was for, when it was booked, the reason for the appointment, which doctor it was with, and when it is scheduled to occur. We might also have a date dimension and a time dimension, storing the various properties of each appointment date and time (such as year or day of week) and appointment-booking date and time.

This would allow us to easily count up how many appointments occurred per time period or determine when the highest volume of appointment-booking calls take place, by grouping the "transactional" fact information by different dimensions.

Figure 1.6 depicts an example dimensional data warehouse design. Can you see why this design is called a star schema?

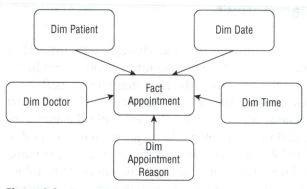

Figure 1.6

There might also be an appointment history log in this data warehouse, with a record of each time the appointment was changed. That way, not only could we tell when the appointment is supposed to take place, but how many times it was modified, whether it was initially assigned to another doctor, etc.

Note that when compared to a normalized relational database, a dimensional model stores a lot more information. Appointment records will appear multiple times in an appointment log table. There may be a record for every calendar date in the date dimension table, even if no appointments are scheduled for that date yet, and the list of dates might extend for decades into the future!

If you're designing a database or data warehouse, you need to understand these concepts in much more detail than we'll cover here. But in order to query the database to build an analytical dataset, you primarily need to understand the data warehouse table *grain* (level of detail; what set of columns makes a row unique) and how the tables are related to one another. Once you have that information, querying a dimensional data warehouse with SQL is much like querying a relational database with SQL.

Asking Questions About the Data Source

Once you find out what type of data source you're working with and learn about the schema design and the relationships between the database tables, there is still a lot of information you should gather about the tables you'll be querying before you dive into writing any SQL.

If you are lucky enough to have access to subject matter experts (SMEs) who know the details of why the database was designed the way it is, how the data is collected and updated, and what to expect in terms of the frequency and types of data that may be updating as you work with the database, stay in communication with them throughout the data exploration and query development process. These might be database administrators (DBAs), ETL engineers (the people who extract, transform, and load data from a source system into a data warehouse), or the people who actually generate or enter the data into the source system in the first place. If you spot some values that don't seem to make sense, you can sometimes look in a data dictionary to learn more (if one exists and is correct), but often going directly to the SMEs to get the details is the best approach. If your questions are easily answered by existing documentation, they will point you to it!

Here are some example questions you might want to ask the SMEs as you're first learning about the data source:

- "Here are the questions I'm being asked to answer in my analysis. Which tables in this database should I look in first for the relevant data? And is there an entity-relationship diagram documenting the relationships between them that I can reference?"

    These questions are especially helpful for large data warehouses with a lot of tables, where being pointed in the right direction from the start can save a lot of time searching for the data you need.

- "What set of fields make up the primary key for this table?" Or, "What is the grain of this fact table?"

  Understanding the level of detail of each table is important in order to know how to filter, group, and summarize the data in the table, and join it to other tables.

- "Are these records imported directly from the source system, or have they been transformed or merged in some way before being stored in this table?"

  This is helpful to know when debugging data that doesn't look like you expected. If the database is "raw" data from the source system, you might talk to those entering the data to learn more about it. If it has gone through a transformation or includes data from several different tables in the system of origin, then the first stop to understand a value would likely be the ETL engineers who programmed the code that modified it.

- "Is this a static snapshot table, or does it update regularly? At what frequency does it update? And are older records expired and kept as new data is added, or is the existing record overwritten when changes occur?"

  If a table you're querying contains "live" data that is being updated as you work, and you are using it to perform calculations or as an input to a machine learning algorithm, you may want to make a copy of it to use while working. That way, you know that changes in the calculations or model output are due to changes in your code, and not due to data that is changing as you debug.

  For datasets updated on a nightly basis, you might want to know what time they refresh, so you can schedule other things that depend on it, like an extract refresh, to occur after the table gets the latest data.

  If old records are maintained in the table as a log, you can use the expiration date to filter out old records if you only want the latest ones, or keep past records if you're reporting on historical trends.

- "Is this data collected automatically as events occur, or are the values entered by people? Do we have documentation on the interface that they can see with the data entry form field labels?"

  Data entered by people may be more prone to error because of manual entry, but the people doing the data entry are often extremely valuable to talk to if you want to understand the business processes that generated the data. You can ask them why certain values were selected, what might trigger an update of a record, or what automated processes are kicked off when they make a change or process a batch.

  It's a good idea to check to see how the values in each field are distributed: What is the range of possible values? If a column contains categorical values, how many rows fall into each category? If the column contains continuous or discrete numeric values, what is the shape of the statistical distribution? I find that it helps to visualize the data at this exploratory stage, called Exploratory Data Analysis (EDA). Histograms are especially useful for this purpose.

Additionally, you might explore the data broken down by time period (such as by fiscal year) to see if those distributions change over time. If you find that they do, you may find out by talking to the SMEs that there is a point at which old records stop being updated, a business process changed, or past values get zeroed out in certain cases, for example.

Knowing how their data entry forms look can also help with communication with SMEs about the data, because they may not know the field names in the underlying database but will be able to describe the data using the labels they can see on the front-end interface.

Knowing the type of database is also important for writing more efficient queries, but that is something you are likely to know from the start, as you will probably need that information in order to connect to it. In some database systems, limiting the number of rows returned will make a query run faster. However, in "columnar" database systems like Redshift, even when limiting results to a single row, returning data from all columns may take longer to complete than summarizing all of the values in a single column across thousands of rows because of how the data is physically stored and compiled behind the scenes before being returned to you.

Additionally, you will need to know the type of database in order to look up SQL syntax details in the official documentation, since syntax can differ slightly between database systems.

Introduction to the Farmer's Market Database

The MySQL database we'll be using for example queries throughout much of this book serves as a tracking system for vendors, products, customers, and sales at a fictional farmer's market. This relational database contains information about each day the farmer's market is open, such as the date, the hours, the day of the week, and the weather. There is data about each vendor, including their booth assignments, products, and prices. We're going to pretend that (unlike at many real farmer's markets) vendors use networked cash registers to ring up individual items, and customers scan farmer's market loyalty cards with every transaction, so we have detailed logs of their purchases (we know who purchased which items and exactly when).

The Farmer's Market database was designed to allow for demonstration of a variety of queries, including those a data analyst might write to answer business questions about the market, such as "How many people visit the market each week throughout the year, and when do our sales peak?" "How much does inclement weather impact attendance?" "When is each type of fresh fruit or vegetable in season, locally?" and "Is this proposed new vendor likely to take business away from existing vendors, or is there enough demand to support another vendor selling these goods?"

We will also prepare datasets based on this database for use with predictive modeling techniques like classification and time-series forecasting, transforming the data into a format that can be used as an input for statistical models and machine learning algorithms. These can help answer questions such as "How many shoppers should we expect to have next month? Next year?" and "Based on what we know about their purchase history, is this customer likely to return in the next month?"

Figure 1.7 shows the ERD for the entire Farmer's Market database. Throughout this book, we will be diving into details of the different tables and relationships depicted in Figure 1.7, as we learn how to write SQL statements that can actually be used to pull data from this database, giving realistic examples of queries that data analysts and data scientists develop.

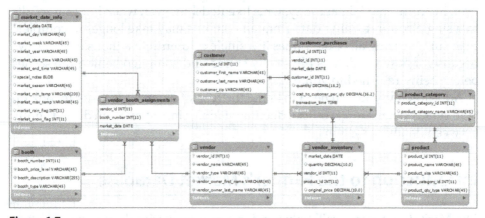

Figure 1.7

A Note on Machine Learning Dataset Terminology

So far, we have defined rows (or records) and columns (or attributes or fields) the way a database developer might. However, if the table is a transformed dataset designed for use in training a predictive model (which is what you will be learning to create throughout this book), a data scientist might use different terminology to describe the rows and columns in that dataset.

In this special use case, the set of values in each row can be used as inputs to train a model, and that row is often called a "training example" (or "instance" or "data point"). And each input column is a "feature" (or "input variable"). A machine learning algorithm might rank important features, letting you know which attributes are most useful to the model for making its prediction. The column that contains the output that the model is trying to predict is called the "target variable."

By the end of this book, you will have learned how to convert "rows and columns" in database tables into "training examples" with "features" for a predictive model to learn from.

Exercises

1. What do you think will happen in the described Books and Authors database depicted in Figure 1.5 if an author changes their name? Which records might be added or updated, and what might be the effect on the results of future queries based on this data?

2. Think of something in your life that you could track using a database. What entities in this database might have one-to-many relationships with one another? Many-to-many?

The SELECT Statement

Before we can discuss designing analytical datasets, you first need to understand the syntax of Structured Query Language (SQL), so the next several chapters will cover SQL basics. Throughout the book, you will see many variations on the themes introduced here, combining these basic concepts with increasing complexity, because even the most complex SQL queries boil down to the same basic concepts.

The SELECT Statement

The majority of the queries in this book will be SELECT statements. A SELECT statement is SQL code that retrieves data from the database. When used in combination with other SQL keywords, SELECT can be used to view data from a set of columns in a database table, combine data from multiple tables, filter the results, perform calculations, and more.

> **NOTE** You'll often see the word SELECT capitalized in SQL code, and I chose to follow that formatting standard in this book, because SELECT is a reserved SQL *keyword*, meaning it is a special instructional word that the code interpreter uses to execute your query. Capitalizing it visually differentiates the keyword from other text in your query, such as field names.

The Fundamental Syntax Structure of a SELECT Query

SQL SELECT queries follow this basic syntax, though most of the clauses are optional:

SELECT [columns to return]

FROM [schema.table]

WHERE [conditional filter statements]

GROUP BY [columns to group on]

HAVING [conditional filter statements that are run after grouping]

ORDER BY [columns to sort on]

The SELECT and FROM clauses are generally required, because those indicate which columns to select and from what table. The words in brackets are place-holders, and as you go through the next several chapters of this book, you will learn what to put in each section.

Selecting Columns and Limiting the Number of Rows Returned

The simplest SELECT statement is

SELECT * FROM [schema.table]

where [schema.table] is the name of the database schema and table you want to retrieve data from.

> **NOTE**   In Chapter 5, "SQL JOINs," you'll learn the syntax for pulling data from multiple tables at once.

For example,

SELECT * FROM farmers_market.product

can be read as "Select everything from the product table in the farmers_market schema." The asterisk really represents "all columns," so technically it's "Select all columns from the product table in the farmers_market schema," but since there are no filters in this query (no WHERE clause, which you'll learn about in Chapter 3, "The WHERE Clause"), it will also return all rows, hence "everything."

There is another optional clause I didn't include in the basic SELECT syntax in the previous section: the LIMIT clause. (The syntax is different in some database systems. See the note about the TOP keyword and WHERE clause.) I frequently use LIMIT while developing queries. LIMIT sets the maximum number of rows that are returned, in cases when you don't want to see all of the results you would otherwise get. It is especially useful when you're developing queries that pull from a large database, when queries take a long time to run, since the query will stop executing and show the output once it's generated the set number of rows.

By using LIMIT, you can get a preview of your current query's results without having to wait for all of the results to be compiled. For example,

```
SELECT *
FROM farmers_market.product
LIMIT 5
```

returns all columns for the first 5 rows of the product table, as shown in Figure 2.1.

product_id	product_name	product_size	product_category_id	product_qty_type
1	Habanero Peppers - Organic	medium	1	lbs
2	Jalapeno Peppers - Organic	small	1	lbs
3	Poblano Peppers - Organic	large	1	unit
4	Banana Peppers - Jar	8 oz	3	unit
5	Whole Wheat Bread	1.5 lbs	3	unit

Figure 2.1

NOTE When querying MS SQL Server databases, there is a keyword similar to MySQL's LIMIT called TOP (which goes before the SELECT statement). For Oracle databases, this is accomplished in the WHERE clause using "WHERE rownum <= [number]". This is one example of the slight differences in SQL syntax across database systems. However, the basic concepts are the same. So, if you learn SQL for one type of database, you will know enough to know what to look up to find the equivalents for other databases. In MySQL syntax, the keyword is LIMIT, which goes at the end of the query.

You might have noticed that I put the FROM clause on the second line in the SELECT query in the preceding example, while the first SELECT query was written as a single line. Line breaks and tabs don't matter to SQL code execution and are treated like spaces, so you can indent your SQL and break it into multiple lines for readability without affecting the output.

To specify which columns you want returned, list the column names immediately after SELECT, separated by commas, instead of using the asterisk. The following query lists five product IDs and their associated product names from the product table, as displayed in Figure 2.2.

```
SELECT product_id, product_name
FROM farmers_market.product
LIMIT 5
```

product_id	product_name
1	Habanero Peppers - Organic
2	Jalapeno Peppers - Organic
3	Poblano Peppers - Organic
4	Banana Peppers - Jar
5	Whole Wheat Bread

Figure 2.2

TIP   Even if you want all columns returned, it's good practice to list the names of the columns instead of using the asterisk, especially if the query will be used as part of a data pipeline (if the query is automatically run nightly and the results are used as an input into the next step of a series of code functions without human review, for example). This is because returning "all" columns may result in a different output if the underlying table is modified, such as when a new column is added, or columns appear in a different order, which could break your automated data pipeline.

The following query lists five rows of farmer's market vendor booth assignments, displaying the market date, vendor ID, and booth number from the vendor_booth_assignments table, depicted in Figure 2.3:

market_date	vendor_id	booth_number
2019-03-13	4	2
2019-03-09	3	1
2019-03-02	4	7
2019-03-02	1	2
2019-03-13	8	6

Figure 2.3

```
SELECT market_date, vendor_id, booth_number
FROM farmers_market.vendor_booth_assignments
LIMIT 5
```

But this output would make a lot more sense if it were sorted by the market date, right? In the next section, we'll learn how to set the sort order of query results.

The ORDER BY Clause: Sorting Results

The ORDER BY clause is used to sort the output rows. In it, you list the columns you want to sort the results by, in order, separated by commas. You can also specify whether you want the sorting to be in ascending (ASC) or descending (DESC) order. ASC sorts text alphabetically and numeric values from low to high, and DESC sorts them in the reverse order. In MySQL, NULL values appear first when sorting in default ascending order.

NOTE   The sort order is ascending by default, so if you want your values sorted in ascending order, the ASC keyword is optional.

The following query sorts the results by product name, even though the product ID is listed first in the output, shown in Figure 2.4:

product_id	product_name
7	Apple Pie
4	Banana Peppers - Jar
8	Cherry Pie
6	Cut Zinnias Bouquet
10	Eggs

Figure 2.4

```
SELECT product_id, product_name
FROM farmers_market.product
ORDER BY product_name
LIMIT 5
```

And the following modification to the ORDER BY clause changes the query to now sort the results by product ID, highest to lowest, as shown in Figure 2.5:

product_id	product_name
11	Pork Chops
10	Eggs
9	Sweet Potatoes
8	Cherry Pie
7	Apple Pie

Figure 2.5

```
SELECT product_id, product_name
FROM farmers_market.product
ORDER BY product_id DESC
LIMIT 5
```

Note that the rows returned display a different set of products than we saw in the previous query. That's because the ORDER BY clause is executed before the LIMIT is imposed. So in addition to limiting the number of rows returned for quicker development (or to conserve space on the page of a book!), a LIMIT clause can also be combined with an ORDER BY statement to sort the results and return the top *x* number of results, for reporting or validation purposes.

To sort the output of the last query in the previous section, we can add an ORDER BY line, specifying that we want it to sort the output first by market date, then by vendor ID.

In Figure 2.6, we only see rows with the earliest market date available in the database, since we sorted by market_date first, there are more than 5 records in the table for that same date, and we limited this query to only return the first 5 rows. After sorting by market date, the records are then sorted by vendor ID in ascending order:

```
SELECT market_date, vendor_id, booth_number
FROM farmers_market.vendor_booth_assignments
ORDER BY market_date, vendor_id
LIMIT 5
```

market_date	vendor_id	booth_number
2019-03-02	1	2
2019-03-02	3	1
2019-03-02	4	7
2019-03-02	7	11
2019-03-02	8	6

Figure 2.6

Introduction to Simple Inline Calculations

In this section, you will see examples of calculations being performed on the data in some columns. We'll dive deeper into calculations throughout later chapters, but this will give you a sense of how calculations look in the basic SELECT query syntax.

Let's say we wanted to do a calculation using the data in two different columns in each row. In the customer_purchases table, we have a quantity column and a cost_to_customer_per_qty column, so we can multiply those to get a price.

In Figure 2.7, you can see how the raw data in the selected columns of the customer_purchases table looks prior to adding any calculations to the following query:

```
SELECT
    market_date,
    customer_id,
    vendor_id,
    quantity,
    cost_to_customer_per_qty
FROM farmers_market.customer_purchases
LIMIT 10
```

market_date	customer_id	vendor_id	quantity	cost_to_customer_per_qty
2019-03-02	4	8	2.00	4.00
2019-03-02	10	8	1.00	4.00
2019-03-09	12	8	1.00	4.00
2019-03-09	5	9	1.00	16.00
2019-03-09	1	9	1.00	18.00
2019-03-02	2	4	4.60	2.00
2019-03-02	3	4	8.40	2.00
2019-03-02	4	4	1.40	2.00
2019-03-09	4	4	9.90	2.00
2019-03-02	1	1	1.00	5.50

Figure 2.7

The following query demonstrates how the values in two different columns can be multiplied by one another by putting an asterisk between them. When used this way, the asterisk represents a multiplication sign. The results of the calculation are shown in the last column in Figure 2.8.

market_date	customer_id	vendor_id	quantity	cost_to_customer_per_qty	quantity * cost_to_customer_per_qty
2019-03-02	4	8	2.00	4.00	8.0000
2019-03-02	10	8	1.00	4.00	4.0000
2019-03-09	12	8	1.00	4.00	4.0000
2019-03-09	5	9	1.00	16.00	16.0000
2019-03-09	1	9	1.00	18.00	18.0000
2019-03-02	2	4	4.60	2.00	9.2000
2019-03-02	3	4	8.40	2.00	16.8000
2019-03-02	4	4	1.40	2.00	2.8000
2019-03-09	4	4	9.90	2.00	19.8000
2019-03-02	1	1	1.00	5.50	5.5000

Figure 2.8

```
SELECT
    market_date,
    customer_id,
    vendor_id,
    quantity,
    cost_to_customer_per_qty,
    quantity * cost_to_customer_per_qty
FROM farmers_market.customer_purchases
LIMIT 10
```

To give the calculated column a meaningful name, we can create an *alias* by adding the keyword AS after the calculation and then specifying the new name. If your alias includes spaces, it should be surrounded by single quotes. I prefer not to use spaces in my aliases, to avoid having to remember to surround them with quotes if I need to reference them later.

Here, we'll give the alias "price" to the result of the "quantity times cost_to_customer_per_qty" calculation. There is no need for the columns used for the calculation to also be included individually like they were in the previous query, so we can remove them in this version.

```
SELECT
    market_date,
    customer_id,
    vendor_id,
    quantity * cost_to_customer_per_qty AS price
FROM farmers_market.customer_purchases
LIMIT 10
```

The column alias is shown in the header of the last column in Figure 2.9.

market_date	customer_id	vendor_id	price
2019-03-02	4	8	8.0000
2019-03-02	10	8	4.0000
2019-03-09	12	8	4.0000
2019-03-09	5	9	16.0000
2019-03-09	1	9	18.0000
2019-03-02	2	4	9.2000
2019-03-02	3	4	16.8000
2019-03-02	4	4	2.8000
2019-03-09	4	4	19.8000
2019-03-02	1	1	5.5000

Figure 2.9

In MySQL syntax, the AS keyword is actually optional, so the following query will return the same results as the previous query. For clarity, we will use the AS convention for assigning column aliases in this book.

```
SELECT
     market_date,
     customer_id,
     vendor_id,
     quantity * cost_to_customer_per_qty price
FROM farmers_market.customer_purchases
LIMIT 10
```

A sensible next step would be to calculate transaction totals (how much the customer paid for all of the products they purchased on that day from each vendor). This could be accomplished by adding up the price per customer per market vendor per market date. In Chapter 6, "Aggregating Results for Analysis," you will learn about aggregate calculations, which calculate summaries across multiple rows. Because we aren't aggregating our results yet, the calculation in the preceding query is applied to the values in each row, as displayed in Figure 2.9, and does not calculate across rows or summarize multiple rows.

More Inline Calculation Examples: Rounding

A SQL function is a piece of code that takes inputs that you give it (which are called parameters), performs some operation on those inputs, and returns a value. You can use functions inline in your query to modify the raw values from the database tables before displaying them in the output. A SQL function call uses the following syntax:

FUNCTION_NAME([parameter 1],[parameter 2], ...[parameter n])

Each bracketed item shown is a placeholder for an input parameter. Parameters go inside the parentheses following the function name and are separated by commas. The input parameter might be a field name or a value that gives the function further instructions. To determine what input parameters a particular function requires, you can look it up in the database documentation, which you can find at dev.mysql.com/doc for MySQL.

To give an example of how functions are used in SELECT statements, we'll use the ROUND() function to round a number. In the query from the previous section, the "price" field was displayed with four digits after the decimal point. Let's say we wanted to display the number rounded to the nearest penny (in US dollars), which is two digits after the decimal. That can be accomplished using the ROUND() function.

The syntax of the ROUND() function is for the first parameter (the first item inside the parentheses) to represent the value to be rounded, followed by a comma, then the second parameter indicating the desired number of digits after the decimal. So ROUND([column name], 3) will round the values in the specified column to 3 digits after the decimal.

We can update our query from the previous section to put the price calculation inside the ROUND() function:

```
SELECT
    market_date,
    customer_id,
    vendor_id,
    ROUND(quantity * cost_to_customer_per_qty, 2) AS price
FROM farmers_market.customer_purchases
LIMIT 10
```

The result of this rounding is shown in the final column of the output, displayed in Figure 2.10.

market_date	customer_id	vendor_id	price
2019-03-02	4	8	8.00
2019-03-02	10	8	4.00
2019-03-09	12	8	4.00
2019-03-09	5	9	16.00
2019-03-09	1	9	18.00
2019-03-02	2	4	9.20
2019-03-02	3	4	16.80
2019-03-02	4	4	2.80
2019-03-09	4	4	19.80
2019-03-02	1	1	5.50

Figure 2.10

TIP   The ROUND() function can also accept negative numbers for the second parameter, to round digits that are to the left of the decimal point. For example, SELECT ROUND(1245, -2) will return a value of 1200.

More Inline Calculation Examples: Concatenating Strings

In addition to performing numeric operations, there are also inline functions that can be used to modify string values in SQL, as well. In our `customer` table, there are separate columns for each customer's first and last names, as shown in Figure 2.11.

customer_id	customer_first_name	customer_last_name	customer_zip
1	Jane	Connor	22801
2	Manuel	Diaz	22803
3	Bob	Wilson	22803
4	Deanna	Washington	22801
5	Abigail	Harris	22801

Figure 2.11

```
SELECT *
FROM farmers_market.customer
LIMIT 5
```

Let's say we wanted to merge each customer's name into a single column that contains the first name, then a space, and then the last name. We can accomplish that by using the CONCAT() function. The list of string values you want to merge together are entered into the CONCAT() function as parameters. A space can be included by surrounding it with quotes. You can see the result of this concatenation in Figure 2.12.

customer_id	customer_name
1	Jane Connor
2	Manuel Diaz
3	Bob Wilson
4	Deanna Washington
5	Abigail Harris

Figure 2.12

```
SELECT
    customer_id,
    CONCAT(customer_first_name, " ", customer_last_name) AS customer_
name
FROM farmers_market.customer
LIMIT 5
```

Note that we can still add an ORDER BY clause and sort by last name first, even though the columns are merged together in the output, as shown in Figure 2.13.

customer_id	customer_name
7	Jessica Armenta
6	Betty Bullard
1	Jane Connor
2	Manuel Diaz
10	Russell Edwards

Figure 2.13

NOTE As we discussed earlier in the "Selecting Columns and Limiting the Number of Rows Returned" section, the LIMIT clause determines how many results we will display. Because more than five names are stored in our table, and we are limiting our results to 5, you see the names change from Figure 2.12 to Figure 2.13 as the sort order changes.

```
SELECT
    customer_id,
    CONCAT(customer_first_name, " ", customer_last_name) AS customer_
name
FROM farmers_market.customer
ORDER BY customer_last_name, customer_first_name
LIMIT 5
```

It's also possible to nest functions inside other functions, which are executed by the SQL interpreter from the "inside" to the "outside." UPPER() is a function that capitalizes string values. We can enclose the CONCAT() function inside it to uppercase the full name. Let's also change the order of the concatenation parameters to put the last name first, and add a comma after the last name (note the comma before the space inside the double quotes). The result is shown in Figure 2.14.

```
SELECT
    customer_id,
    UPPER(CONCAT(customer_last_name, ", ", customer_first_name)) AS
customer_name
FROM farmers_market.customer
ORDER BY customer_last_name, customer_first_name
LIMIT 5
```

Because the CONCAT() function is contained inside the parentheses of the UPPER() function, the concatenation is performed first, and then the combined string is uppercased.

customer_id	customer_name
7	ARMENTA, JESSICA
6	BULLARD, BETTY
1	CONNOR, JANE
2	DIAZ, MANUEL
10	EDWARDS, RUSSELL

Figure 2.14

> **NOTE**   Note that we did not sort on the new derived column alias `customer_name` here, but on columns that exist in the `customer` table. In some cases (depending on what database system you're using, which functions are used, and the execution order of your query) you can't reuse aliases in other parts of the query. It is possible to put some functions or calculations in the ORDER BY clause, to sort by the resulting value. Some other options for referencing derived values will be covered in later chapters.

Evaluating Query Output

When you are developing a SQL SELECT statement, how do you know if the result will include the rows and columns you expect, in the form you expect?

As previously demonstrated, one method is to run the query with a LIMIT each time you make a modification. This gives a quick preview of the first x number of rows to ensure the changes you expect to see are returned, and you can inspect the column names and format of a few output values to verify that they look the way you intended.

However, you still might want to confirm how many rows would have been returned if you hadn't placed the LIMIT on the results. Similarly, there's the concern that your function might not perform as expected on some values that didn't appear in your limited results preview.

I therefore use the query editor to help me review the results of my query a bit further. This method doesn't provide a full quality control of the output (which should be done before putting any query into production), but it can give me a sanity check that the output looks correct enough for me to continue on with my work. To demonstrate, we'll use the "rounded price" query from the earlier "More Inline Calculation Examples: Rounding" section.

First, I remove the LIMIT. Note that your query editor might have a built-in limit (such as 2000 rows) to prevent you from generating a gigantic dataset by accident, so you might need to go into the settings and turn off any pre-set row limits to actually return the full dataset. Figure 2.15 shows the "Don't Limit" option available in MySQL Workbench, under the Query menu.

Then, I'll run the query to generate the output for inspection:

```
SELECT
    market_date,
    customer_id,
    vendor_id,
    ROUND(quantity * cost_to_customer_per_qty, 2) AS price
FROM farmers_market.customer_purchases
```

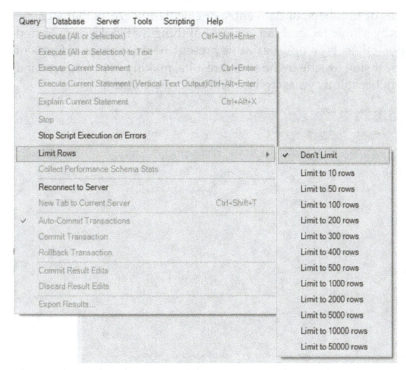

Figure 2.15

The first thing I'll look at in the output is the total count of rows returned, to see if it matches my expectations. This is often displayed at the bottom of the results window or in the output window. In this prototype version of the Farmer's Market database, there are only 21 rows in the `customer_purchases` table, which is indicated in the Message column of the Output section of MySQL Workbench, shown in the lower right of Figure 2.16. (Note that there will be more rows when you run this query yourself, after a more realistic volume of data has been added to the database).

Next, I'll look at the resulting dataset that was generated (which is called the "Result Grid" in MySQL Workbench). I check the column headers, to see if I need to change any aliases. Then, I scroll through and spot-check a few of the values in the output, looking for anything that stands out as incorrect or surprising. If I included an ORDER BY clause (which I did not in this case), I'll also ensure the results are sorted the way I intended.

Then, I can use the editor to manually sort each column first in one direction and then the other. For example, Figures 2.17 and 2.18 show the query results manually sorted in the Result Grid by `market_date` and `vendor_id`, respectively. This allows me to look at the minimum and maximum values in each, because that's often where "edge cases" exist, such as unexpected NULLs, strings that start with spaces or numbers, or data entry or calculation errors that increase numeric values by a large factor. I can explore anything that looks strange, and I might also spot if there is an unusual value present, because series of frequent values will appear side by side in the sorted results, making both frequent and unique values noticeable as you scroll down the sorted column.

market_date	customer_id	vendor_id	price
2019-03-02	4	8	8.00
2019-03-02	10	8	4.00
2019-03-09	12	8	4.00
2019-03-09	5	9	16.00
2019-03-09	1	9	18.00
2019-03-09	12	9	54.00
2019-03-02	2	4	9.20
2019-03-02	3	4	16.80
2019-03-02	4	4	2.80
2019-03-09	4	4	19.80
2019-03-02	1	1	5.50
2019-03-02	1	1	15.00
2019-03-09	1	1	11.00

Figure 2.16

market_date	customer_id	vendor_id	price
2019-03-02	4	8	8.00
2019-03-02	10	8	4.00
2019-03-02	2	4	9.20
2019-03-02	3	4	16.80
2019-03-02	4	4	2.80
2019-03-02	1	1	5.50
2019-03-02	1	1	15.00
2019-03-02	1	1	20.40
2019-03-09	12	8	4.00
2019-03-09	5	9	16.00
2019-03-09	1	9	18.00
2019-03-09	4	4	19.80
2019-03-09	1	1	11.00
2019-03-09	4	1	5.50
2019-03-09	12	1	10.80
2019-03-09	4	7	6.00
2019-03-09	7	7	6.00
2019-03-09	12	7	6.00
2019-03-09	1	7	12.65
2019-03-09	4	7	1.73

Figure 2.17

In Chapter 6, you will learn about aggregate queries, which will provide more options for inspecting your results, but these are a few simple steps you can take, without writing a more complicated query, to make sure your output looks sensible.

market_date	customer_id	vendor_id	price
2019-03-02	1	1	5.50
2019-03-02	1	1	15.00
2019-03-09	1	1	11.00
2019-03-09	4	1	5.50
2019-03-02	1	1	20.40
2019-03-09	12	1	10.80
2019-03-02	2	4	9.20
2019-03-02	3	4	16.80
2019-03-02	4	4	2.80
2019-03-09	4	4	19.80
2019-03-09	4	7	6.00
2019-03-09	7	7	6.00
2019-03-09	12	7	6.00
2019-03-09	1	7	12.65
2019-03-09	4	7	1.73
2019-03-02	4	8	8.00
2019-03-02	10	8	4.00
2019-03-09	12	8	4.00
2019-03-09	5	9	16.00
2019-03-09	1	9	18.00

Figure 2.18

SELECT Statement Summary

In this chapter, you learned basic SQL SELECT statement syntax and how to pull your desired columns from a single table and sort the output. You also learned how simple inline calculations look.

Note that every query in this chapter, even the ones that started to look more complex by including calculations, all followed this basic syntax:

SELECT [columns to return]

FROM [schema.table]

ORDER BY [columns to sort on]

You should now be able to describe what the following two queries do. The results for the following query are shown in Figure 2.19:

```
SELECT * FROM farmers_market.vendor
```

The results for the following query are shown in Figure 2.20:

```
SELECT
    vendor_name,
    vendor_id,
    vendor_type
FROM farmers_market.vendor
ORDER BY vendor_name
```

vendor_id	vendor_name	vendor_type	vendor_owner_first_name	vendor_owner_last_name
1	Chris's Sustainable Eggs & Meats	Eggs & Meats	Chris	Sylvan
3	Hernández Salsa & Veggies	Fresh Variety: Veggies & More	Maria	Hernández
4	Mountain View Vegetables	Fresh Variety: Veggies & More	Joseph	Yoder
6	Seashell Clay Shop	Arts & Jewelry	Karen	Soula
7	Mother's Garlic & Greens	Fresh Variety: Veggies & More	Vera	Gordon
8	Marco's Peppers	Fresh Focused	Marco	Bokashi
9	Annie's Pies	Prepared Foods	Annie	Aquinas
10	Mediterranean Bakery	Prepared Foods	Kani	Hardi
11	Fields of Corn	Fresh Focused	Samuel	Smith

Figure 2.19

vendor_name	vendor_id	vendor_type
Annie's Pies	9	Prepared Foods
Chris's Sustainable Eggs & Meats	1	Eggs & Meats
Fields of Corn	11	Fresh Focused
Hernández Salsa & Veggies	3	Fresh Variety: Veggies & More
Marco's Peppers	8	Fresh Focused
Mediterranean Bakery	10	Prepared Foods
Mother's Garlic & Greens	7	Fresh Variety: Veggies & More
Mountain View Vegetables	4	Fresh Variety: Veggies & More
Seashell Clay Shop	6	Arts & Jewelry

Figure 2.20

Exercises Using the Included Database

The following exercises refer to the customer table. The columns contained in the customer table, and some example rows with data values, are shown in Figure 2.11.

1. Write a query that returns everything in the customer table.

2. Write a query that displays all of the columns and 10 rows from the customer table, sorted by customer_last_name, then customer_first_name.

3. Write a query that lists all customer IDs and first names in the customer table, sorted by first_name.

The WHERE Clause

Now that you have the basic idea of how SQL queries look and have learned how to return the columns of data that you want from a single database table, we can talk about how to filter that result to include only the rows that you want returned.

The WHERE Clause

The WHERE clause is the part of the SELECT statement in which you list conditions that are used to determine which rows in the table should be included in the results set. In other words, the WHERE clause is used for filtering.

If you have programmed in other languages, you have likely encountered other conditional statements such as "IF" statements, which use boolean logic (think "AND" or "OR") to determine what action to take, based on whether certain conditions are met. SQL uses boolean logic to check the available data against conditions in your WHERE clause to determine whether to include each row in the output.

I use the WHERE clause in almost every query I write as a data scientist to accomplish things like narrowing down categories of records to be displayed in a report, or filtering a dataset to a particular date range from the past that will be used to train a predictive model.

Filtering SELECT Statement Results

The WHERE clause goes after the FROM statement and before any GROUP BY, ORDER BY, or LIMIT statements in the SELECT query:

SELECT [columns to return]

FROM [table]

WHERE [conditional filter statements]

ORDER BY [columns to sort on]

For example, to get a list of product IDs and product names that are in product category 1, you could use a conditional statement in the WHERE clause to select only rows from the product table in which the product_category_id is 1, as demonstrated by the following query and the output in Figure 3.1:

```
SELECT
    product_id,
    product_name,
    product_category_id
FROM farmers_market.product
WHERE
    product_category_id = 1
LIMIT 5
```

product_id	product_name	product_category_id
1	Habanero Peppers - Organic	1
2	Jalapeno Peppers - Organic	1
3	Poblano Peppers - Organic	1
9	Sweet Potatoes	1
12	Baby Salad Lettuce Mix - Bag	1

Figure 3.1

One of the queries in Chapter 2 , "The SELECT Statement," returned a list of prices for items purchased by customers at the farmer's market, displaying the market date, customer ID, vendor ID, and calculated price. Let's say we wanted to print a report of everything a particular customer has ever purchased at the farmer's market, sorted by market date, vendor ID, and product ID. We could use a WHERE clause to specify that we want to filter the results of that query to a specified customer ID, and an ORDER BY clause to customize the field sort order:

```
SELECT
    market_date,
    customer_id,
    vendor_id,
```

```
    product_id,
    quantity,
    quantity * cost_to_customer_per_qty AS price
FROM farmers_market.customer_purchases
WHERE customer_id = 4
ORDER BY market_date, vendor_id, product_id
LIMIT 5
```

Figure 3.2 shows the result of this query, which is essentially a line-item receipt of all purchases made at the farmer's market by the customer with an ID of 4. Changing the "4" in the WHERE clause to another customer's ID and re-running the query would result in the same columns, but different rows, listing another customer's purchases.

Note that in order to simplify the query, I did not format the price as currency in the output, but you can refer to the section in Chapter 2 that covers the ROUND() function if you want to format your numeric price output to 2 digits after the decimal.

market_date	customer_id	vendor_id	product_id	quantity	price
2019-03-02	4	4	9	1.40	2.8000
2019-03-02	4	8	4	2.00	8.0000
2019-03-09	4	1	10	1.00	5.5000
2019-03-09	4	4	9	9.90	19.8000
2019-03-09	4	7	12	2.00	6.0000

Figure 3.2

What's actually happening behind the scenes is that each of the conditional statements (like "customer_id = 4") listed in the WHERE clause will evaluate to TRUE or FALSE for each row, and only the rows for which the combination of conditions evaluates to TRUE will be returned.

For example, if a database table contains the transactional data shown in the first six columns of Table 3.1, and the WHERE clause condition is "customer_id = 4" as shown in the previous query, the condition will evaluate to TRUE only for the rows in the table where the customer_id is exactly 4 (as shown in the last column of Table 3.1), and the results will be filtered to only include those six rows, resulting in the output previously shown in Figure 3.2. The customer_id values in the database table are integers, not string characters. If the customer_id values were strings, the comparison value in the WHERE clause would also need to be a string, meaning the `4` would need to be enclosed in single quotes.

Table 3.1

MARKET_ DATE	CUSTOMER_ ID	VENDOR_ID	PRODUCT_ ID	QUANTITY	PRICE	CONDITION: CUSTOMER_ ID = 4
2019-03-02	3	4	4	8.4	16.80	FALSE
2019-03-02	1	1	11	1.7	20.40	FALSE
2019-03-02	4	4	9	1.4	2.80	**TRUE**
2019-03-02	4	8	4	2.0	8.00	**TRUE**
2019-03-09	5	9	7	1.0	16.00	FALSE
2019-03-09	4	1	10	1.0	5.50	**TRUE**
2019-03-09	4	4	9	9.9	19.80	**TRUE**
2019-03-09	4	7	12	2.0	6.00	**TRUE**
2019-03-09	4	7	13	0.3	1.72	**TRUE**
2019-03-16	3	4	9	5.5	11.00	FALSE
2019-03-16	3	9	8	1.0	18.00	FALSE

Filtering on Multiple Conditions

You can combine multiple conditions with boolean operators, such as "AND," "OR," or "AND NOT" between them in order to filter using multiple criteria in the WHERE clause.

Clauses with OR between them will jointly evaluate to TRUE, meaning the row will be returned, if *any* of the clauses are TRUE. Clauses with AND between them will only evaluate to TRUE in combination if *all* of the clauses evaluate to TRUE. Otherwise, the row will not be returned. Remember that NOT flips the following boolean value to its opposite (TRUE becomes FALSE, and vice versa). See Table 3.2.

Table 3.2

CONDITION 1 EVALUATES TO	BOOLEAN OPERATOR	CONDITION 2 EVALUATES TO	ROW RETURNED?
TRUE	OR	FALSE	*TRUE*
TRUE	OR	TRUE	*TRUE*
FALSE	OR	FALSE	*FALSE*
TRUE	AND	FALSE	*FALSE*
TRUE	AND	TRUE	*TRUE*
TRUE	AND NOT	FALSE	*TRUE*

CONDITION 1 EVALUATES TO	BOOLEAN OPERATOR	CONDITION 2 EVALUATES TO	ROW RETURNED?
FALSE	AND NOT	TRUE	*FALSE*
FALSE	AND NOT	FALSE	*FALSE*
FALSE	OR NOT	FALSE	*TRUE*

So if the WHERE clause lists two conditions with OR between them, like "WHERE customer_id = 3 OR customer_id = 4," then each condition will be evaluated for each row, and rows where the customer_id is either 3 or 4 (either condition is met) will be returned, as shown in Table 3.3 (some columns have been removed for readability).

Table 3.3

MARKET_ DATE	CUSTOMER _ID	VENDOR _ID	PRICE	CONDITION: CUSTOMER_ ID = 3	OR	CONDITION: CUSTOMER_ ID = 4	ROW RETURNED?
2019-03-02	3	4	16.80	**TRUE**	OR	FALSE	**TRUE**
2019-03-02	1	1	20.40	FALSE	OR	FALSE	*FALSE*
2019-03-02	4	4	2.80	FALSE	OR	**TRUE**	**TRUE**
2019-03-02	4	8	8.00	FALSE	OR	**TRUE**	**TRUE**
2019-03-09	5	9	16.00	FALSE	OR	FALSE	*FALSE*
2019-03-09	4	1	5.50	FALSE	OR	**TRUE**	**TRUE**
2019-03-09	4	4	19.80	FALSE	OR	**TRUE**	**TRUE**
2019-03-09	4	7	6.00	FALSE	OR	**TRUE**	**TRUE**
2019-03-09	4	7	1.72	FALSE	OR	**TRUE**	**TRUE**
2019-03-16	3	4	11.00	**TRUE**	OR	FALSE	**TRUE**
2019-03-16	3	9	18.00	**TRUE**	OR	FALSE	**TRUE**

Because there is an OR between the two conditions, only one of the conditions has to evaluate to TRUE in order for a row to be returned.

In fact, if there is a long list of conditions, with OR between all of them, only one condition in the entire list has to evaluate to TRUE per row in order for the row to be returned, because it can be read as "Either [Condition 1] is TRUE OR [Condition 2] is TRUE OR [Condition 3] is TRUE," etc. So, only if *all* items in the list of "OR conditions" evaluate to FALSE is a row not returned.

Here is a query containing the conditions illustrated in Table 3.3 in the WHERE clause, and in Figure 3.3, you can see the actual output:

```
SELECT
    market_date,
    customer_id,
    vendor_id,
    product_id,
    quantity,
    quantity * cost_to_customer_per_qty AS price
FROM farmers_market.customer_purchases
WHERE customer_id = 3
    OR customer_id = 4
ORDER BY market_date, customer_id, vendor_id, product_id
```

market_date	customer_id	vendor_id	product_id	quantity	price
2019-03-02	3	4	9	8.40	16.8000
2019-03-02	4	4	9	1.40	2.8000
2019-03-02	4	8	4	2.00	8.0000
2019-03-09	4	1	10	1.00	5.5000
2019-03-09	4	4	9	9.90	19.8000
2019-03-09	4	7	12	2.00	6.0000
2019-03-09	4	7	13	0.30	1.7250
2019-03-16	3	4	9	5.50	11.0000
2019-03-16	3	9	8	1.00	18.0000

Figure 3.3

What would happen if the WHERE clause condition were "customer_id = 3 AND customer_id = 4"? Let's use the same table setup to illustrate what each condition evaluates to for each row. See Table 3.4.

Table 3.4

MARKET_ DATE	CUSTOMER _ID	VENDOR _ID	PRICE	CONDITION: CUSTOMER_ ID = 3	AND	CONDITION: CUSTOMER_ ID = 4	ROW RETURNED?
2019-03-02	3	4	16.80	TRUE	AND	FALSE	FALSE
2019-03-02	1	1	20.40	FALSE	AND	FALSE	FALSE
2019-03-02	4	4	2.80	FALSE	AND	TRUE	FALSE
2019-03-02	4	8	8.00	FALSE	AND	TRUE	FALSE
2019-03-09	5	9	16.00	FALSE	AND	FALSE	FALSE

MARKET_DATE	CUSTOMER _ID	VENDOR _ID	PRICE	CONDITION: CUSTOMER_ ID = 3	AND	CONDITION: CUSTOMER_ ID = 4	ROW RETURNED?
2019-03-09	4	1	5.50	FALSE	AND	**TRUE**	*FALSE*
2019-03-09	4	4	19.80	FALSE	AND	**TRUE**	*FALSE*
2019-03-09	4	7	6.00	FALSE	AND	**TRUE**	*FALSE*
2019-03-09	4	7	1.72	FALSE	AND	**TRUE**	*FALSE*
2019-03-16	3	4	11.00	**TRUE**	AND	FALSE	*FALSE*
2019-03-16	3	9	18.00	**TRUE**	AND	FALSE	*FALSE*

The correct way to read a query with the conditional statement "WHERE cus-tomer_id = 3 AND customer_id = 4" is "Return each row where the customer ID is 3 and the customer ID is 4." But there is only a single customer_id value per row, so it's impossible for the customer_id to be both 3 and 4 at the same time, therefore no rows are returned!

Some people make the mistake of reading the logical AND operator the way we might request in English, "Give me all of the rows with customer IDs 3 and 4," when what we really mean by that phrase is "Give me all of the rows where the customer ID is either 3 or 4," which would require an OR operator in SQL.

When the AND operator is used, *all* of the conditions with AND between them must evaluate to TRUE for a row in order for that row to be returned in the query results.

One example where you could use AND in a WHERE clause referring to only a single column is when you want to return rows with a range of values. If someone requests "Give me all of the rows with a customer ID greater than 3 and less than or equal to 5," the conditions would be written as "WHERE customer_id > 3 AND customer_id <= 5," and would evaluate as shown in Table 3.5.

Because of the AND, both conditions must evaluate to TRUE in order for a row to be returned.

Let's try it in SQL, and see the output in Figure 3.4:

```
SELECT
    market_date,
    customer_id,
    vendor_id,
    product_id,
```

```
    quantity,
    quantity * cost_to_customer_per_qty AS price
FROM farmers_market.customer_purchases
WHERE customer_id > 3
    AND customer_id <= 5
ORDER BY market_date, customer_id, vendor_id, product_id
```

Table 3.5

MARKET_ DATE	CUSTOMER _ID	VENDOR _ID	PRICE	CONDITION: CUSTOMER_ ID > 3	AND	CONDITION: CUSTOMER_ ID <= 5	ROW RETURNED?
2019-03-02	3	4	16.80	FALSE	AND	TRUE	FALSE
2019-03-02	1	1	20.40	FALSE	AND	TRUE	FALSE
2019-03-02	4	4	2.80	TRUE	AND	TRUE	TRUE
2019-03-02	4	8	8.00	TRUE	AND	TRUE	TRUE
2019-03-09	5	9	16.00	TRUE	AND	TRUE	TRUE
2019-03-09	4	1	5.50	TRUE	AND	TRUE	TRUE
2019-03-09	4	4	19.80	TRUE	AND	TRUE	TRUE
2019-03-09	4	7	6.00	TRUE	AND	TRUE	TRUE
2019-03-09	4	7	1.72	TRUE	AND	TRUE	TRUE
2019-03-16	3	4	11.00	FALSE	AND	TRUE	FALSE
2019-03-16	3	9	18.00	FALSE	AND	TRUE	FALSE

```
market_date   customer_id  vendor_id  product_id  quantity   price
2019-03-02    4            4          9           1.40       2.8000
2019-03-02    4            8          4           2.00       8.0000
2019-03-09    4            1          10          1.00       5.5000
2019-03-09    4            4          9           9.90       19.8000
2019-03-09    4            7          12          2.00       6.0000
2019-03-09    4            7          13          0.30       1.7250
2019-03-09    5            9          7           1.00       16.0000
```

Figure 3.4

You can combine multiple AND, OR, and NOT conditions, and control in which order they get evaluated, by using parentheses the same way you would in an algebraic expression to specify the order of operations. The conditions inside the parentheses get evaluated first.

Returning to the `product` table, let's examine a couple of queries and compare their output. First, see this query and its output in Figure 3.5:

```
SELECT
    product_id,
    product_name
FROM farmers_market.product
WHERE
    product_id = 10
    OR (product_id > 3
    AND product_id < 8)
```

product_id	product_name
4	Banana Peppers - Jar
5	Whole Wheat Bread
6	Cut Zinnias Bouquet
7	Apple Pie
10	Eggs

Figure 3.5

Now look at this query and its output in Figure 3.6:

```
SELECT
    product_id,
    product_name
FROM farmers_market.product
WHERE
    (product_id = 10
    OR product_id > 3)
    AND product_id < 8
```

product_id	product_name
4	Banana Peppers - Jar
5	Whole Wheat Bread
6	Cut Zinnias Bouquet
7	Apple Pie

Figure 3.6

When the product ID is 10, the WHERE clause in the first query is evaluated as:

TRUE OR (TRUE AND FALSE) = TRUE **OR** (FALSE) = TRUE

and the WHERE clause in the second query is evaluated as:

(TRUE OR TRUE) AND FALSE = (TRUE) **AND** FALSE = FALSE

Since the OR statement evaluates to TRUE if *any* of the conditions are TRUE, but the AND statement only evaluates to TRUE if *all* of the conditions are true, the row with a `product_id` value of 10 is only returned by the first query.

Multi-Column Conditional Filtering

So far, all of the examples in this chapter have shown combinations of conditions that reference only one field at a time. WHERE clauses can also impose conditions using values in multiple columns.

For example, if we wanted to know the details of purchases made by customer 4 at vendor 7, we could use the following query:

```
SELECT
    market_date,
    customer_id,
    vendor_id,
    quantity * cost_to_customer_per_qty AS price
FROM farmers_market.customer_purchases
WHERE
    customer_id = 4
    AND vendor_id = 7
```

The results of this query are shown in Figure 3.7.

market_date	customer_id	vendor_id	price
2019-03-09	4	7	6.0000
2019-03-09	4	7	1.7250

Figure 3.7

Let's try a WHERE clause that uses an OR condition to apply comparisons across multiple fields. This query will return anyone in the customer table with the first name of "Carlos" or the last name of "Diaz," and its results are shown in Figure 3.8:

```
SELECT
    customer_id,
    customer_first_name,
    customer_last_name
FROM farmers_market.customer
WHERE
    customer_first_name = 'Carlos'
    OR customer_last_name = 'Diaz'
```

customer_id	customer_first_name	customer_last_name
2	Manuel	Diaz
17	Carlos	Diaz

Figure 3.8

And of course the conditions don't both have to be "exact match" filters using equals signs. If you wanted to find out what booth(s) vendor 2 was assigned to on or before (less than or equal to) March 9, 2019, you could use this query (see Figure 3.9 for the output):

```
SELECT *
FROM farmers_market.vendor_booth_assignments
WHERE
    vendor_id = 9
    AND market_date <= '2019-03-09'
ORDER BY market_date
```

vendor_id	booth_number	market_date
9	8	2019-03-02
9	8	2019-03-09

Figure 3.9

More Ways to Filter

The filters you have seen so far in this chapter include numeric, string, and date comparisons to determine if a value in a field is greater than, less than, or equal to a given comparison value. Other ways to filter rows based on the values in that row include checking if a field is NULL, comparing a string against another partial string value using a wildcard comparison, determining if a field value is found within a list of values, and determining if a field value lies between two other values, among others.

BETWEEN

In the previous query, we checked if a date was less than or equal to another date. We can also use the BETWEEN keyword to see if a value, such as a date, is within a specified range of values.

This query will find the booth assignments for vendor 7 for any market date that occurred between March 2, 2019, and March 16, 2019, including either of those two dates. The output is shown in Figure 3.10.

```
SELECT *
FROM farmers_market.vendor_booth_assignments
WHERE
    vendor_id = 7
    AND market_date BETWEEN '2019-03-02' and '2019-03-16'
ORDER BY market_date
```

vendor_id	booth_number	market_date
7	11	2019-03-02
7	11	2019-03-09
7	11	2019-03-13

Figure 3.10

IN

To return a list of customers with selected last names, we could use a long list of OR comparisons, as shown in the first query in the following example. An alternative way to do the same thing, which may come in handy if you had a long list of names, is to use the IN keyword and provide a comma-separated list of values to compare against. This will return TRUE for any row with a customer_last_name that is in the provided list. Both queries in the following example return the same results, shown in Figure 3.11:

```
SELECT
    customer_id,
    customer_first_name,
    customer_last_name
FROM farmers_market.customer
WHERE
    customer_last_name = 'Diaz'
    OR customer_last_name = 'Edwards'
    OR customer_last_name = 'Wilson'
ORDER BY customer_last_name, customer_first_name


SELECT
    customer_id,
    customer_first_name,
    customer_last_name
FROM farmers_market.customer
WHERE
    customer_last_name IN ('Diaz' , 'Edwards', 'Wilson')
ORDER BY customer_last_name, customer_first_name
```

customer_id	customer_first_name	customer_last_name
17	Carlos	Diaz
2	Manuel	Diaz
10	Russell	Edwards
3	Bob	Wilson

Figure 3.11

Another use of the IN list comparison is if you're searching for a person in the customer table, but don't know the spelling of their name. For example, if someone asked you to look up my customer ID, but you didn't know how to spell my name or whether it had any accents (or if it was entered incorrectly), you might try searching against a list with multiple spellings, like this:

```
SELECT
    customer_id,
    customer_first_name,
    customer_last_name
FROM farmers_market.customer
WHERE
    customer_first_name IN ('Renee', 'Rene', 'Renée', 'René', 'Renne')
```

There are not currently any records in the database with any of these names, so the query won't return any results. But there is another way to accomplish the same type of search without typing all of the various spellings.

LIKE

Let's say that there was a farmer's market customer you knew as "Jerry," but you weren't sure if he was listed in the database as "Jerry" or "Jeremy" or "Jeremiah." All you knew for sure was that the first three letters were "Jer." In SQL, instead of listing every variation you can think of, you can search for partially matched strings using a comparison operator called LIKE, and wildcard characters, which serve as a placeholder for unknown characters in a string.

In MS SQL Server–style SQL, the wildcard character % (percent sign) can serve as a stand-in for any number of characters (including none). So the comparison LIKE 'Jer%' will search for strings that start with "Jer" and have any (or no) additional characters after the "r":

```
SELECT
    customer_id,
    customer_first_name,
    customer_last_name
FROM farmers_market.customer
WHERE
    customer_first_name LIKE 'Jer%'
```

In Figure 3.12, you can see that this query returned two customers whose first names matched this pattern, "Jeremy" and "Jeri".

customer_id	customer_first_name	customer_last_name
13	Jeremy	Gruber
18	Jeri	Mitchell

Figure 3.12

IS NULL

It's often useful to find rows in the database where a field is blank or NULL. In the `product` table, the `product_size` field is not required, so it's possible to add a record for a product with no size. If you wanted to find all of the products without sizes, maybe in order to fill in that missing data, you could use the `IS NULL` condition to filter to just those rows (with results shown in Figure 3.13):

```
SELECT *
FROM farmers_market.product
WHERE product_size IS NULL
```

product_id	product_name	product_size	product_category_id	product_qty_type
14	Red Potatoes	NULL	1	NULL

Figure 3.13

Keep in mind that "blank" and NULL are not the same thing in database terms. If someone asked you to find all products that didn't have product sizes, you might also want to check for blank strings, which would equal '' (two single-quotes with nothing between), or rows where someone entered a space or any number of spaces into that field. The `TRIM()` function removes excess spaces from the beginning or end of a string value, so if you use a combination of the `TRIM()` function and blank string comparison, you can find any row that is blank or contains only spaces. In this case, the "Red Potatoes - Small" row, shown in Figure 3.14, has a `product_size` with one space in it, ' ', so could be found using the following query:

```
SELECT *
FROM farmers_market.product
WHERE
    product_size IS NULL
    OR TRIM(product_size) = ''
```

product_id	product_name	product_size	product_category_id	product_qty_type
14	Red Potatoes	NULL	1	NULL
15	Red Potatoes - Small		1	NULL

Figure 3.14

A Warning About Null Comparisons

You might wonder why the comparison operator `IS NULL` is used instead of equals NULL in the previous section. NULL is not actually a value, it's the absence of a value, so it can't be compared to any existing value. If your query were filtered to `WHERE product_size = NULL`, no rows would be returned, even though there is a record with a NULL product_size, because nothing "equals" NULL, even NULL.

This is important for other types of comparisons as well. Look at the following two queries and their output in Figures 3.15 and 3.16:

```
SELECT
    market_date,
    transaction_time,
    customer_id,
    vendor_id,
    quantity
FROM farmers_market.customer_purchases
WHERE
    customer_id = 1
    AND vendor_id = 7
    AND quantity > 1
```

market_date	transaction_time	customer_id	vendor_id	quantity
2019-03-09	08:42:00	1	7	2.20
2019-03-20	08:25:00	1	7	3.10

Figure 3.15

```
SELECT
    market_date,
    transaction_time,
    customer_id,
    vendor_id,
    quantity
FROM farmers_market.customer_purchases
WHERE
    customer_id = 1
    AND vendor_id = 7
    AND quantity <= 1
```

market_date	transaction_time	customer_id	vendor_id	quantity

Figure 3.16

You might think that if you ran both of the queries, you would get all records in the database, since in one case you're looking for quantities over 1, and in the other you're looking for quantities less than or equal to 1, the combination of which appears to contain all possible values. But since NULL values aren't comparable to numbers in that way, there is a record that is never returned when there's a numeric comparison used, because it has a NULL value in the quantity field. You can see that if you run this query, which results in Figure 3.17:

```
SELECT
    market_date,
    transaction_time,
    customer_id,
    vendor_id,
    quantity
FROM farmers_market.customer_purchases
WHERE
    customer_id = 1
    AND vendor_id = 7
```

market_date	transaction_time	customer_id	vendor_id	quantity
2019-03-09	08:42:00	1	7	2.20
2019-03-09	08:43:00	1	7	NULL
2019-03-20	08:25:00	1	7	3.10

Figure 3.17

Ideally, the database should be designed so that the quantity value for a purchase record isn't allowed to be NULL because you can't buy a NULL number of items, but since NULL values weren't prevented, one was entered.

If you wanted to return all records that don't have NULL values in a field, you could use the condition "[field name] IS NOT NULL" in the WHERE clause.

Filtering Using Subqueries

When the IN list comparison was demonstrated earlier, it used a hard-coded list of values. What if you wanted to filter to a list of values that was returned by another query? In other words, you wanted a dynamic list. There is a way to do that in SQL, using a subquery (a query inside a query).

Let's say we wanted to analyze purchases that were made at the farmer's market on days when it rained. There is a value in the market_date_info table called market_rain_flag that has a value of 0 if it didn't rain while the market was open and a value of 1 if it did.

First, let's write a query that gets a list of market dates when it rained, using this query:

```
SELECT market_date, market_rain_flag
FROM farmers_market.market_date_info
WHERE market_rain_flag = 1
```

The results of this query are shown in Figure 3.18.

market_date	market_rain_flag
2019-03-20	1
2019-03-23	1
2019-03-30	1

Figure 3.18

Now let's use the list of dates generated by that query to return purchases made on those dates. Note that when using a query in an IN comparison, you can only return the field you're comparing to, so we will not include the market_rain_flag field in the following subquery. Therefore, the query inside the parentheses just returns the dates shown in Figure 3.18, and the "outer" query looks for customer_purchases records with a market_date value in that list of dates. You can see in the results in Figure 3.19 that all of the purchase records returned occurred on the days it rained.

```
SELECT
    market_date,
    customer_id,
    vendor_id,
    quantity * cost_to_customer_per_qty price
FROM farmers_market.customer_purchases
WHERE
    market_date IN
        (
        SELECT market_date
        FROM farmers_market.market_date_info
        WHERE market_rain_flag = 1
        )
LIMIT 5
```

market_date	customer_id	vendor_id	price
2019-03-20	7	7	9.0000
2019-03-23	4	7	9.0000
2019-03-30	12	7	3.0000
2019-03-20	1	7	17.8250
2019-03-23	4	7	13.8000

Figure 3.19

Creating results that depend on data in more than one table can also be accomplished using something called a JOIN, which you will learn about in Chapter 5, "SQL JOINs."

Exercises Using the Included Database

1. Refer to the data in Table 3.1. Write a query that returns all customer purchases of product IDs 4 and 9.

2. Refer to the data in Table 3.1. Write two queries, one using two conditions with an AND operator, and one using the BETWEEN operator, that will return all customer purchases made from vendors with vendor IDs between 8 and 10 (inclusive).

3. Can you think of two different ways to change the final query in the chapter so it would return purchases from days when it wasn't raining?

CASE Statements

In Chapters 2, "The SELECT Statement," and 3, "The WHERE Clause," you learned how to specify which columns and rows you want to pull from a database table into your dataset. We used the WHERE clause to filter rows using conditional statements that must evaluate to TRUE in order for a row to be returned.

But what if, instead of using conditional statements to filter rows, you want a column or value in your dataset to be based on a conditional statement? For example, instead of filtering your results to purchases over $50, say you just want to return all rows and create a new column that flags each purchase as being above or below $50? Or, maybe the machine learning algorithm you want to use can't accept a categorical string column as an input feature, so you want to encode those categories into numeric values. These are a version of what SQL developers call "derived columns" or "calculated fields," and creating new columns that present the values differently is what data scientists call "feature engineering." This is where CASE statements come in.

> **NOTE** If you're familiar with other scripting languages like Python that use "if" statements, you'll find that SQL handles conditional logic somewhat similarly, just with different syntax.

CASE Statement Syntax

You use conditional reasoning in your daily life any time you think "If [one condition] is true, then [take this action]. Otherwise, [take this other action]." "If the weather forecast predicts it will rain today, then I'll take an umbrella with me. Otherwise, I'll leave the umbrella at home." In SQL, the code to delineate this type of logic is called a CASE statement, which uses the following syntax:

```
CASE
     WHEN [first conditional statement]
        THEN [value or calculation]
     WHEN [second conditional statement]
        THEN [value or calculation]
     ELSE [value or calculation]
END
```

This statement indicates that you want a column to contain different values under different conditions. If we put the umbrella example into this form:

```
CASE
     WHEN weather_forecast = 'rain'
          THEN 'take umbrella'
     ELSE 'leave umbrella at home'
END
```

the WHENs are evaluated in order, from top to bottom, and the first time a condition evaluates to TRUE, the corresponding THEN part of the statement is executed, and no other WHEN conditions are evaluated.

To illustrate, consider this nonsense query:

```
SELECT
     CASE
          WHEN 1=1 THEN 'Yes'
          WHEN 2=2 THEN 'No'
     END
```

This query will always evaluate to "Yes," because 1=1 is always TRUE, and therefore the 2=2 conditional statement is never evaluated, even though it is also true.

The ELSE part of the statement is optional, and that value or calculation result is returned if none of the conditional statements above it evaluate to TRUE. If the ELSE is not included and none of the WHEN conditionals evaluate to TRUE, the resulting value will be NULL.

You should always alias columns that contain CASE statements so the resulting column headers are readable, as demonstrated in the queries in this chapter.

Let's say that we want to know which vendors primarily sell fresh produce and which don't. Figure 4.1 shows the vendor types currently in our Farmer's Market database.

vendor_type
Arts & Jewelry
Eggs & Meats
Fresh Focused
Fresh Variety: Veggies & More
Prepared Foods

Figure 4.1

The vendors we want to label as "Fresh Produce" have the word "Fresh" in the vendor_type column. We can use a CASE statement and the LIKE operator that was covered in Chapter 3 to create a new column, which we'll alias vendor_type_condensed, that condenses the vendor types to just "Fresh Produce" or "Other":

```
SELECT
    vendor_id,
    vendor_name,
    vendor_type,
    CASE
        WHEN LOWER(vendor_type) LIKE '%fresh%'
            THEN 'Fresh Produce'
        ELSE 'Other'
    END AS vendor_type_condensed
FROM farmers_market.vendor
```

In the last two columns of Figure 4.2, you can see how the vendor types were converted to condensed vendor types.

vendor_id	vendor_name	vendor_type	vendor_type_condensed
1	Chris's Sustainable Eggs & Meats	Eggs & Meats	Other
3	Hernández Salsa & Veggies	Fresh Variety: Veggies & More	Fresh Produce
4	Mountain View Vegetables	Fresh Variety: Veggies & More	Fresh Produce
6	Seashell Clay Shop	Arts & Jewelry	Other
7	Mother's Garlic & Greens	Fresh Variety: Veggies & More	Fresh Produce
8	Marco's Peppers	Fresh Focused	Fresh Produce
9	Annie's Pies	Prepared Foods	Other
10	Mediterranean Bakery	Prepared Foods	Other
11	Fields of Corn	Fresh Focused	Fresh Produce

Figure 4.2

We're using the LOWER() function (which does the opposite of the UPPER() function demonstrated in Chapter 2) to lowercase the vendor type string, because we don't want the comparison to fail because of capitalization. UPPER() would have also worked, if we then made the comparison string all caps: '%FRESH%'.

If a new vendor type is added to the database that includes the word "fresh," this query using the LIKE comparison would automatically categorize it as "Fresh Produce" in the vendor_type_condensed column. If we only wanted existing vendor types to be labeled using this logic, we could instead use the IN keyword and explicitly list the existing vendor types we want to label with the "Fresh Produce" category. As a data analyst or data scientist building a dataset that may be refreshed as new data is added to the database, you should always consider what might happen to your transformed columns if the underlying data changes.

Creating Binary Flags Using CASE

A CASE statement can be used to create a "binary flag field," which is a type of field that's often found in machine learning datasets. A binary flag field contains only 1s or 0s, usually indicating a "Yes" or "No" or "exists" or "doesn't exist" type of value. For example, the Farmer's Markets in our database all occur on Wednesday evenings or Saturday mornings. Many machine learning algorithms won't know what to do with the words "Wednesday" and "Saturday" that appear in our database, as shown in the market_day column of Figure 4.3:

```
SELECT
    market_date,
    market_day
FROM farmers_market.market_date_info
LIMIT 5
```

market_date	market_day
2019-03-02	Saturday
2019-03-09	Saturday
2019-03-13	Wednesday
2019-03-16	Saturday
2019-03-20	Wednesday

Figure 4.3

But, the algorithm could use a numeric value as an input. So, how might we turn this string column into a number? One approach we can take to including the market day in our dataset is to generate a binary flag field that indicates whether it's a weekday or weekend market. We can do this with a CASE statement, making a new column that contains a 1 if the market occurs on a Saturday or Sunday, and a 0 if it doesn't, calling the field "weekend_flag," as shown in Figure 4.4.

```
SELECT
    market_date,
```

```
    CASE
        WHEN market_day = 'Saturday' OR market_day = 'Sunday'
            THEN 1
        ELSE 0
    END AS weekend_flag
FROM farmers_market.market_date_info
LIMIT 5
```

market_date	weekend_flag
2019-03-02	1
2019-03-09	1
2019-03-13	0
2019-03-16	1
2019-03-20	0

Figure 4.4

You may have noticed that I included "Sunday" in the OR statement, even though we said earlier that our farmer's markets currently occur on Wednesday evenings and Saturday mornings. I had decided to call the field "weekend_flag" instead of "saturday_flag" because when creating this example, I imagined an analytical question that could be asked: "Do farmers sell more produce at our weekend market or at our weekday market?" If the farmer's market ever changes or expands its schedule to hold a market on a Sunday, this CASE statement will still correctly flag it as a weekend market for the analysis. There is not much downside to making the field aliased "weekend_flag" actually mean what it's called (except for the tiny additional computation done to check the second OR condition when necessary, which is unlikely to make any noticeable difference for data on the scale most farmer's markets could collect) and planning for the future possibility of other market days when designing a dataset to answer this question.

Grouping or Binning Continuous Values Using CASE

In Chapter 3, we had a query that filtered to only customer purchases where an item or quantity of an item cost over $50, by putting a conditional statement in the WHERE clause. But let's say we wanted to return all rows, and instead of using that value as a filter, only indicate whether the cost was over $50 or not. We could write the query like this:

```
SELECT
    market_date,
    customer_id,
    vendor_id,
    ROUND(quantity * cost_to_customer_per_qty, 2) AS price,
```

Continues

(continued)

```
CASE
    WHEN quantity * cost_to_customer_per_qty > 50
        THEN 1
    ELSE 0
END AS price_over_50
FROM farmers_market.customer_purchases
LIMIT 10
```

The final column in Figure 4.5 now contains a flag indicating which item purchases were over $50. The price is displayed here for explanatory purposes, but could be left out if only the flag indicator were important.

market_date	customer_id	vendor_id	price	price_over_50
2019-03-02	4	8	8.00	0
2019-03-02	10	8	4.00	0
2019-03-09	12	8	4.00	0
2019-03-09	5	9	16.00	0
2019-03-09	1	9	18.00	0
2019-03-09	12	9	54.00	1
2019-03-02	2	4	9.20	0
2019-03-02	3	4	16.80	0
2019-03-02	4	4	2.80	0
2019-03-09	4	4	19.80	0

Figure 4.5

CASE statements can also be used to "bin" a continuous variable, such as price. Let's say we wanted to put the line-item customer purchases into bins of under $5.00, $5.00–$9.99, $10.00–$19.99, or $20.00 and over. We could accomplish that with a CASE statement in which we surround the values after the THENs in single quotes to generate a column that contains a string label, as shown in Figure 4.6:

```
SELECT
    market_date,
    customer_id,
    vendor_id,
    ROUND(quantity * cost_to_customer_per_qty, 2) AS price,
    CASE
        WHEN quantity * cost_to_customer_per_qty < 5.00
            THEN 'Under $5'
        WHEN quantity * cost_to_customer_per_qty < 10.00
            THEN '$5-$9.99'
        WHEN quantity * cost_to_customer_per_qty < 20.00
            THEN '$10-$19.99'
        WHEN quantity * cost_to_customer_per_qty >= 20.00
            THEN '$20 and Up'
    END AS price_bin
FROM farmers_market.customer_purchases
LIMIT 10
```

market_date	customer_id	vendor_id	price	price_bin
2019-03-02	4	8	8.00	$5-$9.99
2019-03-02	10	8	4.00	Under $5
2019-03-09	12	8	4.00	Under $5
2019-03-09	5	9	16.00	$10-$19.99
2019-03-09	1	9	18.00	$10-$19.99
2019-03-09	12	9	54.00	$20 and Up
2019-03-02	2	4	9.20	$5-$9.99
2019-03-02	3	4	16.80	$10-$19.99
2019-03-02	4	4	2.80	Under $5
2019-03-09	4	4	19.80	$10-$19.99

Figure 4.6

Or, if the result needs to be numeric, a different approach is to output the bottom end of the numeric range, as shown in Figure 4.7:

```
SELECT
    market_date,
    customer_id,
    vendor_id,
    ROUND(quantity * cost_to_customer_per_qty, 2) AS price,
    CASE
        WHEN quantity * cost_to_customer_per_qty < 5.00
            THEN 0
        WHEN quantity * cost_to_customer_per_qty < 10.00
            THEN 5
        WHEN quantity * cost_to_customer_per_qty < 20.00
            THEN 10
        WHEN quantity * cost_to_customer_per_qty >= 20.00
            THEN 20
    END AS price_bin_lower_end
FROM farmers_market.customer_purchases
LIMIT 10
```

market_date	customer_id	vendor_id	price	price_bin_lower_end
2019-03-02	4	8	8.00	5
2019-03-02	10	8	4.00	0
2019-03-09	12	8	4.00	0
2019-03-09	5	9	16.00	10
2019-03-09	1	9	18.00	10
2019-03-09	12	9	54.00	20
2019-03-02	2	4	9.20	5
2019-03-02	3	4	16.80	10
2019-03-02	4	4	2.80	0
2019-03-09	4	4	19.80	10

Figure 4.7

One of these queries generates a new column of strings, and one generates a new column of numbers. You might actually want to include both columns in your query if you were building it to be used in a report, because the `price_bin` column is a more explanatory label for the bin, but will sort alphabetically instead of in bin value order. With both available to use in your report, you could use the numeric version of the column to sort the bins correctly, and the string version to label the bins.

Remember that because neither of the preceding queries included an ELSE inside the CASE statement, the output will be NULL if the quantity field is blank or the calculation can't be completed with the available values for whatever reason.

If there is a mis-entered price, or perhaps a record of a refund, and the value in the price column turns out to be negative in one row, what do you think will happen? In the preceding queries, the first condition is "less than 5," so negative values will end up in the "Under $5," or 0, bin. Therefore, the name `price_bin_lower_end` is a misnomer, since 0 might not actually represent the lowest value possible in the first bin. It's important when writing CASE statements for analytical purposes to determine what the result will be if there end up being unexpected values in any of the referenced database fields.

Categorical Encoding Using CASE

When developing datasets for machine learning, you will often need to "encode" categorical string variables as numeric variables, in order for a mathematical algorithm to be able to use them as input.

If the categories represent something that can be sorted in a rank order, it might make sense to convert the string variables into numeric values that represent that rank order. For example, the vendor booths at the farmer's market are rented out at different costs, depending on their size and proximity to the entrance. These booth price levels are labeled with the letters "A," "B," and "C," in order by increasing price, which could be converted into either numeric values 1, 2, 3 or the actual booth prices. The following CASE statement converts the booth price levels into numeric values, and the results are shown in Figure 4.8:

```
SELECT
    booth_number,
    booth_price_level,
    CASE
        WHEN booth_price_level = 'A' THEN 1
        WHEN booth_price_level = 'B' THEN 2
        WHEN booth_price_level = 'C' THEN 3
    END AS booth_price_level_numeric
FROM farmers_market.booth
LIMIT 5
```

booth_number	booth_price_level	booth_price_level_numeric
1	A	1
2	A	1
3	B	2
4	C	3
5	C	3

Figure 4.8

If the categories aren't necessarily in any kind of rank order, like our vendor type categories, we might use a method called "one-hot encoding." This helps us avoid inadvertently indicating a sort order when none exists. One-hot encoding means that we create a new column representing each category, assigning it a binary value of 1 if a row falls into that category, and a 0 otherwise. These columns are sometimes called "dummy variables." The following CASE statement one-hot encodes our vendor type categories, and the results are demonstrated in Figure 4.9:

```
SELECT
    vendor_id,
    vendor_name,
    vendor_type,
    CASE WHEN vendor_type =  'Arts & Jewelry'
        THEN 1
        ELSE 0
    END AS vendor_type_arts_jewelry,
    CASE WHEN vendor_type =  'Eggs & Meats'
        THEN 1
        ELSE 0
    END AS vendor_type_eggs_meats,
    CASE WHEN vendor_type =  'Fresh Focused'
        THEN 1
        ELSE 0
    END AS vendor_type_fresh_focused,
    CASE WHEN vendor_type =  'Fresh Variety: Veggies & More'
        THEN 1
        ELSE 0
    END AS vendor_type_fresh_variety,
    CASE WHEN vendor_type = 'Prepared Foods'
        THEN 1
        ELSE 0
    END AS vendor_type_prepared
FROM farmers_market.vendor
```

vendor_id	vendor_name	vendor_type	vendor_type_arts_jewelry	vendor_type_eggs_meats	vendor_type_fresh_focused	vendor_type_fresh_variety	vendor_type_prepared
1	Chris's Sustainable Eggs & Meats	Eggs & Meats	0	1	0	0	0
3	Hernández Salsa & Veggies	Fresh Variety: Veggies & More	0	0	0	1	0
4	Mountain View Vegetables	Fresh Variety: Veggies & More	0	0	0	1	0
6	Seashell Clay Shop	Arts & Jewelry	1	0	0	0	0
7	Mother's Garlic & Greens	Fresh Variety: Veggies & More	0	0	0	1	0
8	Marco's Peppers	Fresh Focused	0	0	1	0	0
9	Annie's Pies	Prepared Foods	0	0	0	0	1
10	Mediterranean Bakery	Prepared Foods	0	0	0	0	1
11	Fields of Corn	Fresh Focused	0	0	1	0	0

Figure 4.9

A situation to be aware of when manually encoding one-hot categorical variables this way is that if a new category is added (a new type of vendor in this case), there will be no column in your dataset for the new vendor type until you add another CASE statement.

CASE Statement Summary

In this chapter, you learned SQL CASE statement syntax for creating new columns with values based on conditions. You also learned how to consolidate categorical values into fewer categories, create binary flags, bin continuous values, and encode categorical values.

You should now be able to describe what the following two queries do. The results for the first query are displayed in Figure 4.10:

```
SELECT
    customer_id,
    CASE
        WHEN customer_zip = '22801' THEN 'Local'
        ELSE 'Not Local'
    END customer_location_type
FROM farmers_market.customer
LIMIT 10
```

customer_id	customer_location_type
1	Local
2	Not Local
3	Not Local
4	Local
5	Local
6	Local
7	Not Local
8	Not Local
9	Local
10	Local

Figure 4.10

The results for the following query are displayed in Figure 4.11:

```
SELECT
    booth_number,
    CASE WHEN booth_price_level = 'A'
        THEN 1
        ELSE 0
    END booth_price_level_A,
    CASE WHEN booth_price_level = 'B'
        THEN 1
        ELSE 0
```

```
        END booth_price_level_B,
        CASE WHEN booth_price_level = 'C'
            THEN 1
            ELSE 0
        END booth_price_level_C
    FROM farmers_market.booth
    LIMIT 5
```

booth_number	booth_price_level_A	booth_price_level_B	booth_price_level_C
1	1	0	0
2	1	0	0
3	0	1	0
4	0	0	1
5	0	0	1

Figure 4.11

Exercises Using the Included Database

Look back at Figure 2.1 in Chapter 2 for sample data and column names for the product table referenced in these exercises.

1. Products can be sold by the individual unit or by bulk measures like lbs. or oz. Write a query that outputs the product_id and product_name columns from the product table, and add a column called prod_qty_type_condensed that displays the word "unit" if the product_qty_type is "unit," and otherwise displays the word "bulk."

2. We want to flag all of the different types of pepper products that are sold at the market. Add a column to the previous query called pepper_flag that outputs a 1 if the product_name contains the word "pepper" (regardless of capitalization), and otherwise outputs 0.

3. Can you think of a situation when a pepper product might not get flagged as a pepper product using the code from the previous exercise?

SQL JOINs

Now that you have learned how to select the data you want from a database table and filter to the rows you want, you might wonder what to do if the data you need exists across multiple related tables in the database. For example, one analytical question mentioned in Chapter 1, "When is each type of fresh fruit or vegetable in season, locally?" requires data from the product_category table (to filter to the categories with fresh fruit and vegetables), the product table (to get details about each specific item, including product names and quantity types), and the vendor_inventory table (to find out when vendors were selling these products). This is where SQL JOINs come in.

Database Relationships and SQL JOINs

In Chapter 1, "Data Sources," we introduced different types of database relationships and the entity-relationship diagram (ERD). The type of relationship between database tables, and the key fields that connect them, give us information we need to combine them using a JOIN statement in SQL.

Let's say we wanted to list each product name along with its product category name. Since only the ID of the product category exists in the product table, and the product category's name is in the product_category table, we have to combine the data in the product and product_category tables together in order to generate this list.

Figure 5.1 shows the one-to-many relationship between these two tables: each product can only belong to one category, but each category can contain many products. The primary key in the `product_category` table is the `product_cate-gory_id`. There is also a `product_category_id` in each row of the `product` table that serves as a foreign key, identifying which category each product belongs to.

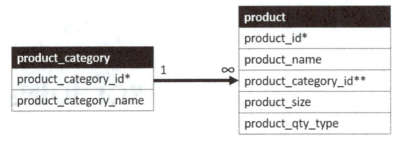

Figure 5.1

> **NOTE**   Remember that in an ERD, an infinity symbol, "N," or "crow's feet" on the end of a line connecting two tables indicates that it is the "many" side of a one-to-many relationship. You can see the infinity symbol next to the product table in Figure 5.1.

In order to combine these tables, we need to figure out which type of JOIN to use. To illustrate the different types of SQL JOINs, we'll use the two tables from the Farmer's Market database found in Figure 5.1, but remove some columns to simplify the illustration, as shown in Figure 5.2.

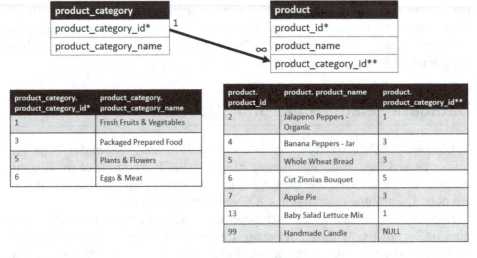

Figure 5.2

Figure 5.2 shows the one-to-many relationship between these tables, as well as some sample data. Their primary keys are each identified with an asterisk, and the foreign key with a double asterisk. Each row in the `product_category` table can be associated with many rows in the `product` table, but each row in the `product` table is associated with only one row in the `product_category` table. The fields that connect the two tables are `product_category.product_category_id` and `product.product_category_id`.

The first type of JOIN we'll cover is the one I've seen used most frequently when building analytical datasets: the LEFT JOIN. This tells the query to pull all records from the table on the "left side" of the JOIN, and only the matching records (based on the criteria specified in the JOIN clause) from the table on the "right side" of the JOIN. See Figure 5.3. Note that the `product` table will be on the left side of the join we're setting up, even though it was on the right side of the relationship diagram!

Left Join

All rows from the "left table", and only rows from the
"right table" with matching values in the specified fields

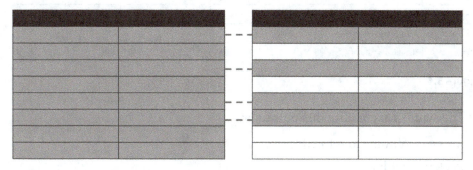

Figure 5.3

In our demonstration tables shown in Figure 5.2, you can see that there are two records in the `product` table that have a `product_category_id` of 1, and only one record in the `product_category` table with the `product_category_id` of 1 (because it is the primary key in this table).

When we LEFT JOIN the `product_category` table to the `product` table, the records with a value of 1 in the `product_category_id` fields of both tables will be joined in the results, as shown in the first two rows of the output in Figure 5.4. Note that the data for `product_category_id` 1 from the `product_category` table is repeated in two rows in the resulting output, even though it was only in one row in the `product_category` table, because it is matched up with two records in the joined product table.

What makes this JOIN a LEFT JOIN is that all of the records from the product table on the *left* side of the join are included in the output, even if they don't have a match in the `product_category` table. But records from the `product_category` table on the right side of the join are only included if they match up with product records on the left side.

In Figure 5.4, you can see that the row with a `product_id` of 99 is included, but the values in the resulting output columns from the `product_category` are NULL (empty) This is because there was no `product_category_id` value on which to join this product to the `product_category` table. However, the row from the `product_category` table with a `product_category_id` of 6 is not included in the output at all, because it was in the "right" table and does not have a matching record on the left side, and this is a LEFT JOIN.

product. product_id	product. product_name	product. product_category_id	product_category. product_category_id	product_category. product_category_name
2	Jalapeno Peppers - Organic	1	1	Fresh Fruits & Vegetables
4	Banana Peppers - Jar	3	3	Packaged Prepared Food
5	Whole Wheat Bread	3	3	Packaged Prepared Food
6	Cut Zinnias Bouquet	5	5	Plants & Flowers
7	Apple Pie	3	3	Packaged Prepared Food
13	Baby Salad Lettuce Mix	1	1	Fresh Fruits & Vegetables
99	Handmade Candle	NULL	NULL	NULL

Figure 5.4

The syntax for creating this output is:

SELECT [columns to return]

FROM [left table]

[JOIN TYPE] [right table]

ON [left table].[field in left table to match] = [right table].[field in right table to match]

Let's look at the actual output of a query that joins our `product` and `product_category` tables from the Farmer's Market database using a LEFT JOIN.

In order to pull a list of all products with each product's category name listed, we make the `product` table the "left" table in this query by listing it first after FROM, and the `product_category` table the "right" side by listing it after the LEFT JOIN, and we'll match up the records using the `product_category_id` fields, as seen after the ON keyword. This is how a query pulling all fields from both tables looks:

```
SELECT * FROM product
    LEFT JOIN product_category
```

```
        ON product.product_category_id = product_category.
    product_category_id
```

This query can be read as "Select everything from the product table, left joined with the product_category table, matched on the product_category_id that's common to both tables," or more specifically: "Select all columns and rows from the product table, and all columns from the product_category table for rows where the product_category's product_category_id matches a product's product_category_id." The first 10 rows of the output from this query are shown in Figure 5.5.

product_id	product_name	product_size	product_category_id	product_qty_type	product_category_id	product_category_name
1	Habanero Peppers - Organic	medium	1	lbs	1	Fresh Fruits & Vegetables
2	Jalapeno Peppers - Organic	small	1	lbs	1	Fresh Fruits & Vegetables
3	Poblano Peppers - Organic	large	1	unit	1	Fresh Fruits & Vegetables
4	Banana Peppers - Jar	8 oz	3	unit	3	Packaged Prepared Food
5	Whole Wheat Bread	1.5 lbs	3	unit	3	Packaged Prepared Food
6	Cut Zinnias Bouquet	medium	5	unit	5	Plants & Flowers
7	Apple Pie	10""	3	unit	3	Packaged Prepared Food
8	Cherry Pie	10""	3	unit	3	Packaged Prepared Food
9	Sweet Potatoes	medium	1	lbs	1	Fresh Fruits & Vegetables
10	Eggs	1 dozen	6	unit	6	Eggs & Meat (Fresh or Frozen)

Figure 5.5

NOTE You may have noticed that there are two columns called product_category_id in Figure 5.5. That is because we selected all fields, using the asterisk, and there are fields in both tables with the same name. To remedy this, we could either specify the list of fields to be returned, and only include the product_category_id from one of the tables, or we could alias the column names to indicate which table each came from, as shown in the next query and pictured in Figure 5.6.

The LEFT JOIN indicates that we want all rows from the product table (which is listed on the left side of the JOIN keyword) and only the associated rows from the product_category table. So, if for some reason there is a category that is not associated with any products, it will not be included in the results. If there were a product without a category (which can't happen in the actual database, because that is a required field), it would be included in the results, with the fields on the product_category side being NULL, as was illustrated in the last row of Figure 5.4.

The ON part of the JOIN clause tells the query to match up the rows in the two tables using the values in the product_category_id field in each table. Note in Figure 5.5 that the product_category_id fields from both tables match on every row. (It would be helpful for us to alias those field names so they don't appear with identical column headers in the output, which we will do in the next query.)

Now, if we want to retrieve specific columns from the merged dataset, we have to specify which table each column is from, since it's possible to have identically named columns in different tables. And we can alias identically named columns to differentiate them. For example, the following code accomplishes the changes shown in Figure 5.6.

product_id	product_name	product_prod_cat_id	category_prod_cat_id	product_category_name
1	Habanero Peppers - Organic	1	1	Fresh Fruits & Vegetables
2	Jalapeno Peppers - Organic	1	1	Fresh Fruits & Vegetables
3	Poblano Peppers - Organic	1	1	Fresh Fruits & Vegetables
4	Banana Peppers - Jar	3	3	Packaged Prepared Food
5	Whole Wheat Bread	3	3	Packaged Prepared Food
6	Cut Zinnias Bouquet	5	5	Plants & Flowers
7	Apple Pie	3	3	Packaged Prepared Food
8	Cherry Pie	3	3	Packaged Prepared Food
9	Sweet Potatoes	1	1	Fresh Fruits & Vegetables
10	Eggs	6	6	Eggs & Meat (Fresh or Frozen)
11	Pork Chops	6	6	Eggs & Meat (Fresh or Frozen)
12	Baby Salad Lettuce Mix - Bag	1	1	Fresh Fruits & Vegetables
13	Baby Salad Lettuce Mix	1	1	Fresh Fruits & Vegetables

Figure 5.6

```
SELECT
    product.product_id,
    product.product_name,
    product.product_category_id AS product_prod_cat_id,
    product_category.product_category_id AS category_prod_cat_id,
    product_category.product_category_name
FROM product
    LEFT JOIN product_category
        ON product.product_category_id = product_category.
product_category_id
```

There is another type of aliasing in a SQL query that is for developer convenience, because it isn't visible in the output: table aliasing. If you don't want to write out the entire table name every time you reference it, you can assign it a short alias in the FROM clause that can then be used to reference it throughout the query, as demonstrated in the following query with the table aliases "p" and "pc." Also, we will also only show a single product_category_id now that we are convinced from the output that they are matching up between tables.

```
SELECT
    p.product_id,
    p.product_name,
    pc.product_category_id,
    pc.product_category_name
FROM product AS p
    LEFT JOIN product_category AS pc
        ON p.product_category_id = pc.product_category_id
ORDER BY pc.product_category_name, p.product_name
```

Again, the AS keyword between the table name and the alias is optional, but I will stick with that standard in this book for consistency. The output from this query is shown in Figure 5.7.

product_id	product_name	product_category_id	product_category_name
10	Eggs	6	Eggs & Meat (Fresh or Frozen)
11	Pork Chops	6	Eggs & Meat (Fresh or Frozen)
13	Baby Salad Lettuce Mix	1	Fresh Fruits & Vegetables
12	Baby Salad Lettuce Mix - Bag	1	Fresh Fruits & Vegetables
1	Habanero Peppers - Organic	1	Fresh Fruits & Vegetables
2	Jalapeno Peppers - Organic	1	Fresh Fruits & Vegetables
3	Poblano Peppers - Organic	1	Fresh Fruits & Vegetables
9	Sweet Potatoes	1	Fresh Fruits & Vegetables
7	Apple Pie	3	Packaged Prepared Food
4	Banana Peppers - Jar	3	Packaged Prepared Food
8	Cherry Pie	3	Packaged Prepared Food
5	Whole Wheat Bread	3	Packaged Prepared Food
6	Cut Zinnias Bouquet	5	Plants & Flowers

Figure 5.7

The next type of SQL JOIN we'll discuss is called a RIGHT JOIN, which is illustrated in Figure 5.8. In a RIGHT JOIN, all of the rows from the "right table" are returned, along with only the matching rows from the "left table," using the fields specified in the ON part of the query.

Right Join

All rows from the "right table", and only rows from the "left table" with matching values in the specified fields

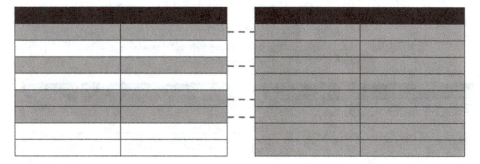

Figure 5.8

If we use a RIGHT JOIN to merge the data in the tables shown in Figure 5.2, the result will look like the table in Figure 5.9. All of the records from the *right* table, product_category, are returned, but only matching records from product. There are no products in this example with a product_category_id value of 6, so the first three columns of the last row are NULL. Note that the record in the product table with a product_id of 99 that was in the last row of Figure 5.4 is now missing, because we performed a RIGHT JOIN this time, and that record does not have a match in the product_category table, since its product_category_id was NULL.

You would use a RIGHT JOIN if you wanted to list all product categories and the products in each. (And you didn't care about products that were not put into a category, but you did care about categories that didn't contain any products.)

product. product_id	product. product_name	product. product_category_id	product_category. product_category_id	product_category. product_category_name
2	Jalapeno Peppers - Organic	1	1	Fresh Fruits & Vegetables
4	Banana Peppers - Jar	3	3	Packaged Prepared Food
5	Whole Wheat Bread	3	3	Packaged Prepared Food
6	Cut Zinnias Bouquet	5	5	Plants & Flowers
7	Apple Pie	3	3	Packaged Prepared Food
13	Baby Salad Lettuce Mix	1	1	Fresh Fruits & Vegetables
NULL	NULL	NULL	6	Eggs & Meat

Figure 5.9

An INNER JOIN only returns records that have matches in both tables. Can you tell which rows from each table in Figure 5.2 will not be returned if we INNER JOIN the `product` and `product_category` tables on `product_category_id`? Figure 5.10 illustrates an INNER JOIN.

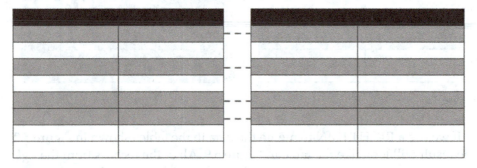

Inner Join

Only rows from the "right table" and "left table" where
values in the specified fields have matches in both tables

Figure 5.10

In Figure 5.4, the fields on the right side of the join (from `product_category`) were NULL in the row where the left side had a NULL `product_category_id`. In Figure 5.9, the fields on the left side of the table (from `product`) were NULL in the row where the `product_category_id` on the right side hadn't been assigned to any products. If we INNER JOIN the tables, neither of those rows will be included in the output, as shown in Figure 5.11.

product. product_id	product. product_name	product. product_category_id	product_category. product_category_id	product_category. product_category_name
2	Jalapeno Peppers - Organic	1	1	Fresh Fruits & Vegetables
4	Banana Peppers - Jar	3	3	Packaged Prepared Food
5	Whole Wheat Bread	3	3	Packaged Prepared Food
6	Cut Zinnias Bouquet	5	5	Plants & Flowers
7	Apple Pie	3	3	Packaged Prepared Food
13	Baby Salad Lettuce Mix	1	1	Fresh Fruits & Vegetables

Figure 5.11

In the INNER JOINed output in Figure 5.11, there is a row for every matched pair of `product_category_ids`, and no rows without a matching `product_category_id` on the other side.

To practice all of these types of JOINs, let's now look at the `customer` and `customer_purchase` tables in the Farmer's Market database. Again, this is a one-to-many type relationship. A customer can have multiple purchases, but each purchase is made by only one customer. The two tables are related via the `customer_id` field, which is the primary key in the `customer` table, and a foreign key in the `customer_purchases` table.

If we do a `LEFT JOIN`, using the following query, we can see in the output in Figure 5.12 that for some rows, the fields that come from the `customer_purchases` table are all NULL. What do you think this means?

```
SELECT *
FROM customer AS c
LEFT JOIN customer_purchases AS cp
    ON c.customer_id = cp.customer_id
```

customer_id	customer_first_name	customer_last_name	customer_zip	product_id	vendor_id	market_date	customer_id	quantity	cost_to_cust	transacti
5	Abigail	Harris	22801	7	9	2019-03-09	5	1.00	16.00	10:41:00
6	Betty	Bullard	22801	NULL	NULL	NULL	NULL	NULL	NULL	NULL
7	Jessica	Armenta	22803	12	7	2019-03-09	7	2.00	3.00	11:40:00
8	Norma	Valenzuela	22803	NULL	NULL	NULL	NULL	NULL	NULL	NULL
9	Janet	Forbes	22801	NULL	NULL	NULL	NULL	NULL	NULL	NULL
10	Russell	Edwards	22801	4	8	2019-03-02	10	1.00	4.00	09:12:00
11	Richard	Paulson	22801	NULL	NULL	NULL	NULL	NULL	NULL	NULL
12	Jack	Wise	22803	4	8	2019-03-09	12	1.00	4.00	13:03:00
12	Jack	Wise	22803	8	9	2019-03-09	12	3.00	18.00	13:18:00
12	Jack	Wise	22803	11	1	2019-03-09	12	0.90	12.00	13:10:00
12	Jack	Wise	22803	12	7	2019-03-09	12	2.00	3.00	13:00:00
13	Jeremy	Gruber	22803	NULL	NULL	NULL	NULL	NULL	NULL	NULL
14	William	Jones	22801	NULL	NULL	NULL	NULL	NULL	NULL	NULL

Figure 5.12

Unlike for the `product-product_category` relationship, there can be customers without any purchases. Such customers were added to the customer table when they signed up for the farmer's market loyalty card, so we have their customer data, but they have not yet purchased any products. Since we did a `LEFT JOIN`, we're getting a list of all customers, and their associated purchases, if there are any. Customers with multiple purchases will show up in the output multiple times—once for each item purchased. Customers without any purchases will have NULL values in all fields displayed that are from the customer_purchases table.

We can use the WHERE clause you learned about in Chapter 3, "The WHERE Clause," to filter the list to only customers with no purchases, if we'd like:

```
SELECT c.*
FROM customer AS c
LEFT JOIN customer_purchases AS cp
    ON c.customer_id = cp.customer_id
WHERE cp.customer_id IS NULL
```

In this case, we only selected columns from the customer table, using c.*, because all of the columns on the customer_purchases side of the relationship will be NULL (since we're filtering to NULL customer_id, and there are no purchases in the customer_purchases table without a customer_id, since it is a required field; remember that in this imaginary farmer's market, every purchase is logged at checkout, and every customer uses their loyalty card).

Figure 5.13 shows what the output of this query looks like, listing all customers who don't have any purchases.

customer_id	customer_first_name	customer_last_name	customer_zip
6	Betty	Bullard	22801
8	Norma	Valenzuela	22803
9	Janet	Forbes	22801
11	Richard	Paulson	22801
13	Jeremy	Gruber	22803
14	William	Lopes	22801
15	Darrell	Messina	22801

Figure 5.13

What if we wanted to list all purchases and the customers associated with them? In that case, we could do a RIGHT JOIN, pulling all records from the customer_purchases table, and only customers from the customer table with a purchase (a record in the customer_purchases table with their ID on it):

```
SELECT *
FROM customer AS c
RIGHT JOIN customer_purchases AS cp
    ON c.customer_id = cp.customer_id
```

The output in Figure 5.14 is truncated to save space and doesn't show all results, but there are no rows returned with NULL values in the customer table columns, because there is no such thing as a purchase without a customer_id. And because we did a RIGHT JOIN, we will no longer get customers without purchases in the results.

customer_id	customer_first_name	customer_last_name	customer_zip	product_id	vendor_id	market_date	customer_id	quantity	cost_to_cust	transacti
4	Deanna	Washington	22801	4	8	2019-03-02	4	2.00	4.00	10:22:00
10	Russell	Edwards	22801	4	8	2019-05-02	10	1.00	4.00	09:12:00
12	Jack	Wise	22803	4	8	2019-03-09	12	1.00	4.00	13:03:00
5	Abigail	Harris	22801	7	9	2019-03-09	5	1.00	16.00	10:41:00
1	Jane	Connor	22801	8	9	2019-03-09	1	1.00	18.00	08:25:00
12	Jack	Wise	22803	8	9	2019-03-09	12	3.00	18.00	13:18:00
2	Manuel	Diaz	22803	9	4	2019-03-02	2	4.60	2.00	10:53:00
3	Bob	Wilson	22803	9	4	2019-03-02	3	8.40	2.00	11:39:00
4	Deanna	Washington	22801	9	4	2019-03-02	4	1.40	2.00	10:31:00
4	Deanna	Washington	22801	9	4	2019-03-09	4	9.90	2.00	13:02:00
1	Jane	Connor	22801	10	1	2019-03-02	1	1.00	5.50	08:59:00
1	Jane	Connor	22801	10	1	2019-03-02	1	3.00	5.00	09:31:00
1	Jane	Connor	22801	10	1	2019-03-09	1	2.00	5.50	08:30:00

Figure 5.14

If you only want records from each table that have matches in both tables, use an INNER JOIN. Using these `customer` and `customer_purchases` tables, an INNER JOIN happens to return the same results as the RIGHT JOIN, because there aren't any records on the "right side" of the join without matches on the "left side"—every purchase is associated with a customer.

A Common Pitfall when Filtering Joined Data

Going back to the LEFT JOIN example between the `customer` and `customer_purchases` tables whose output is depicted in Figure 5.12, how do you think the output of the following query will differ from the original LEFT JOIN query without the added WHERE clause?

```
SELECT *
FROM customer AS c
LEFT JOIN customer_purchases AS cp
    ON c.customer_id = cp.customer_id
WHERE cp.customer_id > 0
```

All `customer_id` values are integers above 0, so it might initially appear like the addition of this WHERE clause will make no difference in the output. However, notice that it is filtering on the `customer_id` on the "right side" table, `customer_purchases` (note the alias cp in the WHERE clause). That means that the customers without purchases will be filtered out, because they wouldn't have matching records in the `customer_purchases` table. The addition of this filter makes the query return results like an INNER JOIN instead of a LEFT JOIN, by filtering out records that return NULL values on the "right side" table columns in the output. So, instead of the output shown in Figure 5.12, this query's output would look like the one shown in Figure 5.14.

If you are using a LEFT JOIN because you want to return all rows from the "left" table, even those that don't have a match on the "right" side of the join, be sure not to filter on any fields from the "right" table without also allowing NULL results on the right side, or you will filter out results you intended to keep.

Let's say we want to write a query that returns a list of all customers who did *not* make a purchase at the March 2, 2019, farmer's market. We will use a LEFT JOIN, since we want to include the customers who have never made a purchase at any farmer's market, so wouldn't have any records in the customer_purchases table:

```
SELECT c.*, cp.market_date
FROM customer AS c
LEFT JOIN customer_purchases AS cp
    ON c.customer_id = cp.customer_id
WHERE cp.market_date <> '2019-03-02'
```

Figure 5.15 displays the output we get with this query. There are multiple problems with this output.

customer_id	customer_first_name	customer_last_name	customer_zip	market_date
1	Jane	Connor	22801	2019-03-09
1	Jane	Connor	22801	2019-03-09
1	Jane	Connor	22801	2019-03-09
2	Manuel	Diaz	22803	2019-03-13
2	Manuel	Diaz	22803	2019-03-13
3	Bob	Wilson	22803	2019-03-16
3	Bob	Wilson	22803	2019-03-16
4	Deanna	Washington	22801	2019-03-09
4	Deanna	Washington	22801	2019-03-09
4	Deanna	Washington	22801	2019-03-09
4	Deanna	Washington	22801	2019-03-09
5	Abigail	Harris	22801	2019-03-09
7	Jessica	Armenta	22803	2019-03-09
10	Russell	Edwards	22801	2019-03-16
12	Jack	Wise	22803	2019-03-09
12	Jack	Wise	22803	2019-03-09
12	Jack	Wise	22803	2019-03-16
12	Jack	Wise	22803	2019-03-09
12	Jack	Wise	22803	2019-03-09

Figure 5.15

The first problem is that we're missing customers who have never made a purchase, like Betty Bullard shown in Figure 5.12, since we filtered to the market_date field in the customer_purchases table, which is on the "right side" of the JOIN, and because (as shown in Chapter 3) SQL doesn't evaluate value comparisons to TRUE when one of the values being compared is NULL. But we need that filter in order to remove customers who made a purchase that day.

One solution that will allow us to filter the results returned using a field in the table on the right side of the join while still returning records that only exist in the left side table is to write the WHERE clause to allow NULL values in the field:

```
SELECT c.*, cp.market_date
FROM customer AS c
LEFT JOIN customer_purchases AS cp
    ON c.customer_id = cp.customer_id
WHERE (cp.market_date <> '2019-03-02' OR cp.market_date IS NULL)
```

customer_id	customer_first_name	customer_last_name	customer_zip	market_date
1	Jane	Connor	22801	2019-03-09
1	Jane	Connor	22801	2019-03-09
1	Jane	Connor	22801	2019-03-09
2	Manuel	Diaz	22803	2019-03-13
2	Manuel	Diaz	22803	2019-03-13
3	Bob	Wilson	22803	2019-03-16
3	Bob	Wilson	22803	2019-03-16
4	Deanna	Washington	22801	2019-03-09
4	Deanna	Washington	22801	2019-03-09
4	Deanna	Washington	22801	2019-03-09
4	Deanna	Washington	22801	2019-03-09
5	Abigail	Harris	22801	2019-03-09
6	Betty	Bullard	22801	NULL
7	Jessica	Armenta	22803	2019-03-09
8	Norma	Valenzuela	22803	NULL
9	Janet	Forbes	22801	NULL
10	Russell	Edwards	22801	2019-03-16
11	Richard	Paulson	22801	NULL
12	Jack	Wise	22803	2019-03-09
12	Jack	Wise	22803	2019-03-09
12	Jack	Wise	22803	2019-03-16

Figure 5.16

Now we see customers without purchases in Figure 5.16, like Betty Bullard, in addition to customers who have made purchases on other dates.

The second problem with this output is that it contains one row per customer per item purchased, because the customer_purchases table has a record for each item purchased, when we just wanted a list of customers. We can resolve this problem by removing the market_date field from the customer_purchases "side" of the relationship, so the purchase dates aren't displayed, then using the DISTINCT keyword, which removes duplicate records in the output, only displaying distinct (unique) results. Figure 5.17 shows the output associated with the following query:

```
SELECT DISTINCT c.*
FROM customer AS c
LEFT JOIN customer_purchases AS cp
    ON c.customer_id = cp.customer_id
WHERE (cp.market_date <> '2019-03-02' OR cp.market_date IS NULL)
```

customer_id	customer_first_name	customer_last_name	customer_zip
1	Jane	Connor	22801
2	Manuel	Diaz	22803
3	Bob	Wilson	22803
4	Deanna	Washington	22801
5	Abigail	Harris	22801
6	Betty	Bullard	22801
7	Jessica	Armenta	22803
8	Norma	Valenzuela	22803
9	Janet	Forbes	22801
10	Russell	Edwards	22801
11	Richard	Paulson	22801
12	Jack	Wise	22803
13	Jeremy	Gruber	22803
14	William	Lopes	22801
15	Darrell	Messina	22801

Figure 5.17

With this approach, we were able to filter out records we didn't want, using values on the `customer_purchases` side of the relationship, without excluding records we did want from the `customer` side of the relationship. And, we only displayed data from one of the tables, even though we were using fields from both in the query.

JOINs with More than Two Tables

Let's say we want details about all farmer's market booths, as well as every vendor booth assignment for every market date. Perhaps we're building an interactive report that lets us filter to a booth, a vendor, or a date, to see the resulting list of booth assignments with additional both and vendor details, so we need a merged dataset that contains all of their records. This requires joining the three tables shown in Figure 5.18 together.

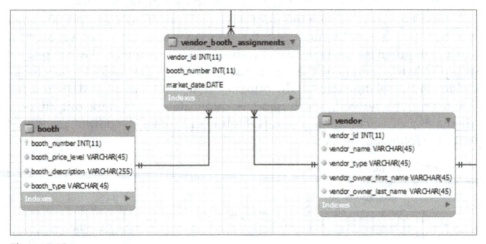

Figure 5.18

What kind of JOINs do you think we could use to ensure that all booths are included, even if they aren't assigned to a vendor yet, and all vendors assigned to booths are included?

We can LEFT JOIN the `vendor_booth_assignments` to `booth`, therefore including all of the booths, and LEFT JOIN `vendor` to `vendor_booth_assignments` in the results. The query to accomplish these joins looks like the following and results in Figure 5.19:

```
SELECT
    b.booth_number,
    b.booth_type,
```

```
        vba.market_date,
        v.vendor_id,
        v.vendor_name,
        v.vendor_type
FROM booth AS b
    LEFT JOIN vendor_booth_assignments AS vba ON b.booth_number = vba.
booth_number
    LEFT JOIN vendor AS v ON v.vendor_id = vba.vendor_id
ORDER BY b.booth_number, vba.market_date
```

booth_number	booth_type	market_date	vendor_id	vendor_name	vendor_type
1	Standard	2019-03-02	3	Hernández Salsa & Veggies	Fresh Variety: Veggies & More
1	Standard	2019-03-09	3	Hernández Salsa & Veggies	Fresh Variety: Veggies & More
1	Standard	2019-03-13	3	Hernández Salsa & Veggies	Fresh Variety: Veggies & More
2	Standard	2019-03-02	1	Chris's Sustainable Eggs & Meats	Eggs & Meats
2	Standard	2019-03-09	1	Chris's Sustainable Eggs & Meats	Eggs & Meats
2	Standard	2019-03-13	4	Mountain View Vegetables	Fresh Variety: Veggies & More
3	Small	NULL	NULL	NULL	NULL
4	Small	NULL	NULL	NULL	NULL
5	Small	NULL	NULL	NULL	NULL
6	Small	2019-03-02	8	Marco's Peppers	Fresh Focused
6	Small	2019-03-09	8	Marco's Peppers	Fresh Focused
6	Small	2019-03-13	8	Marco's Peppers	Fresh Focused
7	Standard	2019-03-02	4	Mountain View Vegetables	Fresh Variety: Veggies & More
7	Standard	2019-03-09	4	Mountain View Vegetables	Fresh Variety: Veggies & More
8	Small	2019-03-02	9	Annie's Pies	Prepared Foods
8	Small	2019-03-09	9	Annie's Pies	Prepared Foods
8	Small	2019-03-13	10	Mediterranean Bakery	Prepared Foods

Figure 5.19

You can think of the second JOIN as being merged into the result of the first JOIN. Because in this case the vendor_id field in the third table, vendor, is joined to the vendor_id field in the second table, vendor_booth_assignments, only vendors that exist in the vendor_booth_assignments table will be included, resembling the diagram shown in Figure 5.20.

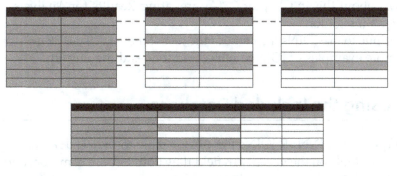

Table LEFT JOINed to a table on the RIGHT
side of an existing LEFT JOIN

All rows from the "left table", only rows from the "middle table" with matching
values in the specified fields of the "left table", and only rows from the "right table"
with matching values in the specified fields of the "middle table".

Figure 5.20

If the third table was instead joined to the first table, using a field common to both of them (which is common, but isn't actually possible using the tables in this Farmer's Market database, because there aren't any other tables joined to the booth table), the arrangement would look like the diagram in Figure 5.21.

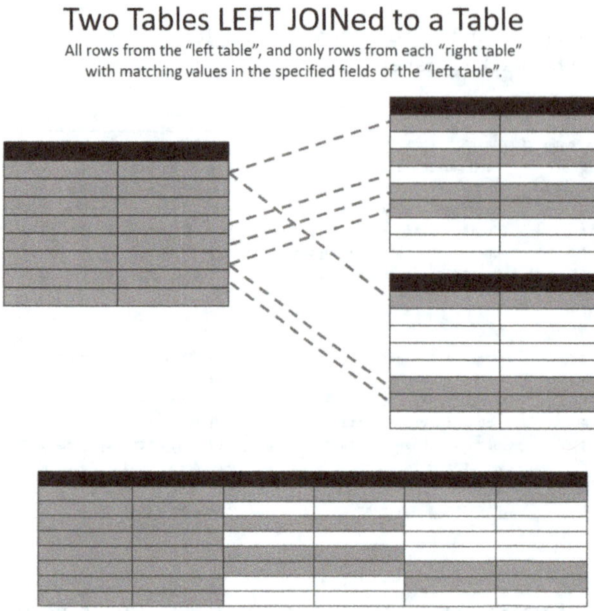

Two Tables LEFT JOINed to a Table
All rows from the "left table", and only rows from each "right table"
with matching values in the specified fields of the "left table".

Figure 5.21

This method of joining multiple tables together is a common one that you will see in machine learning applications, where you have one "primary" table that contains one row per entity record you want data summarized for, with many other tables LEFT JOINed into it. This allows you to pull additional data about the entity in from other tables. Data in these other tables is frequently summarized, so the resulting dataset remains at one row per input example, and data from other tables is represented by counts or sums, for example. You will learn more about this in Chapter 6, "Aggregating Results for Analysis," when we cover aggregation.

We will continue to use JOINs throughout the rest of the book, so look in later chapters for more examples of JOINed tables and the resulting output.

Exercises Using the Included Database

1. Write a query that INNER JOINs the vendor table to the vendor_booth_ assignments table on the vendor_id field they both have in common, and sorts the result by vendor_name, then market_date.

2. Is it possible to write a query that produces an output identical to the output of the following query, but using a LEFT JOIN instead of a RIGHT JOIN?

```
SELECT *
FROM customer AS c
RIGHT JOIN customer_purchases AS cp
    ON c.customer_id = cp.customer_id
```

3. At the beginning of this chapter, the analytical question "When is each type of fresh fruit or vegetable in season, locally?" was asked, and it was explained that the answer requires data from the product_category table, the product table, and the vendor_inventory table. What type of JOINs do you expect would be needed to combine these three tables in order to be able to answer this question?

Aggregating Results for Analysis

SQL starts becoming especially powerful for analysis when you use it to aggregate data. By using the GROUP BY statement, you can specify the level of summarization and then use aggregate functions to summarize values for the records in each group.

Data analysts can use SQL to build dynamic summary reports that can be automatically updated as the database is updated with new data, by simply triggering a refresh that reruns the query. Dashboards and reports built using software like Tableau and Cognos often rely on SQL queries to get the data they need from the underlying database in an aggregated form that can be used for reporting, which we'll cover in Chapter 10, "Building Analytical Reports with SQL." Data scientists can use SQL to summarize data at the level of granularity needed for training a classification model, which we'll get into in more depth in Chapter 12, "SQL for Machine Learning."

But it all starts with basic SQL aggregation.

GROUP BY Syntax

You saw this basic SQL SELECT query syntax in Chapter 2, "The SELECT Statement." Two sections of this query that we haven't yet covered, which are both related to aggregation, are the GROUP BY and HAVING clauses:

SELECT [columns to return]

FROM [table]

WHERE [conditional filter statements]

GROUP BY [columns to group on]

HAVING [conditional filter statements that are run after grouping]

ORDER BY [columns to sort on]

The GROUP BY keywords are followed by a comma-separated list of column names that indicate how you want to summarize the query results.

Using what you've learned so far without grouping, you might write a query like the following to get a list of the customer IDs of customers who made purchases on each market date:

```
SELECT
    market_date,
    customer_id
FROM farmers_market.customer_purchases
ORDER BY market_date, customer_id
```

However, this approach would result in one row per item each customer purchased, displaying duplicates in the output, because you're querying the customer_purchases table with no grouping specified.

To instead get one row per customer per market date, you can group the results by adding a GROUP BY clause that specifies that you want to summarize the results by the customer_id and market_date fields:

```
SELECT
    market_date,
    customer_id
FROM farmers_market.customer_purchases
GROUP BY market_date, customer_id
ORDER BY market_date, customer_id
```

You can also accomplish the same result by using SELECT DISTINCT to remove duplicates, but here we are using GROUP BY with the intention of adding summary columns to the output.

Displaying Group Summaries

Now that you have grouped the data at the desired level, you can add aggregate functions like SUM and COUNT to return summaries of the customer_purchases data per group. This query uses the COUNT() function to count the rows in the customer_purchases table per market date per customer. The output of this query is shown in Figure 6.1.

```
SELECT
    market_date,
    customer_id,
    COUNT(*) AS items_purchased
FROM farmers_market.customer_purchases
GROUP BY market_date, customer_id
ORDER BY market_date, customer_id
LIMIT 10
```

market_date	customer_id	items_purchased
2019-03-02	1	3
2019-03-02	2	1
2019-03-02	3	1
2019-03-02	4	2
2019-03-02	10	1
2019-03-09	1	4
2019-03-09	4	5
2019-03-09	5	1
2019-03-09	7	1
2019-03-09	12	4

Figure 6.1

Now, remember that the granularity of the `customer_purchases` table is such that if a customer were to buy three identical items, such as tomatoes, at once from a vendor, that would show up as 1 in the `items_purchased` column of this query's output, since the item purchase is recorded in one row in the table, with a `quantity` value of 3. (See Figures 1.7 and 2.7 in Chapters 1, "Data Sources," and 2 for reference.) If the customer were to buy three tomatoes, walk away from the stand, then go back and purchase another three tomatoes, that would be counted as two by the preceding query, since the new separate purchase would generate a new line in the database.

If instead of counting up line items, we wanted to add up all quantities purchased, to count all six tomatoes, we can sum up the quantity column using the following query. The output of this query is shown in Figure 6.2.

```
SELECT
    market_date,
    customer_id,
    SUM(quantity) AS items_purchased
FROM farmers_market.customer_purchases
GROUP BY market_date, customer_id
ORDER BY market_date, customer_id
LIMIT 10
```

market_date	customer_id	items_purchased
2019-03-02	1	5.70
2019-03-02	2	4.60
2019-03-02	3	8.40
2019-03-02	4	3.40
2019-03-02	10	1.00
2019-03-09	1	5.20
2019-03-09	4	13.20
2019-03-09	5	1.00
2019-03-09	7	2.00
2019-03-09	12	6.90

Figure 6.2

The `items_purchased` column is no longer an integer, because some of the quantities we're adding up are bulk product weights. After seeing these results and realizing bulk weight quantities are included, you may decide that it doesn't make sense to report the purchases this way, and you instead want to know how many different kinds of items were purchased by each customer. So now you only want to count "1" if they bought tomatoes, no matter how many individual tomatoes they purchased, or how many times they checked out, and only add to that count if they bought other items, such as lettuce.

> **NOTE** Note that this type of modification occurs frequently while designing reports—either by the data analyst or by the requester/customer—so it's important to understand the granularity and structure of the underlying table to ensure that your result means what you think it does. This is why I recommend writing the query without aggregation first to see the values you will be summarizing before grouping the results.

What you want now is a `DISTINCT` count of product IDs, shown in the following query and in Figure 6.3. So instead of counting how many rows there were in the `customer_purchases` table per customer per market date, like we did with `COUNT(*)`, or adding up the quantities, like we did with `SUM(quantity)`, we're identifying how many unique `product_id` values exist across those rows in the group—how many different kinds of products were purchased by each customer on each market date:

```
SELECT
    market_date,
    customer_id,
    COUNT(DISTINCT product_id) AS different_products_purchased
FROM farmers_market.customer_purchases c
GROUP BY market_date, customer_id
ORDER BY market_date, customer_id
LIMIT 10
```

market_date	customer_id	different_products_purchased
2019-03-02	1	2
2019-03-02	2	1
2019-03-02	3	1
2019-03-02	4	2
2019-03-02	10	1
2019-03-09	1	3
2019-03-09	4	4
2019-03-09	5	1
2019-03-09	7	1
2019-03-09	12	4

Figure 6.3

We can also combine these summaries into a single query, as shown here and in Figure 6.4:

```
SELECT
    market_date,
    customer_id,
    SUM(quantity) AS items_purchased,
    COUNT(DISTINCT product_id) AS different_products_purchased
FROM farmers_market.customer_purchases
GROUP BY market_date, customer_id
ORDER BY market_date, customer_id
LIMIT 10
```

market_date	customer_id	items_purchased	different_products_purchased
2019-03-02	1	5.70	2
2019-03-02	2	4.60	1
2019-03-02	3	8.40	1
2019-03-02	4	3.40	2
2019-03-02	10	1.00	1
2019-03-09	1	5.20	3
2019-03-09	4	13.20	4
2019-03-09	5	1.00	1
2019-03-09	7	2.00	1
2019-03-09	12	6.90	4

Figure 6.4

You can include as many different aggregate functions as you want in a single query, and they will all be applied at the same level of grouping—in this case, summarizing per market date per customer ID. Note how we are using column name aliases to describe the different summary values.

If you do want to sum up the quantities but don't like how the "items purchased" column includes both discrete items and bulk weights (some of which may be in pounds and some in ounces, so shouldn't be added together, anyway), we will demonstrate one possible solution later in the chapter in the "CASE Statements Inside Aggregate Functions" section.

Performing Calculations Inside Aggregate Functions

You can also include mathematical operations, which are calculated at the row level prior to summarization, inside the aggregate functions. In Chapter 3, "The WHERE Clause," you learned how to display a list of customer purchases at the farmer's market, using a WHERE clause to filter it to a specific customer. The customer with ID 3 has purchased the items in Figure 6.5, which can be retrieved using the following query that calculates the price per line item:

```
SELECT
    market_date,
    customer_id,
    vendor_id,
    quantity * cost_to_customer_per_qty AS price
FROM farmers_market.customer_purchases
WHERE
    customer_id = 3
ORDER BY market_date, vendor_id
```

market_date	customer_id	vendor_id	price
2019-03-02	3	4	16.8000
2019-03-16	3	4	11.0000
2019-03-16	3	9	18.0000

Figure 6.5

Let's say we wanted to know how much money this customer spent total on each market_date, regardless of item or vendor. We can GROUP BY market_date, and use the SUM aggregate function on the price calculation to add up the prices of the items purchased, as follows:

```
SELECT
    customer_id,
    market_date,
    SUM(quantity * cost_to_customer_per_qty) AS total_spent
FROM farmers_market.customer_purchases
WHERE
    customer_id = 3
GROUP BY market_date
ORDER BY market_date
```

The SUM() function surrounds the "price" calculation, which means that the price will be calculated per row of the table, as we saw in the first query, and then the results will be summed up per group—in this case, per market date.

The summarized results are shown in Figure 6.6, where you can see that the prices of the two line items from March 16, 2019 have been added up, and the alias has been updated to total_spent to better reflect the meaning of the summarized value. We grouped by `customer_id` and `market_date`, so there is now just one summarized row per `customer_id` per `market_date`.

customer_id	market_date	total_spent
3	2019-03-02	16.8000
3	2019-03-16	29.0000

Figure 6.6

Notice that `vendor_id` has been removed from the list of columns to be displayed and from the ORDER BY clause. That's because if we want the aggregation level of one row per customer per date, we can't also include `vendor_id` in the output, because the customer can purchase from multiple vendors on a single date, so the results wouldn't be aggregated at the level we wanted.

Even though it's not required in order to get these results, we should also add `customer_id` to the GROUP BY list, so the query will work without error even when it's not filtered to a single customer. We'll make this change in the next query.

What if we wanted to find out how much this customer had spent at each vendor, regardless of date? Then we can group by `customer_id` and `vendor_id`:

```
SELECT
    customer_id,
    vendor_id,
    SUM(quantity * cost_to_customer_per_qty) AS total_spent
FROM farmers_market.customer_purchases
WHERE
    customer_id = 3
GROUP BY customer_id, vendor_id
ORDER BY customer_id, vendor_id
```

The results of this query are shown in Figure 6.7.

customer_id	vendor_id	total_spent
3	4	27.8000
3	9	18.0000

Figure 6.7

We can also remove the `customer_id` filter—in this case by removing the entire WHERE clause since there are no other filter values—and GROUP BY `customer_id` only, to get a list of every customer and how much they have ever spent at the farmer's market. The results of the following query are shown in Figure 6.8:

```
SELECT
    customer_id,
    SUM(quantity * cost_to_customer_per_qty) AS total_spent
FROM farmers_market.customer_purchases
```

Continues

(continued)

```
GROUP BY customer_id
ORDER BY customer_id
```

customer_id	total_spent
1	100.3750
2	25.4000
3	45.8000
4	66.6250
5	16.0000
7	15.0000
10	8.0000
12	95.8000

Figure 6.8

So far, we have been doing all of this aggregation on a single table, but it can be done on joined tables, as well. It's a good idea to join the tables without the aggregate functions first, to make sure the data is at the level of granularity you expect (and not generating duplicates) before adding the GROUP BY.

Let's say that for the query that was grouped by customer_id and vendor_id, we want to bring in some customer details, such as first and last name, and the vendor name. We can first join the three tables together, select columns from all of the tables, and inspect the output before grouping, as shown in Figure 6.9:

```
SELECT
    c.customer_first_name,
    c.customer_last_name,
    cp.customer_id,
    v.vendor_name,
    cp.vendor_id,
    cp.quantity * cp.cost_to_customer_per_qty AS price
FROM farmers_market.customer c
    LEFT JOIN farmers_market.customer_purchases cp
        ON c.customer_id = cp.customer_id
    LEFT JOIN farmers_market.vendor v
        ON cp.vendor_id = v.vendor_id
WHERE
    cp.customer_id = 3
ORDER BY cp.customer_id, cp.vendor_id
```

customer_first_name	customer_last_name	customer_id	vendor_name	vendor_id	price
Bob	Wilson	3	Mountain View Vegetables	4	16.8000
Bob	Wilson	3	Mountain View Vegetables	4	11.0000
Bob	Wilson	3	Annie's Pies	9	18.0000

Figure 6.9

To summarize at the level of one row per customer per vendor, we will have to group by a lot more fields, including all of the customer table fields and all of the vendor table fields. Basically, we want to group by all of the displayed fields that don't include aggregate functions. The following query shows the list of fields used for grouping, and the output of this query is shown in Figure 6.10. The ROUND() function was added here to format the total_spent calculation nicely in dollar form:

```
SELECT
    c.customer_first_name,
    c.customer_last_name,
    cp.customer_id,
    v.vendor_name,
    cp.vendor_id,
    ROUND(SUM(quantity * cost_to_customer_per_qty), 2) AS total_spent
FROM farmers_market.customer c
    LEFT JOIN farmers_market.customer_purchases cp
        ON c.customer_id = cp.customer_id
    LEFT JOIN farmers_market.vendor v
        ON cp.vendor_id = v.vendor_id
WHERE
    cp.customer_id = 3
GROUP BY
    c.customer_first_name,
    c.customer_last_name,
    cp.customer_id,
    v.vendor_name,
    cp.vendor_id
ORDER BY cp.customer_id, cp.vendor_id
```

customer_first_name	customer_last_name	customer_id	vendor_name	vendor_id	total_spent
Bob	Wilson	3	Mountain View Vegetables	4	27.80
Bob	Wilson	3	Annie's Pies	9	18.00

Figure 6.10

We can also keep the same level of aggregation and filter to a single vendor instead of a single customer, to get a list of customers per vendor instead of vendors per customer, as shown in the following code. Note that the only line of code that is changed is the WHERE clause condition, because even though we're changing the filter, we want the grouping level and the output fields to stay the same. You can see in Figure 6.11 that the customer_id column now has values other than 3, and the vendor_id column now is limited to vendor 9:

```
SELECT
    c.customer_first_name,
    c.customer_last_name,
    cp.customer_id,
    v.vendor_name,
    cp.vendor_id,
    ROUND(SUM(quantity * cost_to_customer_per_qty), 2) AS total_spent
FROM farmers_market.customer c
```

Continues

(continued)

```
    LEFT JOIN farmers_market.customer_purchases cp
        ON c.customer_id = cp.customer_id
    LEFT JOIN farmers_market.vendor v
        ON cp.vendor_id = v.vendor_id
WHERE
    cp.vendor_id = 9
GROUP BY
    c.customer_first_name,
    c.customer_last_name,
    cp.customer_id,
    v.vendor_name,
    cp.vendor_id
ORDER BY cp.customer_id, cp.vendor_id
```

customer_first_name	customer_last_name	customer_id	vendor_name	vendor_id	total_spent
Jane	Connor	1	Annie's Pies	9	18.00
Bob	Wilson	3	Annie's Pies	9	18.00
Abigail	Harris	5	Annie's Pies	9	16.00
Jack	Wise	12	Annie's Pies	9	72.00

Figure 6.11

Or, we could remove the WHERE clause altogether and get one row for every customer-vendor pair in the database. This would be useful as a query to support a reporting system that allows for front-end filtering, such as Tableau. The query can provide a list of any customer that has shopped at any vendor and the sum of how much they have spent, and the reporting tool can then allow the user to choose any customer or vendor, to narrow down the results dynamically.

You can now see how all of the basic SQL components you have learned in previous chapters are coming together to build analytical reports!

MIN and MAX

If we wanted to get the most and least expensive items per product category, considering the fact that each vendor sets their own prices and can adjust prices per customer (which is why the customer_purchases table has a cost_to_customer_per_qty field, so the original price can be overridden at the time of purchase, if needed), we will use the vendor_inventory table, which has a field for the original price the vendors set for each item they bring to market on each market date.

First, let's look at all of the available fields in the vendor_inventory table by using the following SELECT * query. The output is shown in Figure 6.12.

```
SELECT *
FROM farmers_market.vendor_inventory
ORDER BY original_price
LIMIT 10
```

market_date	quantity	vendor_id	product_id	original_price
2019-03-09	10.00	9	5	5.00
2019-03-30	17.00	7	13	6.00
2019-03-23	8.00	7	13	6.00
2019-03-02	13.00	1	10	6.00
2019-03-09	17.00	1	10	6.00
2019-03-09	8.00	7	13	6.00
2019-03-20	13.00	7	13	6.00
2019-03-02	28.00	1	11	12.00
2019-03-09	10.00	1	11	12.00
2019-03-20	15.00	1	11	13.00

Figure 6.12

We can get the least and most expensive item prices in the entire table by using the MIN() and MAX() functions without grouping in MySQL, as shown here and in Figure 6.13:

```
SELECT
    MIN(original_price) AS minimum_price,
    MAX(original_price) AS maximum_price
FROM farmers_market.vendor_inventory
ORDER BY original_price
```

minimum_price	maximum_price
2.00	18.00

Figure 6.13

But if we want to get the lowest and highest prices within each product category, we have to group by the product_category_id (and product_category_name, if we want to display it), then the summary values will be calculated per group, as shown in the following query and in Figure 6.14. Table aliases were added here since we're referencing multiple tables and need to distinguish which table each field is from:

```
SELECT
    pc.product_category_name,
    p.product_category_id,
    MIN(vi.original_price) AS minimum_price,
    MAX(vi.original_price) AS maximum_price
FROM farmers_market.vendor_inventory AS vi
    INNER JOIN farmers_market.product AS p
        ON vi.product_id = p.product_id
    INNER JOIN farmers_market.product_category AS pc
        ON p.product_category_id = pc.product_category_id
GROUP BY pc.product_category_name, p.product_category_id
```

product_category_name	product_category_id	minimum_price	maximum_price
Fresh Fruits & Vegetables	1	2.00	6.00
Packaged Prepared Food	3	4.00	18.00
Eggs & Meat (Fresh or Frozen)	6	6.00	13.00

Figure 6.14

If we were to also add columns for MIN(product_name) and MAX(product_name), we would not get the product names associated with the lowest and highest prices; instead, we would get the first and last product names, sorted alphabetically. If we wanted to get the products associated with these min and max prices per category, we would use window functions, which will be covered in the next chapter.

COUNT and COUNT DISTINCT

Suppose we wanted to count how many products were for sale on each market date, or how many different products each vendor offered. We can determine these values using COUNT and COUNT DISTINCT.

COUNT will count up the rows within a group when used with GROUP BY, and COUNT DISTINCT will count up the unique values present in the specified field within the group.

To determine how many products are offered for sale each market date, we can count up the rows in the vendor_inventory table, grouped by date. This doesn't tell us what quantity of each product was offered or sold (because we're not adding up the quantity column, or counting customer purchases), but counts the number of products available, because there is a row in this table for each product for each vendor for each market date.

Of course, the values shown in the screenshots are too small to be realistic numbers, because the database has only been populated with a small number of sample rows per table, but you can see in Figure 6.15 that the result is a count for each market_date.

```
SELECT
    market_date,
    COUNT(product_id) AS product_count
FROM farmers_market.vendor_inventory
GROUP BY market_date
ORDER BY market_date
```

If we wanted to know how many different products—with unique product IDs—each vendor brought to market during a date range, we could use COUNT DISTINCT on the product_id field, like so:

market_date	product_count
2019-03-02	4
2019-03-09	9
2019-03-13	2
2019-03-16	3
2019-03-20	3
2019-03-23	2
2019-03-30	2

Figure 6.15

```
SELECT
    vendor_id,
    COUNT(DISTINCT product_id) AS different_products_offered
FROM farmers_market.vendor_inventory
WHERE market_date BETWEEN '2019-03-02' AND '2019-03-16'
GROUP BY vendor_id
ORDER BY vendor_id
```

Note that the DISTINCT goes inside the parentheses for the COUNT() aggregate function. The results of the query are shown in Figure 6.16.

vendor_id	different_products_offered
1	2
4	1
7	2
8	1
9	3

Figure 6.16

Average

What if, in addition to the count of different products per vendor, we also want the average original price of a product per vendor? We can add a line to the preceding query, and use the AVG() function, like we do in the following query, with results shown in Figure 6.17:

```
SELECT
    vendor_id,
    COUNT(DISTINCT product_id) AS different_products_offered,
    AVG(original_price) AS average_product_price
FROM farmers_market.vendor_inventory
WHERE market_date BETWEEN '2019-03-02' AND '2019-03-16'
GROUP BY vendor_id
ORDER BY vendor_id
```

vendor_id	different_products_offered	average_product_price
1	2	9.000000
4	1	2.000000
7	2	4.500000
8	1	4.000000
9	3	14.750000

Figure 6.17

However, we have to think about what we're actually averaging here. Is it fair to call it "average product price" when the underlying table has one row per type of product? If the vendor brought 100 tomatoes to market, those would all be in one line of the underlying vendor inventory table, so the price of a tomato would only be included in the average once. Then if that same vendor also sold bouquets of flowers for $20, no matter how many bouquets they brought, that would only be included in the average once. If you calculated the "average product price" for the vendor this way, you would just get the average of the price of one tomato and one bouquet.

To get an actual average price of items in each vendor's inventory between the specified dates, it might make more sense to multiply the quantity of each type of item times the price of that item, which is a calculation that would occur per row, then sum that up and divide by the total quantity of items, which is a calculation that would occur per vendor. Let's try a calculation that includes these two summary values. We also surrounded the calculation with a ROUND() function to format the output in dollars, as shown in Figure 6.18.

```
SELECT
    vendor_id,
    COUNT(DISTINCT product_id) AS different_products_offered,
    SUM(quantity * original_price) AS value_of_inventory,
    SUM(quantity) AS inventory_item_count,
    ROUND(SUM(quantity * original_price) / SUM(quantity), 2) AS
average_item_price
FROM farmers_market.vendor_inventory
WHERE market_date BETWEEN '2019-03-02' AND '2019-03-16'
GROUP BY vendor_id
ORDER BY vendor_id
```

vendor_id	different_products_offered	value_of_inventory	inventory_item_count	average_item_price
1	2	636.0000	68.00	9.35
4	1	258.0000	129.00	2.00
7	2	105.0000	27.00	3.89
8	1	400.0000	100.00	4.00
9	3	410.0000	30.00	13.67

Figure 6.18

The multiplication of `quantity * original_price` inside the aggregate function is performed per row, then the aggregate SUMs are calculated, then the division of one SUM into the other to determine the "average item price" is calculated. So we're performing mathematical operations both before and after the GROUP BY summarization occurs.

Filtering with HAVING

Filtering is another thing that can be done in the query after summarization occurs.

In previous chapters and in the following query, we filtered rows using the WHERE clause. Here, we're filtering to a date range in the WHERE clause prior to grouping.

If you want to filter values after the aggregate functions are applied, you can add a HAVING clause to the query. This filters the groups based on the summary values.

So, modifying the previous query, let's filter to vendors who brought at least 100 items to the farmer's market over the specified time period. You can see the HAVING clause usage in the following code, and the results in Figure 6.19:

```
SELECT
    vendor_id,
    COUNT(DISTINCT product_id) AS different_products_offered,
    SUM(quantity * original_price) AS value_of_inventory,
    SUM(quantity) AS inventory_item_count,
    SUM(quantity * original_price) / SUM(quantity) AS average_item_price
FROM farmers_market.vendor_inventory
WHERE market_date BETWEEN '2019-03-02' AND '2019-03-16'
GROUP BY vendor_id
HAVING inventory_item_count >= 100
ORDER BY vendor_id
```

vendor_id	different_products_offered	value_of_inventory	inventory_item_count	average_item_price
4	1	258.0000	129.00	2.00000000
8	1	400.0000	100.00	4.00000000

Figure 6.19

TIP   If you GROUP BY all of the fields that are supposed to be distinct in your resulting dataset, then add a HAVING clause that filters to aggregated rows with a COUNT(*) > 1, any results returned indicate that there is more than one row with your "unique" combination of values, highlighting the existence of unwanted duplicates in your database or query results!

CASE Statements Inside Aggregate Functions

Earlier in this chapter, in the query that generated the output in Figure 6.4, we added up the quantity value in the `customer_purchases` table, which included discrete items sold individually as well as bulk items sold by ounce or pound, and it was awkward to add those quantities together. In Chapter 4, "Conditionals / CASE Statements," you learned about conditional `CASE` statements. Here, we'll use a `CASE` statement to specify which type of item quantities to add together using each `SUM` aggregate function.

First, we'll need to `JOIN` the `customer_purchases` table to the `product` table to pull in the `product_qty_type` column, which currently only contains the values "unit" and "lbs," as shown in Figure 6.20.

```
SELECT
      cp.market_date,
      cp.vendor_id,
      cp.customer_id,
      cp.product_id,
      cp.quantity,
      p.product_name,
      p.product_size,
      p.product_qty_type
FROM farmers_market.customer_purchases AS cp
      INNER JOIN farmers_market.product AS p
          ON cp.product_id = p.product_id
```

market_date	vendor_id	customer_id	product_id	quantity	product_name	product_size	product_qty_type
2019-03-02	8	10	4	1.00	Banana Peppers - Jar	8 oz	unit
2019-03-09	8	12	4	1.00	Banana Peppers - Jar	8 oz	unit
2019-03-13	8	2	4	2.00	Banana Peppers - Jar	8 oz	unit
2019-03-16	8	10	4	1.00	Banana Peppers - Jar	8 oz	unit
2019-03-02	4	2	9	4.60	Sweet Potatoes	medium	lbs
2019-03-02	4	3	9	8.40	Sweet Potatoes	medium	lbs
2019-03-02	4	4	9	1.40	Sweet Potatoes	medium	lbs
2019-03-09	4	4	9	9.90	Sweet Potatoes	medium	lbs
2019-03-13	4	2	9	4.10	Sweet Potatoes	medium	lbs
2019-03-16	4	3	9	5.50	Sweet Potatoes	medium	lbs
2019-03-02	1	1	10	1.00	Eggs	1 dozen	unit
2019-03-02	1	1	10	3.00	Eggs	1 dozen	unit
2019-03-09	1	1	10	2.00	Eggs	1 dozen	unit
2019-03-09	1	4	10	1.00	Eggs	1 dozen	unit
2019-03-02	1	1	11	1.70	Pork Chops	1 lb	lbs
2019-03-09	1	12	11	0.90	Pork Chops	1 lb	lbs

Figure 6.20

To create one column that only adds up quantities of products that are sold by unit, another column that adds up quantities of products sold by the pound, and a third for any products that may be entered in the future that are sold by other units (like bulk ounces), we'll put `CASE` statements inside the `SUM` functions to indicate which values to add up in each summary column.

First, we'll review the results with the `CASE` statements included before grouping or using aggregate functions. Notice in Figure 6.21 that the `CASE` statements have separated the quantity values into three different columns, by product_qty_type. These are the values we'll be adding up per group in the next step:

```
SELECT
    cp.market_date,
    cp.vendor_id,
    cp.customer_id,
    cp.product_id,
    CASE WHEN product_qty_type = "unit" THEN quantity ELSE 0 END AS
quantity_units,
    CASE WHEN product_qty_type = "lbs" THEN quantity ELSE 0 END AS
quantity_lbs,
    CASE WHEN product_qty_type NOT IN ("unit","lbs") THEN quantity ELSE
0 END AS quantity_other,
    p.product_qty_type
FROM farmers_market.customer_purchases cp
    INNER JOIN farmers_market.product p
        ON cp.product_id = p.product_id
```

market_date	vendor_id	customer_id	product_id	quantity_units	quantity_lbs	quantity_other	product_qty_type
2019-03-02	8	4	4	2.00	0	0	unit
2019-03-02	8	10	4	1.00	0	0	unit
2019-03-09	8	12	4	1.00	0	0	unit
2019-03-13	8	2	4	2.00	0	0	unit
2019-03-16	8	10	4	1.00	0	0	unit
2019-03-02	4	2	9	0	4.60	0	lbs
2019-03-02	4	3	9	0	8.40	0	lbs
2019-03-02	4	4	9	0	1.40	0	lbs
2019-03-09	4	4	9	0	9.90	0	lbs
2019-03-13	4	2	9	0	4.10	0	lbs
2019-03-16	4	3	9	0	5.50	0	lbs
2019-03-02	1	1	10	1.00	0	0	unit
2019-03-02	1	1	10	3.00	0	0	unit
2019-03-09	1	1	10	2.00	0	0	unit
2019-03-09	1	4	10	1.00	0	0	unit
2019-03-02	1	1	11	0	1.70	0	lbs
2019-03-09	1	12	11	0	0.90	0	lbs

Figure 6.21

Now we can add the SUM functions around each CASE statement to add up these values per market date per customer, as defined in the GROUP BY clause. The results are shown in Figure 6.22. (The prior screenshot was just a subset of the full results, so there may be values added into the rows in Figure 6.22 that are not visible in Figure 6.21.)

```
SELECT
    cp.market_date,
    cp.customer_id,
    SUM(CASE WHEN product_qty_type = "unit" THEN quantity ELSE 0 END) AS
qty_units_purchased,
    SUM(CASE WHEN product_qty_type = "lbs" THEN quantity ELSE 0 END) AS
qty_lbs_purchased,
    SUM(CASE WHEN product_qty_type NOT IN ("unit","lbs") THEN quantity
ELSE 0 END) AS qty_other_purchased
```

Continues

(continued)

```
FROM farmers_market.customer_purchases cp
    INNER JOIN farmers_market.product p
        ON cp.product_id = p.product_id
GROUP BY market_date, customer_id
ORDER BY market_date, customer_id
```

market_date	customer_id	qty_units_purchased	qty_lbs_purchased	qty_other_purchased
2019-03-02	1	4.00	1.70	0.00
2019-03-02	2	0.00	4.60	0.00
2019-03-02	3	0.00	8.40	0.00
2019-03-02	4	2.00	1.40	0.00
2019-03-02	10	1.00	0.00	0.00
2019-03-09	1	2.00	2.20	0.00
2019-03-09	4	3.00	10.20	0.00
2019-03-09	7	2.00	0.00	0.00
2019-03-09	12	3.00	0.90	0.00
2019-03-13	2	2.00	4.10	0.00
2019-03-16	3	0.00	5.50	0.00
2019-03-16	10	1.00	0.00	0.00
2019-03-20	1	0.00	3.10	0.00
2019-03-20	7	3.00	0.00	0.00
2019-03-23	4	3.00	2.40	0.00

Figure 6.22

So now you have seen examples of how to use COUNT, COUNT DISTINCT, SUM, AVG, MIN, and MAX aggregate SQL functions, as well as CASE statements and calculations inside the functions, and calculations performed with the summarized values. I hope that by now you are starting to dream up how to apply these skills to your own work!

Exercises Using the Included Database

1. Write a query that determines how many times each vendor has rented a booth at the farmer's market. In other words, count the vendor booth assignments per vendor_id.

2. In Chapter 5, "SQL Joins," Exercise 3, we asked "When is each type of fresh fruit or vegetable in season, locally?" Write a query that displays the product category name, product name, earliest date available, and latest date available for every product in the "Fresh Fruits & Vegetables" product category.

3. The Farmer's Market Customer Appreciation Committee wants to give a bumper sticker to everyone who has ever spent more than $50 at the market. Write a query that generates a list of customers for them to give stickers to, sorted by last name, then first name. (HINT: This query requires you to join two tables, use an aggregate function, and use the HAVING keyword.)

Window Functions and Subqueries

All of the functions that have been covered in this book so far, like ROUND(), return one value in each row of the results dataset. When GROUP BY is used, the functions operate on multiple values in an aggregated group of records, summarizing across multiple rows in the underlying dataset, like AVG(), but each value returned is associated with a single row in the results.

Window functions operate across multiple records, as well, but those records don't have to be grouped in the output. This gives the ability to put the values from one row of data into context compared to a group of rows, or partition, enabling an analyst to write queries that answer questions like: If the dataset were sorted, where would this row land in the results? How does a value in this row compare to a value in the prior row? How does a value in the current row compare to the average value for its group?

So, window functions return group aggregate calculations alongside individual row-level information for items in that group, or partition. They can also be used to rank or sort values within each partition.

One use for window functions in data science is to include some information from a past record alongside the most recent detail record related to an entity. For example, we could use window functions to get the date of the first purchase a person made at the farmer's market, to be returned alongside their detailed purchase records, which could then be used to determine how long they had been a customer at the time each purchase was made.

ROW NUMBER

Based on what you've learned in previous chapters, if you wanted to determine how much the most expensive product sold by each vendor costs, you could group the records in the `vendor_inventory` table by `vendor_id`, and return the maximum `original_price` value using the following query:

```
SELECT
    vendor_id,
    MAX(original_price) AS highest_price
FROM farmers_market.vendor_inventory
GROUP BY vendor_id
ORDER BY vendor_id
```

But this just gives you the price of the most expensive item per vendor. If you wanted to know which item was the most expensive, how would you determine which `product_id` was associated with that `MAX(original_price)` per vendor?

There is a window function that enables you to rank rows by a value—in this case, ranking products per vendor by price—called `ROW_NUMBER()`. This approach will allow you to maintain the detail-level information that you would otherwise lose by aggregating like we did in the preceding query:

```
SELECT
    vendor_id,
    market_date,
    product_id,
    original_price,
    ROW_NUMBER() OVER (PARTITION BY vendor_id ORDER BY original_price DESC) AS
price_rank
FROM farmers_market.vendor_inventoryORDER BY vendor_id, original_price DESC
```

Let's break that syntax down a bit. I would interpret the `ROW_NUMBER()` line as "number the rows of inventory per vendor, sorted by original price, in descending order." The part inside the parentheses says how to apply the `ROW_NUMBER()` function. We're going to `PARTITION BY vendor_id` (you can think of this like a `GROUP BY` without actually combining the rows, so we're telling it how to split the rows into groups, without aggregating). Then within the partition, the `ORDER BY` indicates how to sort the rows. So, we'll sort the rows by price, high to low, within each `vendor_id` partition, and number each row. That means the highest-priced item per vendor will be first, and assigned row number 1.

You can see in Figure 7.1 that for each vendor, the products are sorted by `original_price`, high to low, and the row numbering column is called `price_rank`. The row numbering starts over when you get to the next `vendor_id`, so the most expensive item per vendor has a `price_rank` of 1.

vendor_id	market_date	product_id	original_price	price_rank
1	2019-03-20	11	13.00	1
1	2019-03-02	11	12.00	2
1	2019-03-09	11	12.00	3
1	2019-03-02	10	6.00	4
1	2019-03-09	10	6.00	5
4	2019-03-16	9	2.00	4
4	2019-03-02	9	2.00	1
4	2019-03-09	9	2.00	2
4	2019-03-13	9	2.00	3
7	2019-03-09	13	6.00	1
7	2019-03-20	13	6.00	2
7	2019-03-23	13	6.00	3
7	2019-03-30	13	6.00	4
7	2019-03-20	12	3.00	6
7	2019-03-23	12	3.00	7
7	2019-03-30	12	3.00	8
7	2019-03-09	12	3.00	5

Figure 7.1

To return only the record of the highest-priced item per vendor, you can query the results of the previous query (which is called a subquery), and limit the output to the #1 ranked item per vendor_id. With this approach, you're not using a GROUP BY to aggregate the records. You're sorting the records within each partition (a set of records that share a value or combination of values—vendor_id in this case), then filtering to a value (the row number called price_rank here) that was evaluated over that partition. Figure 7.2 shows the highest-priced product per vendor using the following query:

```
SELECT * FROM
(
    SELECT
        vendor_id,
        market_date,
        product_id,
        original_price,
        ROW_NUMBER() OVER (PARTITION BY vendor_id ORDER BY original_price DESC) AS
price_rank
    FROM farmers_market.vendor_inventory
    ORDER BY vendor_id) x
WHERE x.price_rank = 1
```

vendor_id	market_date	product_id	original_price	price_rank
1	2019-03-20	11	13.00	1
4	2019-03-02	9	2.00	1
7	2019-03-09	13	6.00	1
8	2019-03-02	4	4.00	1
9	2019-03-09	7	18.00	1

Figure 7.2

This will only return one row per vendor, even if there are multiple products with the same price. To return all products with the highest price per vendor when there is more than one with the same price, use the RANK function found in the next section. If you want to determine which one of the multiple items gets returned by this ROW_NUMBER function, you can add additional sorting columns in the ORDER BY section of the ROW_NUMBER function. For example, you can sort by both original_price (descending) and market_date (ascending) to get the product brought to market by each vendor the earliest that had this top price.

You'll notice that the preceding query has a different structure than the queries we have written so far. There is one query embedded inside the other! Sometimes this is called "querying from a derived table," but is more commonly called a "subquery." What we're doing is treating the results of the "inner" SELECT statement like a table, here given the table alias x, selecting all columns from it, and filtering to only the rows with a particular ROW_NUMBER. Our ROW_NUMBER column is aliased price_rank, and we're filtering to price_rank = 1, because we numbered the rows by original_price in descending order, so the most expensive item will have the lowest row number.

The reason we have to structure this as a subquery is that the entire dataset has to be processed in order for the window function to find the highest price per vendor. So we can't filter the results using a WHERE clause (which you'll remember evaluates the conditional statements row by row) because when that filtering is applied, the ROW_NUMBER has not yet been calculated for every row.

Figure 7.3 illustrates which parts of the SQL statement are considered the "inner" and "outer" queries. The "outer" part of a subquery is processed *after* the "inner" query is complete, so the row numbers have been determined, and we can then filter by the values in the price_rank column.

```
 1 •   SELECT * FROM                    "outer" query
 2   ⊖ (
 3         SELECT                                                          "inner" query
 4             vi.vendor_id,
 5             vi.market_date,
 6             vi.product_id,
 7             vi.original_price,
 8             ROW_NUMBER() OVER (PARTITION BY vendor_id ORDER BY original_price DESC) AS price_rank
 9         FROM farmers_market.vendor_inventory vi
10         ORDER BY vi.vendor_id
11     ) x
12     WHERE x.price_rank = 1          "outer" query
```

Figure 7.3

TIP   Many SQL editors allow you to run the inner query by itself, by highlighting it and executing the selected SQL only. This allows you to preview the results of the inner query that will then be used by the outer query.

If we didn't use a subquery, and had attempted to filter based on the values in the `price_rank` field by adding a WHERE clause to the first query with the ROW_NUMBER function, we would get an error. The `price_rank` value is unknown at the time the WHERE clause conditions are evaluated per row, because the window functions have not yet had a chance to check the entire dataset to determine the ranking. If we tried to put the ROW_NUMBER function in the WHERE clause, instead of referencing the `price_rank` alias, we would get a different error, but for the same reason.

You will see the subquery format throughout this chapter, because if you want to do anything with the results of most window functions, you have to allow them to calculate across the entire dataset first. Then, by treating the results like a table, you can query from and filter by the results returned by the window functions.

Note that you can also use ROW_NUMBER without a PARTITION BY clause, to number every record across the whole result (instead of numbering per partition). If you were to use the same ORDER BY clause we did earlier, and eliminate the PARTITION BY clause, then only one item with the highest price in the entire results set would get the `price_rank` of 1, instead of one item per vendor.

RANK and DENSE RANK

Two other window functions are very similar to ROW_NUMBER and have the same syntax, but provide slightly different results.

The RANK function numbers the results just like ROW_NUMBER does, but gives rows with the same value the same ranking. If we run the same query as before, but replace ROW_NUMBER with RANK, we get the output shown in Figure 7.4.

```
SELECT
    vendor_id,
    market_date,
    product_id,
    original_price,
    RANK() OVER (PARTITION BY vendor_id ORDER BY original_price DESC) AS
price_rank
    FROM farmers_market.vendor_inventory
ORDER BY vendor_id, original_price DESC
```

If we used subquery structure and embedded this query inside another SELECT statement like we did previously, and filtered to `price_rank = 1`, multiple rows per vendor would be returned.

Notice in Figure 7.4 that the ranking for `vendor_id` 1 goes from 1 to 2 to 4, skipping 3. That's because there's a tie for second place, so there's no third place. If you don't want to skip numbers like this in your ranking when there is a tie

vendor_id	market_date	product_id	original_price	price_rank
1	2019-03-20	11	13.00	1
1	2019-03-02	11	12.00	2
1	2019-03-09	11	12.00	2
1	2019-03-02	10	6.00	4
1	2019-03-09	10	6.00	4
4	2019-03-16	9	2.00	1
4	2019-03-02	9	2.00	1
4	2019-03-09	9	2.00	1
4	2019-03-13	9	2.00	1
7	2019-03-09	13	6.00	1
7	2019-03-20	13	6.00	1
7	2019-03-23	13	6.00	1
7	2019-03-30	13	6.00	1
7	2019-03-20	12	3.00	5
7	2019-03-23	12	3.00	5
7	2019-03-30	12	3.00	5
7	2019-03-09	12	3.00	5

Figure 7.4

(so the items for vendor_id in the example would be numbered 1 and 2 instead of 1 and 5), use the DENSE_RANK function. If you don't want any ties in your numbering at all, and want each row to have its own number, use the ROW_NUMBER function (compare the output in Figure 7.4 to the output in Figure 7.1).

NTILE

The ROW_NUMBER() and RANK() functions can help answer a question that asks something like "What are the top 10 items sold at the farmer's market, by price?" (by filtering the results to rows numbered less than or equal to 10). But what if you were asked to return the "top tenth" of the inventory, when sorted by price? You could start by running a query that used the COUNT() function, dividing the number returned by 10, then writing another query that numbers the rows, and filtering to those with a row number less than or equal to the number you just determined. But that isn't a dynamic solution, and you'd have to modify it as the number of rows in the database changed.

The dynamic solution is to use the NTILE function. With NTILE, you specify a number inside the parentheses, NTILE(n), to indicate that you want the results broken up into n blocks. So, to get the top tenth, you could put 10 in the parentheses, with no partition (segmenting the entire results set), then filter to the rows in NTILE 1, like so:

```
SELECT
    vendor_id,
    market_date,
```

```
      product_id,
      original_price,
      NTILE(10) OVER (ORDER BY original_price DESC) AS price_ntile
      FROM farmers_market.vendor_inventory
  ORDER BY original_price DESC
```

If the number of rows in the results set can be divided evenly, the results will be broken up into *n* equally sized groups, labeled 1 to *n*. If they can't be divided up evenly, some groups will end up with one more row than others.

Note that the NTILE is only using the count of rows to split the groups (or to split the partition into groups, if you specify a partition), and is not using a field value to determine where to make the splits. Therefore, it's possible that two rows with the same value specified in the ORDER BY clause (two products with the same original_price, in this case) will end up in two different NTILE groups.

You can sort on additional fields if you want a little more control over how the rows are split into NTILE groups. But if you want to ensure that all items with the same price are grouped together, for example, then it would make more sense to use RANK than NTILE, because in that case, you aren't looking for evenly sized groupings.

Aggregate Window Functions

You learned about aggregate SQL functions like SUM() in Chapter 6, "Aggregating Results for Analysis," and in this chapter you have learned about window functions that partition the results set. Can you imagine how they might be used together? It turns out that you can use most aggregate functions across partitions like the window functions, returning an aggregate calculation for a partition on every row in that partition (or, for the whole results set, if you don't use the PARTITION BY clause). One way this approach can be used is to compare each row's value to the aggregate value for that grouped category.

For example, what if you are a farmer selling products at the market, and you want to know which of your products were above the average price per product on each market date? (Remember that because of the way our database is designed, this isn't a true average for the full inventory, because we're not multiplying by a quantity, but you can think of it as the average display price in a product catalog.) We can use the AVG() function as a window function, partitioned by market_date, and compare each product's price to that value. First, let's try using AVG() as a window function. The output of the following query is shown in Figure 7.5:

```
  SELECT
      vendor_id,
      market_date,
```

Continues

(continued)

```
            product_id,
            original_price,
            AVG(original_price) OVER (PARTITION BY market_date ORDER BY
    market_date)
                AS average_cost_product_by_market_date
        FROM farmers_market.vendor_inventory
```

vendor_id	market_date	product_id	original_price	average_cost_product_by_market_date
8	2019-03-02	4	4.00	6.000000
4	2019-03-02	9	2.00	6.000000
1	2019-03-02	10	6.00	6.000000
1	2019-03-02	11	12.00	6.000000
8	2019-03-09	4	4.00	8.222222
9	2019-03-09	5	5.00	8.222222
9	2019-03-09	7	18.00	8.222222
9	2019-03-09	8	18.00	8.222222
4	2019-03-09	9	2.00	8.222222
1	2019-03-09	10	6.00	8.222222
1	2019-03-09	11	12.00	8.222222
7	2019-03-09	12	3.00	8.222222
7	2019-03-09	13	6.00	8.222222
8	2019-03-13	4	4.00	3.000000
4	2019-03-13	9	2.00	3.000000

Figure 7.5

The AVG() function in this query is structured as a window function, meaning it has "OVER (PARTITION BY __ ORDER BY __)" syntax, so instead of returning a single row per group with the average for that group, like you would get with GROUP BY, this function displays the average for the partition on every row within the partition. You can see in Figure 7.5 that when you get to a new market_date value in the results dataset, the average_cost_product_by_market_date value changes.

Now, let's wrap that query inside another query (use it as a subquery) so we can compare the original price per item to the average cost of products on each market date that has been calculated by the window function. In this example, we are comparing the values in the last two columns of Figure 7.5. Remember that we can't compare the two values in the original query, because the window function is calculated over multiple rows and won't have a value for the partition yet when the WHERE clause filters are being applied row by row.

Using a subquery, we can filter the results to a single vendor, with vendor_id 1, and only display products that have prices above the market date's average product cost. Here we will also format the average_cost_product_by_market_date to two digits after the decimal point using the ROUND() function:

```
SELECT * FROM
(
    SELECT
        vendor_id,
        market_date,
```

```
        product_id,
        original_price,
        ROUND(AVG(original_price) OVER (PARTITION BY market_date ORDER BY
market_date), 2)
            AS average_cost_product_by_market_date
    FROM farmers_market.vendor_inventory
) x
WHERE x.vendor_id = 1
    AND x.original_price > x.average_cost_product_by_market_date
ORDER BY x.market_date, x.original_price DESC
```

Note that we will get different (and incorrect) results if we put the WHERE clause filtering by vendor_id inside the parentheses with the original query in this case. That's because the results set of the inner SELECT statement would be filtered to vendor_id 1 before the window function was calculated, we would only be calculating the average price of vendor 1's products! Since we want to compare vendor 1's prices on each market date to the average price of all vendors' products on each market date, we don't want to filter to vendor_id 1 until after the averages have been calculated, so we put the WHERE clause on the "outer" query outside the parentheses.

The results of the preceding query are shown in Figure 7.6. So vendor_id 1 had a single product, with product_id 11, that was above the average product cost on each of the market dates listed.

vendor_id	market_date	product_id	original_price	average_cost_product_by_market_date
1	2019-03-02	11	12.00	6.00
1	2019-03-09	11	12.00	8.22
1	2019-03-20	11	13.00	7.33

Figure 7.6

Another use of an aggregate window function is to count how many items are in each partition. The following is a query that counts how many different products each vendor brought to market on each date, and displays that count on each row. This way, even if the results weren't sorted in a way that let you quickly determine how many inventory rows there are for each vendor, you would know that the row you're looking at represents just one of the products in a counted set:

```
SELECT
    vendor_id,
    market_date,
    product_id,
    original_price,
    COUNT(product_id) OVER (PARTITION BY market_date, vendor_id)
vendor_product_count_per_market_date
    FROM farmers_market.vendor_inventory
ORDER BY vendor_id, market_date, original_price DESC
```

The output for this query is shown in Figure 7.7. You can see that even if I'm only looking at one row for vendor 9 on March 9, 2019, I would know that it is one of three products that vendor had in their inventory on that market date.

vendor_id	market_date	product_id	original_price	vendor_product_count_per_market_date
1	2019-03-02	11	12.00	2
1	2019-03-02	10	6.00	2
1	2019-03-09	11	12.00	2
1	2019-03-09	10	6.00	2
1	2019-03-20	11	13.00	1
4	2019-03-02	9	2.00	1
4	2019-03-09	9	2.00	1
4	2019-03-13	9	2.00	1
4	2019-03-16	9	2.00	1

Figure 7.7

You can also use aggregate window functions to calculate running totals. In the first query shown next, we're not using a PARTITION BY clause, so the running total of the price is calculated across the entire results set, in the sort order specified in the ORDER BY clause of the SUM() window function. The results are displayed in Figure 7.8.

```
SELECT customer_id,
    market_date,
    vendor_id,
    product_id,
    quantity * cost_to_customer_per_qty AS price,
    SUM(quantity * cost_to_customer_per_qty) OVER (ORDER BY market_date,
transaction_time, customer_id, product_id) AS running_total_purchases
FROM farmers_market.customer_purchases
```

customer_id	market_date	vendor_id	product_id	price	running_total_purchases
10	2019-03-02	8	4	4.0000	29.9000
1	2019-03-02	1	10	15.0000	44.9000
4	2019-03-02	8	4	8.0000	52.9000
4	2019-03-02	4	9	2.8000	55.7000
2	2019-03-02	4	9	9.2000	64.9000
3	2019-03-02	4	9	16.8000	81.7000
1	2019-03-09	9	8	18.0000	99.7000
1	2019-03-09	1	10	11.0000	110.7000
1	2019-03-09	7	13	12.6500	123.3500
1	2019-03-09	7	13	NULL	123.3500
4	2019-03-09	7	13	1.7250	125.0750
4	2019-03-09	7	13	NULL	125.0750
5	2019-03-09	9	7	16.0000	141.0750
7	2019-03-09	7	12	6.0000	147.0750

Figure 7.8

In this next query, we are calculating the same running total, but it is partitioned by customer_id. That means that each time we get to a new customer_id, the running total resets. So we're getting a running total of the cost of items purchased by each customer, sorted by the date and time, and the product ID (in case any two items have identical purchase times). The result is shown in Figure 7.9.

```
SELECT customer_id,
    market_date,
    vendor_id,
    product_id,
    quantity * cost_to_customer_per_qty AS price,
    SUM(quantity * cost_to_customer_per_qty) OVER (PARTITION BY
customer_id ORDER BY market_date, transaction_time, product_id) AS
customer_spend_running_total
FROM farmers_market.customer_purchases
```

customer_id	market_date	vendor_id	product_id	price	customer_spend_running_total
1	2019-03-09	9	8	18.0000	58.9000
1	2019-03-09	1	10	11.0000	69.9000
1	2019-03-09	7	13	12.6500	82.5500
1	2019-03-09	7	13	NULL	82.5500
1	2019-03-20	7	13	17.8250	100.3750
2	2019-03-02	4	9	9.2000	9.2000
2	2019-03-13	4	9	8.2000	17.4000
2	2019-03-13	8	4	8.0000	25.4000
3	2019-03-02	4	9	16.8000	16.8000
3	2019-03-16	9	8	18.0000	34.8000
3	2019-03-16	4	9	11.0000	45.8000

Figure 7.9

This SUM functions as a running total because of the combination of the PARTITION BY and ORDER BY clauses in the window function. We showed what happens when there is only an ORDER BY clause, and when both clauses are present. What do you expect to happen when there is only a PARTITION BY clause (and no ORDER BY clause)?

```
SELECT customer_id,
    market_date,
    vendor_id,
    product_id,
    ROUND(quantity * cost_to_customer_per_qty, 2) AS price,
    ROUND(SUM(quantity * cost_to_customer_per_qty) OVER (PARTITION BY
customer_id), 2) AS customer_spend_total
FROM farmers_market.customer_purchases
```

As hinted at by the field name alias, this version with no in-partition sorting calculates the total spent by the customer and displays that summary total on every row. So, without the ORDER BY, the SUM is calculated across the entire partition, instead of as a per-row running total, as shown in Figure 7.10. We also added the ROUND() function so this final output displays the prices with two numbers after the decimal point.

customer_id	market_date	vendor_id	product_id	price	customer_spend_total
1	2019-03-09	9	8	18.0000	100.3750
1	2019-03-02	1	10	5.5000	100.3750
1	2019-03-02	1	10	15.0000	100.3750
1	2019-03-09	1	10	11.0000	100.3750
1	2019-03-02	1	11	20.4000	100.3750
1	2019-03-09	7	13	12.6500	100.3750
1	2019-03-09	7	13	NULL	100.3750
1	2019-03-20	7	13	17.8250	100.3750
2	2019-03-13	8	4	8.0000	25.4000
2	2019-03-02	4	9	9.2000	25.4000
2	2019-03-13	4	9	8.2000	25.4000
3	2019-03-16	9	8	18.0000	45.8000
3	2019-03-02	4	9	16.8000	45.8000
3	2019-03-16	4	9	11.0000	45.8000

Figure 7.10

LAG and LEAD

With the running total example in the previous section, you can start to see how SQL can be used to calculate changes in a value over time.

Using the vendor_booth_assignments table in the Farmer's Market database, we can display each vendor's booth assignment for each market_date alongside their previous booth assignments using the LAG() function.

LAG retrieves data from a row that is a selected number of rows back in the dataset. You can set the number of rows (offset) to any integer value x to count x rows backwards, following the sort order specified in the ORDER BY section of the window function:

```
SELECT
    market_date,
    vendor_id,
    booth_number,
    LAG(booth_number,1) OVER (PARTITION BY vendor_id ORDER BY market_date,
vendor_id) AS previous_booth_number
FROM farmers_market.vendor_booth_assignments
ORDER BY market_date, vendor_id, booth_number
```

In this case, for each vendor_id for each market_date, we're pulling the booth_number the vendor had 1 market date in the past. As you can see in Figure 7.11, the values are all NULL for the first market date, because there is no prior market date to pull values from.

market_date	vendor_id	booth_number	previous_booth_number
2019-04-03	3	1	NULL
2019-04-03	4	7	NULL
2019-04-03	7	11	NULL
2019-04-03	8	6	NULL
2019-04-03	9	8	NULL
2019-04-06	1	2	2
2019-04-06	3	1	1
2019-04-06	4	7	7
2019-04-06	7	11	11
2019-04-06	8	6	6
2019-04-06	9	8	8
2019-04-10	1	7	2
2019-04-10	3	1	1
2019-04-10	4	2	7
2019-04-10	7	11	11
2019-04-10	8	6	6
2019-04-10	9	8	8

Figure 7.11

The recipient of a report like this, such as the manager of the farmer's market, may want to filter these query results to a specific market date to determine which vendors are new or changing booths that day, so we can contact them and ensure setup goes smoothly. We will create this report by wrapping the query with the LAG function in another query, which we can use to filter the results to a market_date and vendors whose current booth_number is different from their previous_booth_number:

```
SELECT * FROM
(
    SELECT
        market_date,
        vendor_id,
        booth_number,
        LAG(booth_number,1) OVER (PARTITION BY vendor_id ORDER BY market_
date, vendor_id) AS previous_booth_number
        FROM farmers_market.vendor_booth_assignments
        ORDER BY market_date, vendor_id, booth_number
) x
WHERE x.market_date = '2019-04-10'
        AND (x.booth_number <> x.previous_booth_number OR x.previous_
booth_number IS NULL)
```

If you look closely at Figure 7.11, you can see that for the April 10, 2019 market, vendor 1 and vendor 4 have swapped booths compared to the previous market date. This would be hard to spot from a printout of this output, but using the preceding query, we can return just the rows with booth changes on the specified date, as shown in Figure 7.12.

market_date	vendor_id	booth_number	previous_booth_number
2019-04-10	4	2	7
2019-04-10	1	7	2

Figure 7.12

To show another example use case, let's say we want to find out if the total sales on each market date are higher or lower than they were on the previous market date. In this example, we are going to use the `customer_purchases` table from the Farmer's Market database, and also add in a GROUP BY function, which the previous examples did not include. The window functions are calculated after the grouping and aggregation occurs.

First, we need to get the total sales per market date, using a GROUP BY and regular aggregate SUM. The results of the following query are shown in Figure 7.13:

```
SELECT
    market_date,
    SUM(quantity * cost_to_customer_per_qty) AS market_date_total_sales
FROM farmers_market.customer_purchases
GROUP BY market_date
ORDER BY market_date
```

market_date	market_date_total_sales
2019-03-02	81.7000
2019-03-09	171.4750
2019-03-13	16.2000
2019-03-16	51.0000
2019-03-20	26.8250
2019-03-23	22.8000
2019-03-30	3.0000

Figure 7.13

Then, we can add the LAG() window function to output the previous market_date's calculated sum on each row. We ORDER BY market_date in the window function to ensure it's the previous market date we're comparing to and not another date. You can see in Figure 7.14 that each row has a new total value (for that market date), as well as the previous market date's total:

```
SELECT
    market_date,
    SUM(quantity * cost_to_customer_per_qty) AS market_date_total_sales,
    LAG(SUM(quantity * cost_to_customer_per_qty), 1) OVER (ORDER BY
market_date) AS previous_market_date_total_sales
FROM farmers_market.customer_purchases
GROUP BY market_date
ORDER BY market_date
```

market_date	market_date_total_sales	previous_market_date_total_sales
2019-03-02	81.7000	NULL
2019-03-09	171.4750	81.7000
2019-03-13	16.2000	171.4750
2019-03-16	51.0000	16.2000
2019-03-20	26.8250	51.0000
2019-03-23	22.8000	26.8250
2019-03-30	3.0000	22.8000

Figure 7.14

LEAD works the same way as LAG, but it gets the value from the next row instead of the previous row (assuming the offset integer is 1). You can set the offset integer to any value x to count x rows forward, following the sort order specified in the ORDER BY section of the window function. If the rows are sorted by a time value, LAG would be retrieving data from the past, and LEAD would be retrieving data from the future (relative to the current row). These values can also now be used in calculations; for example, to determine the change in sales week to week.

This chapter just covers the tip of the iceberg when it comes to window functions! Look in the documentation for the type of database you're working with to see what other functions are available, and what caveats to be aware of for each. Some database systems offer additional capabilities. For example, PostgreSQL supports something called "window naming," Oracle has additional useful aggregate functions like LISTAGG (which operates on string values), and some database systems allow for additional clauses like RANGE.

Once you understand the concept of a window function and how to use it in your query, you have the knowledge you need to research and apply the many variations.

Exercises Using the Included Database

1. Do the following two steps:

    a. Write a query that selects from the customer_purchases table and numbers each customer's visits to the farmer's market (labeling each market date with a different number). Each customer's first visit is labeled 1, second visit is labeled 2, etc. (We are of course not counting visits where no purchases are made, because we have no record of those.) You can either display all rows in the customer_purchases table, with the counter changing on each new market date for each customer, or select only the unique market dates per customer (without purchase details) and number those visits. HINT: One of these approaches uses ROW_NUMBER() and one uses DENSE_RANK().

b. Reverse the numbering of the query from a part so each customer's most recent visit is labeled 1, then write another query that uses this one as a subquery and filters the results to only the customer's most recent visit.

2. Using a COUNT() window function, include a value along with each row of the customer_purchases table that indicates how many different times that customer has purchased that product_id.

3. In the last query associated with Figure 7.14 from the chapter, we used LAG and sorted by market_date. Can you think of a way to use LEAD in place of LAG, but get the exact same output?

CHAPTER 8

Date and Time Functions

Data scientists use date and time functions many different ways in our queries. We may use two dates to calculate a duration, for example. Many machine learning algorithms are "trained" to identify patterns in data from the past and use those patterns to predict future outcomes. In order to build a dataset for that purpose, we have to be able to filter queries by time range.

Often, datasets that are built for predictive models include summaries of activities within dynamic date ranges—for example, a count of some activity occurrence during each of the past three months. Or, in the case of time-series analysis, an input dataset might include one row per time period (hour, day, week, month) with a count of something associated with each time period; for example, the number of patients a doctor sees per week.

Many predictive models are time-bound. For example, the question "Will this first-time customer become a repeat customer?" will be further refined as "What is the likelihood that each first-time customer at today's farmer's market will return and make a second purchase within the next month?" To answer this question, we could create a dataset with a row for every customer, columns containing data values as of the time of their first purchase, and a binary "target variable" that indicates whether that customer made another purchase within a month of their first purchase date.

Let's look at some different ways to work with date and time values in our Farmer's Market database.

Setting datetime Field Values

The Farmer's Market `market_date_info` table doesn't include any fields stored as datetime values, so in order to demonstrate date and time functions without having to combine fields in every query, I'm going to first create a demonstration table with datetimes created by combining the `market_date` and `market_start_time` fields in the `market_date_info` table using the following query:

```
CREATE TABLE farmers_market.datetime_demo AS
(
    SELECT market_date,
        market_start_time,
        market_end_time,
        STR_TO_DATE(CONCAT(market_date, ' ', market_start_time), '%Y-%m-%d
%h:%i %p')
            AS market_start_datetime,
        STR_TO_DATE(CONCAT(market_date, ' ', market_end_time), '%Y-%m-%d
%h:%i %p')
            AS market_end_datetime
    FROM farmers_market.market_date_info
)
```

We will go over table creation in Chapter 14, "Storing Machine Learning Results," but I want to explain what the functions here are doing. Refer to Figure 8.1 to see data in the table generated by this query.

market_date	market_start_time	market_end_time	market_start_datetime	market_end_datetime
2019-03-02	8:00 AM	2:00 PM	2019-03-02 08:00:00	2019-03-02 14:00:00
2019-03-09	9:00 AM	2:00 PM	2019-03-09 09:00:00	2019-03-09 14:00:00
2019-03-13	4:00 PM	7:00 PM	2019-03-13 16:00:00	2019-03-13 19:00:00
2019-03-16	8:00 AM	2:00 PM	2019-03-16 08:00:00	2019-03-16 14:00:00
2019-03-20	4:00 PM	7:00 PM	2019-03-20 16:00:00	2019-03-20 19:00:00
2019-03-23	8:00 AM	2:00 PM	2019-03-23 08:00:00	2019-03-23 14:00:00
2019-03-27	4:00 PM	7:00 PM	2019-03-27 16:00:00	2019-03-27 19:00:00
2019-03-30	8:00 AM	2:00 PM	2019-03-30 08:00:00	2019-03-30 14:00:00

Figure 8.1

The innermost part of the nested functions in the line of the query used to create the `market_start_datetime` field concatenates the `market_date` and `market_start_time` into a single string value, using `CONCAT()`. The surrounding `STR_TO_DATE()` function, as you might guess, converts string values to date values. The string of percent signs and letters in single quotes at the end is an input parameter that tells the function how the date and time are formatted.

`%Y` is a 4-digit year, `%m` is a 2-digit month, `%d` is a 2-digit day, `%h` is the hour, `%i` represents the minutes, and `%p` indicates there is an AM/PM indicator in the time string. Every database system has some codes for the date and time formatting, which can be found in the documentation, but these values are common, originating from the C programming language.

NOTE   You can find the SQL date and time function documentation for any database system by searching the internet for "[database system] date and time functions." For MySQL 8.0, you can find this documentation at dev.mysql.com/doc/refman/8.0/en/date-and-time-functions.html.

The combination of functions in the query associated with Figure 8.1 is taking each date and time string, concatenating them into a combined datetime string, and converting that to a datetime data type. So, the final market_start_datetime and market_end_datetime fields are actually stored as datetime values, which we can then use to perform calculations, like finding the difference between two datetimes. The STR_TO_DATE() function does the type conversion to a date, time, or datetime, depending on the input. It will return a NULL value if the input string isn't formatted in a way it can interpret.

You'll notice that the dates in the final two columns in Figure 8.1 are formatted as YYYY-MM-DD, and the times are in 24-hour time (HH:MM:SS), which is one indication that the fields are datetimes (though I should note it would also be possible to format a string to look like a datetime using the DATE_FORMAT() function and a particular formatting string).

EXTRACT and DATE_PART

You will encounter datetime data types, such as timestamps, in the databases you work with and might only need a portion of the stored date and time value. For example, you might only want the month and day from a full date, in one field, with the year stripped out into a second field, to create a year-over-year comparison (to align and visualize daily totals from different years by month and day).

Depending on the database system you are using, the function that retrieves different portions of a datetime value may be called EXTRACT (MySQL), DATE_PART (Redshift), or DATEPART (Oracle and SQL Server). The example Farmer's Market database is in MySQL, so these examples use EXTRACT(), but the concepts are the same for the other functions, even though the syntax will vary. The market_start_datetime field in Figure 8.2 is an example of a MySQL datetime type field.

In addition to EXTRACT(), MySQL offers the functions DATE() and TIME() to extract the date and time parts of a datetime field, respectively (you put the datetime value inside the parentheses, and just the date or time portion is returned).

Using datetime values established in the datetime_demo table created in the previous section, we can EXTRACT date and time parts from the fields.

The following query demonstrates five different "date parts" that can be extracted from the datetime and results in the output shown in Figure 8.2. Using the time intervals allowed by the database system (see the documentation for others), you can extract portions of a datetime field as needed:

```
SELECT market_start_datetime,
    EXTRACT(DAY FROM market_start_datetime) AS mktsrt_day,
    EXTRACT(MONTH FROM market_start_datetime) AS mktsrt_month,
    EXTRACT(YEAR FROM market_start_datetime) AS mktsrt_year,
    EXTRACT(HOUR FROM market_start_datetime) AS mktsrt_hour,
    EXTRACT(MINUTE FROM market_start_datetime) AS mktsrt_minute
FROM farmers_market.datetime_demo
WHERE market_start_datetime = '2019-03-02 08:00:00'
```

market_start_datetime	mktsrt_day	mktsrt_month	mktsrt_year	mktsrt_hour	mktsrt_minute
2019-03-02 08:00:00	2	3	2019	8	0

Figure 8.2

There are also shortcuts for extracting the entire date and entire time from the datetime field, so you don't have to extract each part and re-concatenate it together. The following query and the output in Figure 8.3 demonstrate the DATE() and TIME() functions:

```
SELECT market_start_datetime,
    DATE(market_start_datetime) AS mktsrt_date,
    TIME(market_start_datetime) AS mktsrt_time
FROM farmers_market.datetime_demo
WHERE market_start_datetime = '2019-03-02 08:00:00'
```

market_start_datetime	mktsrt_date	mktsrt_time
2019-03-02 08:00:00	2019-03-02	08:00:00

Figure 8.3

DATE_ADD and DATE_SUB

The powerful thing about storing string dates as datetime values (or converting them using SQL) is that you can do date calculations, which is not possible when they are stored as numbers and punctuation and letters in a string field. Date math can get complex when dealing with multiple time zones, so in this case we're assuming that all datetimes we're working with are from the same time zone. Here, we'll use the market_start_datetime and market_end_datetime fields to demonstrate.

If you wanted to determine how many sales occurred within the first 30 minutes after the farmer's market opened, how would you dynamically determine what cutoff time to use (automatically calculate it for every market date in your database)? This is where the DATE_ADD function comes in. We can use SQL to add 30 minutes to the start time by passing the datetime, the interval (minutes, in this case), and the number of minutes we want to add into the DATE_ADD function, as shown in the second line of the following query:

```
SELECT market_start_datetime,
    DATE_ADD(market_start_datetime, INTERVAL 30 MINUTE) AS mktstrt_date_
plus_30min
FROM farmers_market.datetime_demo
WHERE market_start_datetime = '2019-03-02 08:00:00'
```

I filtered the results to a single market date for clarity. You can see in Figure 8.4 that the calculated mktstrt_date_plus_30min is 30 minutes after the displayed market_start_datetime.

market_start_datetime	mktstrt_date_plus_30min
2019-03-02 08:00:00	2019-03-02 08:30:00

Figure 8.4

If we instead wanted to do a calculation that required looking 30 days past a date (like the example analysis mentioned in the introduction, which would require calculating 30 days past a customer's first purchase to determine if they made a second purchase within that time frame), we could change the interval parameter from MINUTE to DAY, and add 30 days instead:

```
SELECT market_start_datetime,
    DATE_ADD(market_start_datetime, INTERVAL 30 DAY) AS mktstrt_date_
plus_30days
FROM farmers_market.datetime_demo
WHERE market_start_datetime = '2019-03-02 08:00:00'
```

You can see in Figure 8.5 that the calculated mktstrt_date_plus_30min is 30 days after market_start_datetime.

market_start_datetime	mktstrt_date_plus_30days
2019-03-02 08:00:00	2019-04-01 08:00:00

Figure 8.5

There is also a related function called DATE_SUB() that subtracts intervals from datetimes. However, instead of switching to DATE_SUB(), you could also just add a negative number to the datetime if you prefer. The following query demonstrates that using DATE_ADD() to add –30 days to a date has the same effect as using DATE_SUB() to subtract 30 days from a date, and the results are shown in Figure 8.6:

```
SELECT market_start_datetime,
    DATE_ADD(market_start_datetime, INTERVAL -30 DAY) AS mktstrt_date_
plus_neg30days,
    DATE_SUB(market_start_datetime, INTERVAL 30 DAY) AS mktstrt_date_
minus_30days
FROM farmers_market.datetime_demo
WHERE market_start_datetime = '2019-03-02 08:00:00'
```

market_start_datetime	mktstrt_date_plus_neg30days	mktstrt_date_minus_30days
2019-03-02 08:00:00	2019-01-31 08:00:00	2019-01-31 08:00:00

Figure 8.6

DATEDIFF

In the previous section we added 30 days to a date using DATE_ADD(), and I mentioned that the result could be used to determine if an action occurs within 30 days of the first purchase date. However, there is another way to determine whether two dates are within 30 days of one another: DATEDIFF()!

DATEDIFF is a SQL function available in most database systems that accepts two dates or datetime values, and returns the difference between them in days.

Here, the inner query (by which I mean the query inside parentheses, aliased "x") returns the first and last market dates from the datetime_demo table, and the outer query (which is selecting from "x") calculates the difference between those two dates using DATEDIFF. The output of this query is shown in Figure 8.7:

```
SELECT
    x.first_market,
    x.last_market,
    DATEDIFF(x.last_market, x.first_market) days_first_to_last
FROM
(
    SELECT
        min(market_start_datetime) first_market,
        max(market_start_datetime) last_market
    FROM farmers_market.datetime_demo
) x
```

first_market	last_market	days_first_to_last
2019-03-02 08:00:00	2019-03-30 08:00:00	28

Figure 8.7

There are additional examples using DATEDIFF later in this chapter.

TIMESTAMPDIFF

The DATEDIFF function returns the difference in days, but there is also a function in MySQL called TIMESTAMPDIFF that returns the difference between two date-times in any chosen interval. Here, we calculate the hours and minutes between the market start and end times on each market date. The results are shown in Figure 8.8:

```
SELECT market_start_datetime, market_end_datetime,
    TIMESTAMPDIFF(HOUR, market_start_datetime, market_end_datetime)
        AS market_duration_hours,
    TIMESTAMPDIFF(MINUTE, market_start_datetime, market_end_datetime)
        AS market_duration_mins
  FROM farmers_market.datetime_demo
```

market_start_datetime	market_end_datetime	market_duration_hours	market_duration_mins
2019-03-02 08:00:00	2019-03-02 14:00:00	6	360
2019-03-09 09:00:00	2019-03-09 14:00:00	5	300
2019-03-13 16:00:00	2019-03-13 19:00:00	3	180
2019-03-16 08:00:00	2019-03-16 14:00:00	6	360
2019-03-20 16:00:00	2019-03-20 19:00:00	3	180
2019-03-23 08:00:00	2019-03-23 14:00:00	6	360
2019-03-27 16:00:00	2019-03-27 19:00:00	3	180
2019-03-30 08:00:00	2019-03-30 14:00:00	6	360

Figure 8.8

In Oracle SQL, you can simply subtract two datetimes from one another and use the EXTRACT function to specify which interval you want the result returned in.

In Redshift and MS SQL Server, the TIMESTAMPDIFF doesn't exist and isn't necessary, because the DATEDIFF function allows for specification of a datepart interval as a parameter.

NOTE An interesting note about the timestamp values in many database (and other) systems is that they are stored as 32-bit integers "under the hood" that represent the number of seconds since January 1, 1970. Because of this, the latest timestamp that can be stored that fits within 32 bits is 2038-01-19 03:14:07. Timestamps above this value will cause an integer overflow (similar to the "Y2K" issue) until database systems are updated to use a new timestamp standard.

Date Functions in Aggregate Summaries and Window Functions

In this section, we'll explore a few ways that you can use date functions when summarizing data.

Let's say we wanted to get a profile of each farmer's market customer's habits over time. So, we'll want to group the results at the customer level and include some date-related summary information in the output. Our database isn't very heavily populated with example purchases over a long time period yet, but we can use the sample data to demonstrate these concepts.

First, let's get each customer's purchase detail records, particularly the dates on which each customer made purchases. We'll start by querying the database for the records for customer_id 1:

```
SELECT customer_id, market_date
FROM farmers_market.customer_purchases
WHERE customer_id = 1
```

Figure 8.9 shows all of the purchases made by customer 1 over time. Let's summarize this data and get their earliest purchase date, latest purchase date, and number of different days on which they made a purchase.

customer_id	market_date
1	2019-03-09
1	2019-03-02
1	2019-03-02
1	2019-03-09
1	2019-03-02
1	2019-03-09
1	2019-03-09
1	2019-03-20

Figure 8.9

We'll GROUP BY customer_id, use MIN and MAX to get the lowest (earliest) and highest (latest) purchase dates, and COUNT DISTINCT to determine on how many different dates they made purchases:

```
SELECT customer_id,
    MIN(market_date) AS first_purchase,
    MAX(market_date) AS last_purchase,
    COUNT(DISTINCT market_date) AS count_of_purchase_dates
FROM farmers_market.customer_purchases
WHERE customer_id = 1
GROUP BY customer_id
```

Figure 8.10 shows the output of this query.

customer_id	first_purchase	last_purchase	count_of_purchase_dates
1	2019-03-02	2019-03-20	3

Figure 8.10

If we wanted to determine for how long this person has been a customer of the farmer's market, we can get the difference between the first and last purchase. Note that in this query, we're using a DATEDIFF on the aggregate MIN and MAX dates. Those are still date values, so are therefore valid parameters to pass to the DATEDIFF function. I'll also remove the customer filter here, so we can see the results for all customers in Figure 8.11:

```
SELECT customer_id,
    MIN(market_date) AS first_purchase,
    MAX(market_date) AS last_purchase,
    COUNT(DISTINCT market_date) AS count_of_purchase_dates,
    DATEDIFF(MAX(market_date), MIN(market_date)) AS days_between_first_
last_purchase
FROM farmers_market.customer_purchases
GROUP BY customer_id
```

customer_id	first_purchase	last_purchase	count_of_purchase_dates	days_between_first_last_purchase
1	2019-03-02	2019-03-20	3	18
2	2019-03-02	2019-03-13	2	11
3	2019-03-02	2019-03-16	2	14
4	2019-03-02	2019-03-23	3	21
5	2019-03-09	2019-03-09	1	0
7	2019-03-09	2019-03-20	2	11
10	2019-03-02	2019-03-16	2	14
12	2019-03-09	2019-03-30	3	21

Figure 8.11

If we wanted to also know how long it's been since the customer last made a purchase, we can use the CURDATE() function (which may be called CURRENT_DATE, TODAY(), SYSDATE, or GETDATE() in your particular database system's SQL syntax; check the documentation). The following query demonstrates its usage. CUR-DATE() can be used to represent the current system date in any calculation that requires a date or datetime parameter. Keep in mind that the server's current time might differ from your local time, depending on what time zone it is set to:

```
SELECT customer_id,
    MIN(market_date) AS first_purchase,
    MAX(market_date) AS last_purchase,
    COUNT(DISTINCT market_date) AS count_of_purchase_dates,
    DATEDIFF(MAX(market_date), MIN(market_date)) AS days_between_first_
last_purchase,
    DATEDIFF(CURDATE(), MAX(market_date)) AS days_since_last_purchase
FROM farmers_market.customer_purchases
GROUP BY customer_id
```

Going back to the window functions covered in Chapter 7, "Window Functions Frequently Used by Data Scientists," we can also write a query that gives us the days between each purchase a customer makes. Let's go back to customer 1's detailed purchases (previously shown in Figure 8.9) and use both the RANK and LAG window functions to retrieve each purchase date, along with the next purchase date, so we can have both values per row to enable us to display both and calculate the time between each:

```
SELECT customer_id, market_date,
    RANK() OVER (PARTITION BY customer_id ORDER BY market_date) AS
purchase_number,
    LEAD(market_date,1) OVER (PARTITION BY customer_id ORDER BY market_
date) AS next_purchase
FROM farmers_market.customer_purchases
WHERE customer_id = 1
```

The results of this query are shown in Figure 8.12.

customer_id	market_date	purchase_number	next_purchase
1	2019-03-02	1	2019-03-02
1	2019-03-02	1	2019-03-02
1	2019-03-02	1	2019-03-09
1	2019-03-09	4	2019-03-09
1	2019-03-09	4	2019-03-09
1	2019-03-09	4	2019-03-09
1	2019-03-09	4	2019-03-20
1	2019-03-20	8	NULL

Figure 8.12

You can see that we didn't quite accomplish the goal of retrieving each purchase date and the previous purchase date in order to show the time between them, because there are multiple rows with the same date in cases where the customer purchased multiple items on the same date. We can resolve this a few ways.

One approach is to remove the duplicates by using the DISTINCT keyword, and then use a WHERE clause filter to remove rows where the two dates (current and next purchase) are the same (because multiple purchases were made on the same date).

Another is to remove duplicates in the initial dataset and use a subquery (a query inside a query) to get the date differences. Doing this and moving the window functions to the outer query will also fix the issue of the RANK counting each purchase, when we really want to count each purchase date.

This is what that second approach looks like:

```
SELECT
    x.customer_id,
    x.market_date,
    RANK() OVER (PARTITION BY x.customer_id ORDER BY x.market_date) AS
purchase_number,
    LEAD(x.market_date,1) OVER (PARTITION BY x.customer_id ORDER BY
x.market_date) AS next_purchase
```

```
FROM
    (
        SELECT DISTINCT customer_id, market_date
        FROM farmers_market.customer_purchases
        WHERE customer_id = 1
    ) x
```

and we can now add a line to the query to use that `next_purchase` date in a `DATEDIFF` calculation:

```
SELECT
    x.customer_id,
    x.market_date,
    RANK() OVER (PARTITION BY x.customer_id ORDER BY x.market_date)
        AS purchase_number,
    LEAD(x.market_date,1) OVER (PARTITION BY x.customer_id ORDER BY
x.market_date) AS next_purchase,
    DATEDIFF(
        LEAD(x.market_date,1) OVER
        (PARTITION BY x.customer_id ORDER BY x.market_date),
        x.market_date
        ) AS days_between_purchases
FROM
    (
        SELECT DISTINCT customer_id, market_date
        FROM farmers_market.customer_purchases
        WHERE customer_id = 1
    ) x
```

This may look confusing, but we used the same exact `LEAD` function inside the `DATEDIFF` as we used in the `next_purchase` field above it, and the second `DATEDIFF` parameter is just `market_date`, so we are calculating the days between the current row's `market_date` and `next_purchase` columns. We can't just insert the `next_purchase` column name into the query there; we have to calculate it for the `days_between_purchases` field as well, because the calculations don't happen sequentially and are at the same level (the outer query).

The results of the preceding query are shown in Figure 8.13. You might notice that the final `days_between_purchases` value is NULL. That's because that row's `next_purchase` date is NULL, since there are no more purchases for customer 1 after March 20, 2019.

customer_id	market_date	purchase_number	next_purchase	days_between_purchases
1	2019-03-02	1	2019-03-09	7
1	2019-03-09	2	2019-03-20	11
1	2019-03-20	3	NULL	NULL

Figure 8.13

If we wanted to use the next_purchase field name inside the DATEDIFF() function to avoid inserting that LEAD() calculation twice, we could use another query layer and have a query of a query of a query, as shown in the following code. Here, we'll remove the customer_id filter to return all customers, then filter to each customer's first purchase by adding a filter on the calculated purchase_number. This query answers the question "How many days pass between each customer's first and second purchase?" The results of this query are shown in Figure 8.14.

```
SELECT
    a.customer_id,
    a.market_date AS first_purchase,
    a.next_purchase AS second_purchase,
    DATEDIFF(a.next_purchase, a.market_date) AS time_between_1st_2nd_
purchase
FROM
(
    SELECT
        x.customer_id,
        x.market_date,
        RANK() OVER (PARTITION BY x.customer_id ORDER BY x.market_date)
AS purchase_number,
        LEAD(x.market_date,1) OVER (PARTITION BY x.customer_id ORDER BY
x.market_date) AS next_purchase
        FROM
        (
            SELECT DISTINCT customer_id, market_date
            FROM farmers_market.customer_purchases
        ) x
) a
WHERE a.purchase_number = 1
```

customer_id	first_purchase	second_purchase	time_between_1st_2nd_purchase
1	2019-03-02	2019-03-09	7
2	2019-03-02	2019-03-13	11
3	2019-03-02	2019-03-16	14
4	2019-03-02	2019-03-09	7
5	2019-03-09	NULL	NULL
7	2019-03-09	2019-03-20	11
10	2019-03-02	2019-03-16	14
12	2019-03-09	2019-03-16	7

Figure 8.14

In Chapter 10, "Building Analytical Reports with SQL," we will cover a concept called Common Table Expression, also known as a CTE or "WITH clause," which offers another way to select from precalculated values instead of nesting multiple queries inside one another as we did earlier, which you can imagine will get increasingly complex and difficult to read as we attempt to answer more complex questions.

To get back to simpler aggregate functions that use dates, we will again return to customer 1's purchase history (originally shown in Figure 8.9). Let's say that today's date is March 31, 2019, and the marketing director of the farmer's market wants to give infrequent customers an incentive to return to the market in April. The director asks you for a list of everyone who only made a purchase at one market event during the previous month, because they want to send an email to all of those customers with a coupon to receive a discount on a purchase made in April. How would you pull up that list?

Well, first we have to find everyone who made a purchase in the 31 days prior to March 31, 2019. Then, we need to filter that list to those who only made a purchase on a single market date during that time.

This query would retrieve a list of one row per market date per customer within that date range:

```
SELECT DISTINCT customer_id, market_date
FROM farmers_market.customer_purchases
WHERE DATEDIFF('2019-03-31', market_date) <= 31
```

Then, we could query the results of that query, count the distinct market_date values per customer during that time, and filter to those with exactly one market date, using the HAVING clause (which remember is like the WHERE clause, but calculated after the GROUP BY aggregation):

```
SELECT x.customer_id,
    COUNT(DISTINCT x.market_date) AS market_count
FROM
(
    SELECT DISTINCT customer_id, market_date
    FROM farmers_market.customer_purchases
    WHERE DATEDIFF('2019-03-31', market_date) <= 31
) x
GROUP BY x.customer_id
HAVING COUNT(DISTINCT market_date) = 1
```

customer_id	market_count
5	1

Figure 8.15

The results of this query are shown in Figure 8.15

If we were actually fulfilling a report request, we would want to next join these results to the customer table to get the customer name and contact information, but here we have shown how to use date calculations to filter a list of customers by the actions they took.

Exercises

1. Get the `customer_id`, month, and year (in separate columns) of every purchase in the `farmers_market.customer_purchases` table.

2. Write a query that filters to purchases made in the past two weeks, returns the earliest `market_date` in that range as a field called `sales_since_date`, and a sum of the sales (`quantity * cost_to_customer_per_qty`) during that date range.

   Your final answer should use the `CURDATE()` function, but if you want to test it out on the Farmer's Market database, you can replace your `CURDATE()` with the value `'2019-03-31'` to get the report for the two weeks prior to March 31, 2019 (otherwise your query will not return any data, because none of the dates in the database will have occurred within two weeks of you writing the query).

3. In MySQL, there is a `DAYNAME()` function that returns the full name of the day of the week on which a date occurs. Query the Farmer's Market database `market_date_info` table, return the `market_date`, the `market_day`, and your calculated day of the week name that each `market_date` occurred on. Create a calculated column using a `CASE` statement that indicates whether the recorded day in the database differs from your calculated day of the week. This is an example of a quality control query that could be used to check manually entered data for correctness.

Exploratory Data Analysis with SQL

Exploratory Data Analysis (EDA) is often discussed in a data science context as a first step in the predictive modeling process, when a data scientist explores what the data in a provided dataset looks like prior to using it to build a predictive model. The SQL we'll be using in this chapter could be used at that point in the process, to explore an already-prepared dataset. But what if you don't have a dataset to work with yet?

Here we'll show examples that could occur even earlier in the data pipeline, as we explore raw data straight from the database tables (as opposed to an already-aggregated dataset in which the raw data has been combined and transformed using SQL that is ready to be ingested into a model). If you are given access to a database for the first time, these are the types of queries you can run to familiarize yourself with the tables and data in it.

There are of course many ways to conduct EDA, including in a Jupyter notebook with Python code, in a Tableau workbook, or using SQL. (I regularly do all three in my job as a data scientist.) In the later EDA, once a dataset has been prepared, the focus is often on distributions of values, relationships between columns, and identifying correlations between input features and the target variable (column with values to be predicted by the model). Here, we will use the types of queries we've covered so far in this book to explore some tables in the Farmer's Market database, as a demonstration of a real EDA focusing on familiarizing ourselves with the data in the database for the first time.

Demonstrating Exploratory Data Analysis with SQL

Let's start with a real-world scenario for this example Exploratory Data Analysis: Let's say the Director of the Farmer's Market asks us to help them build some reports to use throughout the year, and gives us access to the database referenced in this book. They haven't yet given us any specific report requirements, but they have told us that they'll be asking questions related to general product availability and purchase trends, and have given us the E-R diagram found in Chapter 1, "Data Sources," so we know the relationships between the tables.

Based on the little information we have, we might guess that we should familiarize ourselves with the product, vendor_inventory, and customer_purchases tables, because we've been told we'll be building reports on "product availability" and "purchase trends."

Some sensible questions to ask via query are:

- How large are the tables, and how far back in time does the data go?

- What kind of information is available about each product and each purchase?

- What is the granularity of each of these tables; what makes a row unique?

- Since we'll be looking at trends over time, what kind of date and time dimensions are available, and how do the different values look when summarized over time?

- How is the data in each table related to the other tables? How might we join them together to summarize the details for reporting?

Exploring the Products Table

Some databases (like MySQL) offer a function called DESCRIBE [table name] or DESC [table name], or have a special schema to select from to list the columns, data types, and other settings for fields in tables, but this function isn't available in every database system and doesn't show a preview of the data, so we'll take a more universal approach here to preview data in a table.

Let's start with the product table first. We'll select everything in the table, to see what kind of data is in each column, but limit it to 10 rows in case it is a large table:

```
SELECT * FROM farmers_market.product
LIMIT 10
```

The output from this query is shown in Figure 9.1. What do we notice in this output? We can see that there is a product_id, product_name, product_size, `product_category_id`, and `product_qty_type` on each row, and at least in this small subset, it appears that most of the fields are populated (there aren't a lot of NULL values). This table looks like a catalog of products, with product metadata like name and category. It doesn't list individual items for sale by vendors or purchased by customers, like a transactional table would. The `product_category_id` is an integer, and we know there is a `product_category` table, so we might assume that is a foreign key and check out that relationship later in the EDA. There are many `product_name` and `product_size` values, but in this preview, only two `product_qty_type` values, "lbs" and "unit."

product_id	product_name	product_size	product_category_id	product_qty_type
1	Habanero Peppers - Organic	medium	1	lbs
2	Jalapeno Peppers - Organic	small	1	lbs
3	Poblano Peppers - Organic	large	1	unit
4	Banana Peppers - Jar	8 oz	3	unit
5	Whole Wheat Bread	1.5 lbs	3	unit
6	Cut Zinnias Bouquet	medium	5	unit
7	Apple Pie	10"	3	unit
8	Cherry Pie	10"	3	unit
9	Sweet Potatoes	medium	1	lbs
10	Eggs	1 dozen	6	unit

Figure 9.1

The `product_id` appears to be the primary key. What if we didn't know whether it was a unique identifier? To check to see if any two rows have the same `product_id`, we can write a query that groups by the `product_id` and returns any groups with more than one record. This isn't a guarantee that it is the primary key, but can tell you whether, at least currently, the `product_id` is unique per record:

```
SELECT product_id, count(*)
FROM farmers_market.product
GROUP BY product_id
HAVING count(*) > 1
```

There are no results returned, so no `product_id` groups have more than one row, meaning each `product_id` is unique, and we can say that this table has a *granularity* of one row per product

What about the product categories we see IDs for in the `product` table? How many different categories are there, and what do those look like? Let's see what's in the `product_category` table:

```
SELECT * FROM farmers_market.product_category
```

The results of this query are shown in Figure 9.2, and the listing of categories gives a sense of how the Farmer's Market groups its different types of products. This might be useful when we need to write reports, because we could report on inventory and trends by product category.

product_category_id	product_category_name
1	Fresh Fruits & Vegetables
2	Packaged Pantry Goods
3	Packaged Prepared Food
4	Freshly Prepared Food
5	Plants & Flowers
6	Eggs & Meat (Fresh or Frozen)
7	Non-Edible Products

Figure 9.2

How many different products are there in the catalog-like product metadata table?

```
SELECT count(*) FROM farmers_market.product
```

As you can see in Figure 9.3, only 23 products have been entered into this database so far. If this were a report, we would want to give this column a header besides `count(*)`, but during an Exploratory Data Analysis, you are often moving quickly and writing queries for your own information and not for display purposes, so there is not a need to alias the columns in every query.

count(*)
23

Figure 9.3

We might next ask, "How many products are there per product category?" We'll quickly join the `product` table and the `product_category` table to pull in the category names that we think go with the IDs here, and count up the products in each category:

```
SELECT pc.product_category_id, pc.product_category_name,
    count(product_id) AS count_of_products
FROM farmers_market.product_category AS pc
LEFT JOIN farmers_market.product AS p
    ON pc.product_category_id = p.product_category_id
GROUP BY pc.product_category_id
```

In Figure 9.4, you can see that the IDs did all match up with categories, and the most common product category is "Fresh Fruits & Vegetables." The "Freshly Prepared Food" category does not yet have any products in it.

product_category_id	product_category_name	count_of_products
1	Fresh Fruits & Vegetables	13
2	Packaged Pantry Goods	1
3	Packaged Prepared Food	4
4	Freshly Prepared Food	0
5	Plants & Flowers	1
6	Eggs & Meat (Fresh or Frozen)	2
7	Non-Edible Products	2

Figure 9.4

Exploring Possible Column Values

To further familiarize ourselves with the range of values in a column that appears to contain string values that represent categories, we might ask, "What is in the product_qty_type field we saw in our first preview of the product table? And how many different quantity types are there?" which could be answered with this query using the DISTINCT keyword:

```
SELECT DISTINCT product_qty_type
FROM farmers_market.product
```

As you can see in Figure 9.5, the two quantity types we saw in the 10-row preview turned out to be the only two values in the column, though some products have a NULL product_qty_type, so we'll have to remember that when doing any sort of filtering or calculation based on this column.

product_qty_type
lbs
unit
NULL

Figure 9.5

Let's take a look at some of the data in the vendor_inventory table next:

```
SELECT * FROM farmers_market.vendor_inventory
LIMIT 10
```

In the output shown in Figure 9.6, we can see that it looks like there is one row per market_date, vendor_id, and product_id, with the quantity of that product that the vendor brought to each market, and the original_price. We might need to ask the Director what the "original price" of an item is, but with that name, we might guess that it is the item price before any sales or special deals. And it is tracked per market date, so changes over time would be recorded. We can also see that the quantity is a decimal value, at least for the product displayed.

market_date	quantity	vendor_id	product_id	original_price
2019-07-03	7.38	7	1	6.99
2019-07-06	10.96	7	1	6.99
2019-07-10	13.08	7	1	6.99
2019-07-13	10.22	7	1	6.99
2019-07-17	10.59	7	1	6.99
2019-07-20	9.04	7	1	6.99
2019-07-24	10.66	7	1	6.99
2019-07-27	6.76	7	1	6.99
2019-07-31	11.23	7	1	6.99
2019-08-03	10.72	7	1	6.99

Figure 9.6

We should confirm our assumption about the primary key. If your database system offers the DESCRIBE function or a schema to query from to see table properties, that could give definite confirmation that a field is set to be a unique primary key. (See your database's documentation.) Otherwise, we can group by the fields we expect are unique and use HAVING to check whether there is more than one record with each combination, like we did previously with the product_id in the product table:

```
SELECT market_date, vendor_id, product_id, count(*)
FROM farmers_market.vendor_inventory
GROUP BY market_date, vendor_id, product_id
HAVING count(*) > 1
```

There are no combinations of these three values that occur on more than one row, so at least with the currently entered data, this combination of fields is indeed unique, and the vendor_inventory table has a granularity of one record per market date, vendor, and product. It is not visible in the version of the E-R diagram displayed in Chapter 1, but it's possible to highlight the primary key of a table in MySQL Workbench, as shown in Figure 9.7. Here, we confirm that it is a composite primary key, made up of the three fields we guessed.

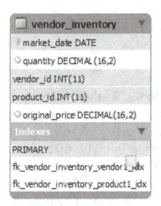

Figure 9.7

We also saw in Figure 9.6 that there are dates in this table, in the `market_date` field. So we might ask, "How far back does the data go: When was the first market that was tracked in this database, and how recent is the latest data?" To answer this, we can get the minimum (earliest) and maximum (latest) values from that field:

```
SELECT min(market_date), max(market_date)
FROM farmers_market.vendor_inventory
```

As you can see in Figure 9.8, it looks like we have about one and a half years' worth of records. So, if we're asked to build any kind of forecast involving an annual seasonality, we will have to explain that we have limited training data for that, since we don't have multiple complete years of seasonal trends yet. It would be good to check to see if purchases were tracked during that entire period, as well.

min(market_date)	max(market_date)
2019-04-03	2020-10-10

Figure 9.8

Another question we might ask to better understand the Farmer's Market and the data it generates is: How many different vendors are there, and when did they each start selling at the market? And which are still selling at the most recent `market_date`? We can do that by grouping the previous query by `vendor_id` to get the earliest and latest dates for which each vendor had inventory. We will also sort by these dates, to see which vendors were selling the longest ago, and the most recently:

```
SELECT vendor_id, min(market_date), max(market_date)
FROM farmers_market.vendor_inventory
GROUP BY vendor_id
ORDER BY min(market_date), max(market_date)
```

The output in Figure 9.9 shows that the inventories of only three vendors have been added to the database so far. Vendors 7 and 8 have been selling since April 3, 2019, and most recently brought inventory to the October 10, 2020 market. Vendor 4 started later and was last at the market on September 30, 2020.

vendor_id	min(market_date)	max(market_date)
7	2019-04-03	2020-10-10
8	2019-04-03	2020-10-10
4	2019-06-01	2020-09-30

Figure 9.9

Exploring Changes Over Time

One thought that comes to mind looking at the dates during this exploration is that we should check to find out if there is an indicator in the database showing whether the market changed format, perhaps allowing online orders during the COVID-19 pandemic in 2020, since that might have impacted sales, and that indicator could be valuable for predictive modeling.

Another question we might ask the database after seeing the output in Figure 9.9 is: Do most vendors sell at the market year-round, or is there a certain time of year when there are different numbers of vendors at the farmer's market? We'll extract the month and year from each market date and look at the counts of vendors that appear in the data each month:

```
SELECT
EXTRACT(YEAR FROM market_date) AS market_year,
EXTRACT(MONTH FROM market_date) AS market_month,
COUNT(DISTINCT vendor_id) AS vendors_with_inventory
FROM farmers_market5.vendor_inventory
GROUP BY EXTRACT(YEAR FROM market_date), EXTRACT(MONTH FROM market_date)
ORDER BY EXTRACT(YEAR FROM market_date), EXTRACT(MONTH FROM market_date)
```

Since only three vendors have inventory entered into this example database, there isn't much variation seen in this output, but you can see in Figure 9.10 that there are three vendors in June through September, and two vendors per month the rest of the year. So one of the vendors (likely vendor 4, from the date ranges we saw in Figure 9.9) may be a seasonal vendor.

market_year	market_month	vendors_with_inventory
2019	4	2
2019	5	2
2019	6	3
2019	7	3
2019	8	3
2019	9	3
2019	10	2
2019	11	2
2019	12	2
2020	3	2
2020	4	2
2020	5	2
2020	6	3
2020	7	3
2020	8	3
2020	9	3
2020	10	2

Figure 9.10

Perhaps surprisingly, we can also see in Figure 9.10 that there are no months 1 and 2 listed in this output, only months 3–12, so the farmer's market must be closed in January and February. (We'll have to remember to check with the Director to see whether that is true, because if not, there might be an issue with the data.) These are the aspects of the data that we want to discover during EDA instead of later when we're doing analysis, so we know what to expect in the report output.

Next, let's look at the details of what a particular vendor's inventory looks like. We saw a vendor with an ID of 7 in a previous query, so we'll explore their inventory first:

```
SELECT * FROM farmers_market.vendor_inventory
WHERE vendor_id = 7
ORDER BY market_date, product_id
```

Part of the output of this query is shown in Figure 9.11. In the limited amount of data visible in the screenshot, we can see that this vendor was only selling one product through most of May and June, then there are some other products (with IDs 1–3) that appear in July. We can also see that product 4 has not changed price at all and is $4.00 throughout the period visible in Figure 9.11.

market_date	quantity	vendor_id	product_id	original_price
2019-05-15	30.00	7	4	4.00
2019-05-18	30.00	7	4	4.00
2019-05-22	40.00	7	4	4.00
2019-05-25	30.00	7	4	4.00
2019-05-29	40.00	7	4	4.00
2019-06-01	30.00	7	4	4.00
2019-06-05	40.00	7	4	4.00
2019-06-08	30.00	7	4	4.00
2019-06-12	30.00	7	4	4.00
2019-06-15	40.00	7	4	4.00
2019-06-19	40.00	7	4	4.00
2019-06-22	40.00	7	4	4.00
2019-06-26	40.00	7	4	4.00
2019-06-29	30.00	7	4	4.00
2019-07-03	7.38	7	1	6.99
2019-07-03	33.63	7	2	3.49
2019-07-03	70.00	7	3	0.50
2019-07-03	40.00	7	4	4.00

Figure 9.11

Exploring Multiple Tables Simultaneously

Some of the products have round quantities, and some appear to be continuous numbers, possibly products sold by weight. This vendor always brings either 30 or 40 of product 4 to each market. It would be interesting to see how many of those items are sold at each market, in comparison.

Let's jump over to the `customer_purchases` table to get a sense of what the purchases of that product look like, compared to the vendor's inventory. First, we need to see what data is available in that table, so we'll select all fields and 10 rows to get a preview:

```
SELECT * FROM farmers_market.customer_purchases
LIMIT 10
```

As shown in Figure 9.12, each row has a `product_id`, `vendor_id`, `market_date`, `customer_id`, `quantity`, `cost_to_customer_per_qty`, and `transaction_time`. We can see that each product purchased by a customer is in its own row, but multiple units of the same product can be recorded in one row, as indicated by the quantity field. We might also guess from the `cost_to_customer_per_qty` field in this output that the reason the `original_price` is recorded in the `vendor_inventory` table is because different customers might pay different prices for the same items. We also notice that the quantity and `cost_to_customer_per_qty` values are numeric values with two digits after the decimal point.

product_id	vendor_id	market_date	customer_id	quantity	cost_to_customer_per_qty	transaction_time
1	7	2019-07-03	2	2.77	6.99	18:11:00
1	7	2019-07-03	14	0.99	6.99	17:32:00
1	7	2019-07-03	14	2.18	6.99	18:23:00
1	7	2019-07-03	15	1.53	6.99	18:41:00
1	7	2019-07-03	16	2.02	6.99	18:18:00
1	7	2019-07-03	17	4.75	6.99	17:27:00
1	7	2019-07-06	4	0.27	6.99	12:20:00
1	7	2019-07-06	12	3.60	6.99	09:33:00
1	7	2019-07-06	14	3.04	6.99	13:05:00
1	7	2019-07-10	3	2.48	6.99	18:40:00

Figure 9.12

It's also interesting that each individual purchase's `transaction_time` is recorded, in addition to the date. This could allow us to build reports on the flow of customers to the market throughout the day, or to estimate how long each customer spends at the market, by looking for their earliest and latest purchase times.

Since we see `vendor_id` and `product_id` are both included here, we can look closer at purchases of vendor 7's product #4:

```
SELECT * FROM farmers_market.customer_purchases
WHERE vendor_id = 7 AND product_id = 4
ORDER BY market_date, transaction_time
```

Glancing at this data in Figure 9.13, we can see that for the two market dates that are visible, most customers are buying between 1 and 5 of these items at a time and spending $4 per item.

product_id	vendor_id	market_date	customer_id	quantity	cost_to_customer_per_qty	transaction_time
4	7	2019-04-03	7	5.00	4.00	17:59:00
4	7	2019-04-03	4	1.00	4.00	18:09:00
4	7	2019-04-03	12	3.00	4.00	18:35:00
4	7	2019-04-03	3	1.00	4.00	18:44:00
4	7	2019-04-03	6	4.00	4.00	18:49:00
4	7	2019-04-03	5	3.00	4.00	18:54:00
4	7	2019-04-03	16	2.00	4.00	18:58:00
4	7	2019-04-06	12	5.00	4.00	08:12:00
4	7	2019-04-06	12	5.00	4.00	08:41:00
4	7	2019-04-06	2	5.00	4.00	09:34:00
4	7	2019-04-06	5	1.00	4.00	11:51:00
4	7	2019-04-06	16	2.00	4.00	13:08:00
4	7	2019-04-06	16	5.00	4.00	13:12:00
4	7	2019-04-06	14	2.00	4.00	13:16:00

Figure 9.13

I see `customer_id` 12 in Figure 9.13 several times, and out of curiosity, we might run the same query but filtered to, or sorted by, the `customer_id` to explore one customer's purchase history of a product in more detail:

```
SELECT * FROM farmers_market.customer_purchases
WHERE vendor_id = 7 AND product_id = 4 AND customer_id = 12
ORDER BY customer_id, market_date, transaction_time
```

This is simulated (generated) data, and I know this result shown in Figure 9.14 occurred because there are a limited number of customer IDs in the database to associate with purchases so far, but it looks like customer 12 really likes this product. They first purchased it on April 3, then came back and bought five more three days later on April 6, only to come back 30 minutes later on the same day to buy five more! Sorting and filtering the data different ways—by market date and time, by `vendor_id`, by `customer_id`—you can get a sense of the processes that the data represents and see if anything stands out that might be worth following up on with the subject matter experts.

product_id	vendor_id	market_date	customer_id	quantity	cost_to_customer_per_qty	transaction_time
4	7	2019-04-03	12	3.00	4.00	18:35:00
4	7	2019-04-06	12	5.00	4.00	08:12:00
4	7	2019-04-06	12	5.00	4.00	08:41:00

Figure 9.14

We can see by looking at this detailed view of the `customer_purchases` data that there are multiple sales recorded per vendor per product per day, but we can't get a good sense of what that looks like in summary. And since we wanted to compare the sales per day to the inventory that the vendor brought to each market, we'll want to aggregate these sales by market date. So, we can group by market_date, vendor_id, and product_id, and add up the quantities sold and each row's quantity (?): multiplied by the cost to get the total sales for each group:

```
SELECT market_date,
    vendor_id,
    product_id,
    SUM(quantity) quantity_sold,
    SUM(quantity * cost_to_customer_per_qty) total_sales
FROM farmers_market.customer_purchases
WHERE vendor_id = 7 and product_id = 4
GROUP BY market_date, vendor_id, product_id
ORDER BY market_date, vendor_id, product_id
```

You can see the results of this in Figure 9.15.

market_date	vendor_id	product_id	quantity_sold	total_sales
2019-04-03	7	4	19.00	76.0000
2019-04-06	7	4	30.00	120.0000
2019-04-10	7	4	23.00	92.0000
2019-04-13	7	4	30.00	120.0000
2019-04-17	7	4	39.00	156.0000
2019-04-20	7	4	20.00	80.0000
2019-04-24	7	4	27.00	108.0000
2019-04-27	7	4	29.00	116.0000
2019-05-01	7	4	22.00	88.0000
2019-05-04	7	4	25.00	100.0000
2019-05-08	7	4	22.00	88.0000
2019-05-11	7	4	30.00	120.0000
2019-05-15	7	4	35.00	140.0000
2019-05-18	7	4	30.00	120.0000

Figure 9.15

Again, if we were building a report, we would probably want to round those dollars in the last column to two numbers after the decimal, but since this is an exploration for our own information, I won't spend the extra time on formatting.

Exploring Inventory vs. Sales

Now we have all of the information we need to answer our question about the sales of this product compared to the inventory except the inventory counts!

Throughout the EDA so far, we have gotten a sense of what the data in each of these related tables looks like, and now we can start joining them together to get a better sense of the relationship between entities. For example, now that we have aggregated the customer_purchases to the same granularity of the vendor_inventory table—one row per market_date, vendor_id, and product_id— we can join the two tables together to view inventory side by side with sales.

First, we'll join the two tables (the details of one and the summary of the other) and display all columns to check to make sure it's combining the way we expect it to. We'll give the `customer_purchases` summary table the alias "sales," and limit the output to 10 rows since we haven't filtered to a vendor or product yet, so this query will return a lot of rows:

```
SELECT * FROM farmers_market.vendor_inventory AS vi
    LEFT JOIN
        (
        SELECT market_date,
            vendor_id,
            product_id,
            SUM(quantity) AS quantity_sold,
            SUM(quantity * cost_to_customer_per_qty) AS total_sales
        FROM farmers_market.customer_purchases
        GROUP BY market_date, vendor_id, product_id
        ) AS sales
        ON vi.market_date = sales.market_date
            AND vi.vendor_id = sales.vendor_id
            AND vi.product_id = sales.product_id
ORDER BY vi.market_date, vi.vendor_id, vi.product_id
LIMIT 10
```

We can see in Figure 9.16 that the `vendor_id`, `product_id`, and `market_date` do match on every row, and the summary values for `vendor_id` 8 and `product_id` 4 match what we saw when looking at the `customer_purchases` table alone. This confirms that our join looks right, and we can remove these redundant columns by specifying which columns we want to display from each table. We'll make sure to pull these columns in from the `vendor_inventory` table, which we made the "left" side of the JOIN relationship because a customer can't buy inventory that doesn't exist (Theoretically! We should check the data to make sure that never happens, which might indicate a vendor made a mistake in entering their available inventory.) But there could be inventory that doesn't get purchased, which we would want to see in the output, but would be missing if we chose a RIGHT JOIN instead.

market_date	quantity	vendor_id	product_id	original_price	market_date	vendor_id	product_id	quantity_sold	total_sales
2019-04-03	40.00	7	4	4.00	2019-04-03	7	4	19.00	76.0000
2019-04-03	16.00	8	5	6.50	2019-04-03	8	5	20.00	130.0000
2019-04-03	8.00	8	7	18.00	2019-04-03	8	7	8.00	144.0000
2019-04-03	10.00	8	8	18.00	2019-04-03	8	8	8.00	144.0000
2019-04-06	40.00	7	4	4.00	2019-04-06	7	4	30.00	120.0000
2019-04-06	23.00	8	5	6.50	2019-04-06	8	5	20.00	130.0000
2019-04-06	8.00	8	7	18.00	2019-04-06	8	7	7.00	126.0000
2019-04-06	8.00	8	8	18.00	2019-04-06	8	8	6.00	108.0000
2019-04-10	30.00	7	4	4.00	2019-04-10	7	4	23.00	92.0000
2019-04-10	23.00	8	5	6.50	2019-04-10	8	5	25.00	162.5000

Figure 9.16

We can also join in additional "lookup" tables to convert the various IDs to human-readable values, pulling in the vendor name and product names.

Then, we can filter to vendor 7 and product 4 to get the information we were looking for earlier, comparing this vendor's inventory of this product to the sales made at each market:

```
SELECT vi.market_date,
    vi.vendor_id,
    v.vendor_name,
    vi.product_id,
    p.product_name,
    vi.quantity AS quantity_available,
    sales.quantity_sold,
    vi.original_price,
    sales.total_sales
FROM farmers_market.vendor_inventory AS vi
    LEFT JOIN
        (
        SELECT market_date,
            vendor_id,
            product_id,
            SUM(quantity) AS quantity_sold,
            SUM(quantity * cost_to_customer_per_qty) AS total_sales
        FROM farmers_market.customer_purchases
        GROUP BY market_date, vendor_id, product_id
        ) AS sales
    ON vi.market_date = sales.market_date
        AND vi.vendor_id = sales.vendor_id
        AND vi.product_id = sales.product_id
    LEFT JOIN farmers_market.vendor v
        ON vi.vendor_id = v.vendor_id
    LEFT JOIN farmers_market.product p
        ON vi.product_id = p.product_id
WHERE vi.vendor_id = 7
    AND vi.product_id = 4
ORDER BY vi.market_date, vi.vendor_id, vi.product_id
```

Now we can see in a sample of this query's output in Figure 9.17 that this vendor is called Marco's Peppers, and the product we were looking at is jars of Banana Peppers. He brings 30–40 jars each time and sells between 1 and 40 jars per market (which we quickly determined by sorting the output in the SQL editor ascending and descending by the quantity_sold, but we could've also done by adding quantity_sold to the ORDER BY clause of the query and scrolling to the top and bottom of the output or surrounding this query with another query that calculated the MIN and MAX quantity_sold).

market_date	vendor_id	vendor_name	product_id	product_name	quantity_available	quantity_sold	original_price	total_sales
2019-04-03	7	Marco's Peppers	4	Banana Peppers - Jar	40.00	19.00	4.00	76.0000
2019-04-06	7	Marco's Peppers	4	Banana Peppers - Jar	40.00	30.00	4.00	120.0000
2019-04-10	7	Marco's Peppers	4	Banana Peppers - Jar	30.00	23.00	4.00	92.0000
2019-04-13	7	Marco's Peppers	4	Banana Peppers - Jar	30.00	30.00	4.00	120.0000
2019-04-17	7	Marco's Peppers	4	Banana Peppers - Jar	40.00	39.00	4.00	156.0000
2019-04-20	7	Marco's Peppers	4	Banana Peppers - Jar	40.00	20.00	4.00	80.0000
2019-04-24	7	Marco's Peppers	4	Banana Peppers - Jar	40.00	27.00	4.00	108.0000
2019-04-27	7	Marco's Peppers	4	Banana Peppers - Jar	30.00	29.00	4.00	116.0000
2019-05-01	7	Marco's Peppers	4	Banana Peppers - Jar	40.00	22.00	4.00	88.0000
2019-05-04	7	Marco's Peppers	4	Banana Peppers - Jar	30.00	25.00	4.00	100.0000
2019-05-08	7	Marco's Peppers	4	Banana Peppers - Jar	40.00	22.00	4.00	88.0000
2019-05-11	7	Marco's Peppers	4	Banana Peppers - Jar	40.00	30.00	4.00	120.0000

Figure 9.17

To take a closer look at the distribution of sales and continue our EDA visually, or to easily filter to different combinations of vendors and products, we can remove the WHERE clause filter and pull the dataset generated by this query into reporting software such as Tableau, building dashboards and reports. Figure 9.18 shows a dashboard with the inventory and sales of the selected products during the selected date range. Figure 9.19 shows a histogram with how many different market dates each count of jars of Banana Peppers were sold.

We could also do a lot more calculations in SQL using this dataset, such as calculating the percent of each vendor's inventory sold at each market, but the purpose of this demonstration was to show how much you can learn about the data in a database using the types of SQL queries you have learned in this book so far.

In the next chapter, we'll explore more analytical queries for building reports using SQL that go beyond simple data previews and basic summaries.

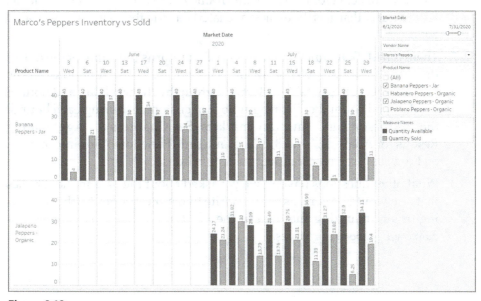

Figure 9.18

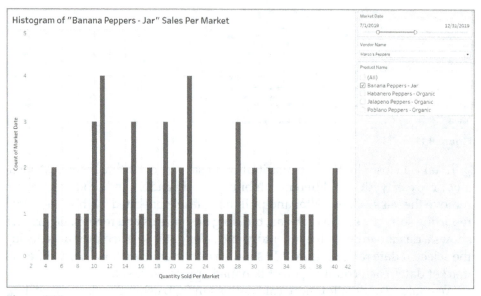

Figure 9.19

Exercises

1. In the chapter, it was suggested that we should see if the `customer_purchases` data was collected for the same time frame as the `vendor_inventory` table. Write a query that gets the earliest and latest dates in the `customer_purchases` table.

2. There is a MySQL function `DAYNAME()` that returns the name of the day of the week for a date. Using the `DAYNAME` and `EXTRACT` functions on the `customer_purchases` table, select and group by the weekday and hour of the day, and count the distinct number of customers during each hour of the Wednesday and Saturday markets. See Chapters 6, "Aggregating Results for Analysis," and 8, "Date and Time Functions," for information on the `COUNT DISTINCT` and `EXTRACT` functions.

3. What other questions haven't we yet asked about the data in these tables that you would be curious about? Write two more queries further exploring or summarizing the data in the `product`, `vendor_inventory`, or `customer_purchases` tables.

Building SQL Datasets for Analytical Reporting

In previous chapters, we covered basic SQL SELECT syntax and started to use SQL to construct datasets to answer specific questions. In the data analysis world, being asked questions, exploring a database, writing SQL statements to find and pull the data needed to determine the answers, and conducting the analysis of that data to calculate the answers to the questions, is called *ad-hoc reporting*.

I often say in my data science conference presentations that the process depicted in Figure 10.1 is what is expected of any data analyst or data scientist: to be able to listen to a question from a business stakeholder, determine how it might be answered using data from the database, retrieve the data needed to answer it, calculate the answers, and present that result in a form that the business stakeholder can understand and use to make decisions.

You now know enough SQL to answer some basic ad-hoc questions about what is occurring at the fictional farmer's market using the demonstration database by filtering, joining, and summarizing the data.

In the remaining chapters, we'll take those skills to the next level and demonstrate how to think through multiple analysis questions, simulating what it might be like to write queries to answer a question posed by a business stakeholder. We'll design and develop analytical datasets that can be used repeatedly to facilitate ad-hoc reporting, build dashboards, and serve as inputs into predictive models.

Figure 10.1

Thinking Through Analytical Dataset Requirements

In this chapter, we'll walk through some examples of designing reusable datasets that can be queried to build many report variations. An experienced analyst who goes through the steps in Figure 10.1 won't only think about writing a query to answer the immediate question at hand but will think more generally about "Building Datasets for Analysis" (we're finally getting to this book's subtitle!) and designing SQL queries that combine and summarize data in a way that can then be used to answer many similar questions that might arise as offshoots of the original question.

You can think of a dataset as being like a table, already summarized at the desired level of detail, with multiple measures and dimensions that you can break down those metrics by. An analytical dataset is designed for use in reports and predictive models, and usually combines data from several tables summarized at a granularity (row level of detail) that lends itself to multiple analyses. If the dataset is meant to be used in a visual report or dashboard, it's a good idea to join in all fields that could be used for human-readable report labels (like vendor names instead of just IDs), measures (the numeric values you'll want to summarize and report on, such as sales), and dimensions (for grouping and slicing and dicing the measures, like product category).

Because I know that the first question I'm asked to answer with an ad-hoc query is almost never the only question, I will use any remaining project time to try to anticipate follow-up questions and design a dataset that may be useful for answering them. Adding additional relevant columns or calculations to a query also makes the resulting dataset reusable for future reporting purposes.

Anticipating potential follow-up questions is a skill that analysts develop over time, through experience. For example, if the manager of the farmer's market asked me "What were the total sales at the market last week?" I would expect to be asked more questions after delivering the answer to that one, such as,

"How many sales were at the Wednesday market versus the Saturday market last week?" or "Can you calculate the total sales over another time period?" or "Let's track these weekly market sales over time," or "Now that we have the total sales for last week, can we break this down by vendor?" Given time, I could build a single dataset that could be imported into a reporting system like Tableau and used to answer all of these questions.

Since we're talking about summary sales and time, I would first think about all of the different time periods by which someone might want to "slice and dice" market sales. Someone could ask to summarize sales by minute, hour, day, week, month, year, and so on. Then I would think about dimensions other than time that people might want to filter or summarize sales by, such as vendor or customer zip code.

Whatever granularity I choose to make the dataset (at what level of detail I choose to summarize it) dictates the lowest level of detail at which I can then filter or summarize a report based on that dataset. So, for example, if I build a dataset that summarizes the data by week, I will not be able to produce a daily sales report from that dataset, because weeks are less granular than days.

Conversely, the granularity I choose means I will always need to write summary queries for any question that's at a higher level of aggregation than the dataset. For example, if I create a dataset that summarizes sales per minute, I will always have to use GROUP BY in the query, or use a reporting tool to summarize sets of rows, to answer any question that needs those minutes combined into a longer time period like hours or days.

If you are developing a dataset for use in a reporting tool that makes aggregation simple, such as Tableau, you may want to keep it as granular as possible, so you can drill down to as small of a time period as is available in the data. In Tableau, measures are automatically summarized by default as you build a report, and you have to instead break down the summary measures by adding dimensions. Summarizing by date in Tableau is as simple as dragging any datetime value into a report and choosing at what timescale you want to view that date field, regardless of whether the underlying dataset has one row per day or one row per second.

However, if you are primarily going to be querying the dataset with SQL, you will have to use GROUP BY and structure your queries to summarize at the desired level every time you use it to build a report. So, if you anticipate that you will frequently be summarizing by day, it would make sense to build a dataset that is already summarized to one row per day. You can always go back to the source data and write a custom query for that rare case when you're expected to report on sales per hour, but reuse the pre-summarized daily sales dataset as a shortcut for the more common report requests in this case.

Let's say that for this example, I can safely assume that most reports will be summarized at the daily or weekly level, so I will choose to build a dataset that has one row per day. In each row, I can summarize not only the total daily sales but also include other summary metrics and attributes that sales might be reported by. Once I think it through, I realize that the reports I'm asked to provide are often broken down by vendor, so I will revise my design to be one row per day per vendor. This will allow us to filter any report built on this dataset to any date range and to a specific vendor, or set of vendors.

In the Farmer's Market database, the sales are tracked in the `customer_purchases` table, which has one row per item purchased (with multiples of the same item potentially included in a single row, since there is a quantity column). Each row in `customer_purchases` contains the ID of the product purchased, the ID of the vendor the product was purchased from, the ID of the customer making the purchase, the transaction date and time, and the quantity and cost per quantity. Because I am designing my dataset to have one row per date and vendor, I do not need to include detailed information about the customers or products. And because my most granular time dimension is `market_date`, I do not need to consider the field that tracks the time of purchase.

I will start by writing a `SELECT` statement that pulls only the fields I need, leaving out unnecessary information, and allowing me to summarize at the selected level of detail. I don't need to include the quantity of an item purchased in this dataset, only the final sale amount, so I'll multiply the `quantity` and the `cost_to_customer_per_qty` fields, like we did in Chapter 3, "The WHERE Clause":

```
SELECT
    market_date,
    vendor_id,
    quantity * cost_to_customer_per_qty
FROM farmers_market.customer_purchases
```

After reviewing the output without aggregation, to ensure that these are the fields and values I expected to see, I'll group and sort by `vendor_id` and `market_date`, SUM the calculated cost column, round it to two decimal places, and give it an alias of `sales`. The resulting output is shown in Figure 10.2.

market_date	vendor_id	sales
2019-04-03	7	76.00
2019-04-03	8	255.00
2019-04-06	7	120.00
2019-04-06	8	292.00
2019-04-10	7	92.00
2019-04-10	8	214.00
2019-04-13	7	120.00
2019-04-13	8	204.50
2019-04-17	7	136.50
2019-04-17	8	281.00
2019-04-20	7	80.00
2019-04-20	8	210.50

Figure 10.2

```
SELECT
    market_date,
    vendor_id,
    ROUND(SUM(quantity * cost_to_customer_per_qty),2) AS sales
FROM farmers_market.customer_purchases
GROUP BY market_date, vendor_id
ORDER BY market_date, vendor_id
```

This is a good time to review whether my results will allow me to answer the other questions I assumed I might be asked in the future and to determine what other information might be valuable to add to the dataset for reporting purposes. Let's go through each one:

- **What were the total sales at the market last week?** There are multiple ways to accomplish this. A simple option is to filter the results by last week's date range and sum the sales. If we wanted the report to update dynamically as data is added, always adding up sales "over the last week," we could have our query subtract 7 days from the current date and filter to only sales in rows with a `market_date` value that occurred after that date. We have the fields necessary to accomplish this.

- **How many of last week's sales were at the Wednesday market versus the Saturday market?** In addition to the approach to answering the previous question, we can use the `DAYNAME()` function in MySQL to return the name of the day of the week of each market date. It might be a good idea to add the day of the week to the dataset so it's easily accessible for report labeling and grouping. If we explore the `market_date_info` table, we'll find that there is a field called `market_day` that already includes the weekday label of each market date, so there is actually no need to calculate it; we can join it in.

- **Can we calculate the total sales over another time period?** Yes, we can filter the results of the existing query to any date range and sum up the sales.

- **Can we track the weekly market sales over time?** We can use the MySQL functions `WEEK()` and `YEAR()` on the `market_date` field to pull those values into the dataset and group rows by week number (which could be especially useful for year over year comparisons) or by year and week (for a weekly summary time series). However, these values are also already in the `market_date_info` table, so we can join those in to allow reporting by that information.

▪ **Can we break down the weekly sales by vendor?** Because we included `vendor_id` in the output, we can group or filter any of the preceding approaches by vendor. It might be a good idea to join in the vendor name and type in this dataset in case we end up grouping by vendor in a report, so we can label those rows with more than just the numeric vendor ID.

While evaluating whether the dataset includes the data that we need to answer the expected questions, we identified some additional information that might be valuable to have on hand for reporting from other tables, including `market_day`, `market_week`, and `market_year` from the `market_date_info` table (which also contains fields indicating properties of that date such as whether it was raining, which might be a dimension someone wants to summarize by in the future), and `vendor_name` and `vendor_type` from the `vendor` table. Let's LEFT JOIN those into our dataset, so we keep all of the existing rows, and add in more columns where available. A sample of the dataset generated by this query is shown in Figure 10.3:

market_date	market_day	market_week	market_year	vendor_id	vendor_name	vendor_type	sales
2019-04-03	Wednesday	14	2019	7	Marco's Peppers	Fresh Focused	76.00
2019-04-03	Wednesday	14	2019	8	Annie's Pies	Prepared Foods	255.00
2019-04-06	Saturday	14	2019	7	Marco's Peppers	Fresh Focused	120.00
2019-04-06	Saturday	14	2019	8	Annie's Pies	Prepared Foods	292.00
2019-04-10	Wednesday	15	2019	7	Marco's Peppers	Fresh Focused	92.00
2019-04-10	Wednesday	15	2019	8	Annie's Pies	Prepared Foods	214.00
2019-04-13	Saturday	15	2019	7	Marco's Peppers	Fresh Focused	120.00
2019-04-13	Saturday	15	2019	8	Annie's Pies	Prepared Foods	204.50
2019-04-17	Wednesday	16	2019	7	Marco's Peppers	Fresh Focused	136.50
2019-04-17	Wednesday	16	2019	8	Annie's Pies	Prepared Foods	281.00
2019-04-20	Saturday	16	2019	7	Marco's Peppers	Fresh Focused	80.00
2019-04-20	Saturday	16	2019	8	Annie's Pies	Prepared Foods	210.50
2019-04-24	Wednesday	17	2019	7	Marco's Peppers	Fresh Focused	108.00

Figure 10.3

```
SELECT
    cp.market_date,
    md.market_day,
    md.market_week,
    md.market_year,
    cp.vendor_id,
    v.vendor_name,
    v.vendor_type,
    ROUND(SUM(cp.quantity * cp.cost_to_customer_per_qty),2) AS sales
FROM farmers_market.customer_purchases AS cp
    LEFT JOIN farmers_market.market_date_info AS md
        ON cp.market_date = md.market_date
    LEFT JOIN farmers_market.vendor AS v
        ON cp.vendor_id = v.vendor_id
GROUP BY cp.market_date, cp.vendor_id
ORDER BY cp.market_date, cp.vendor_id
```

Now we can use this custom dataset to create reports and conduct further analysis.

Using Custom Analytical Datasets in SQL: CTEs and Views

There are multiple ways to store queries (and the results of queries) for reuse in reports and other analyses. Some techniques, such as creating new database tables, will be covered in later chapters. Here, we will cover two approaches for more easily querying from the results of custom dataset queries you build: *Common Table Expressions* and *views*.

Most database systems, including MySQL since version 8.0, support Common Table Expressions (CTEs), also known as "WITH clauses." CTEs allow you to create an alias for an entire query, which allows you to reference it in other queries like you would any database table.

The syntax for CTEs is:

WITH [query_alias] AS

(

  [query]

) ,

[query_2_alias] AS

(

  [query_2]

)

SELECT [column list]

FROM [query_alias]

  . . . [remainder of query that references aliases created above]

where "[query_alias]" is a placeholder for the name you want to use to refer to a query later, and "[query]" is a placeholder for the query you want to reuse. If you want to alias multiple queries in the WITH clause, you put each query inside its own set of parentheses, separated by commas. You only use the WITH keyword once at the top, and enter "[alias_name] AS" before each new query you want to later reference. (The AS is not optional in this case.) Each query in the WITH clause can reference any query that preceded it, by using its alias.

Then below the WITH clause, you start your SELECT statement like you normally would, and use the query aliases to refer to the results of each of them. They are run before the rest of your queries that rely on their results, the same way they would be if you put them inside the SELECT statement as subqueries, which were covered in Chapter 7, "Window Functions Frequently Used by Data Scientists."

For example, if we wanted to reuse the previous query we wrote to generate the dataset of sales summarized by date and vendor for a report that summarizes sales by market week, we could put that query inside a WITH clause, then query from it using another SELECT statement, like so:

```
WITH sales_by_day_vendor AS
(
    SELECT
        cp.market_date,
        md.market_day,
        md.market_week,
        md.market_year,
        cp.vendor_id,
        v.vendor_name,
        v.vendor_type,
        ROUND(SUM(cp.quantity * cp.cost_to_customer_per_qty),2) AS sales
    FROM farmers_market.customer_purchases AS cp
        LEFT JOIN farmers_market.market_date_info AS md
            ON cp.market_date = md.market_date
        LEFT JOIN farmers_market.vendor AS v
            ON cp.vendor_id = v.vendor_id
    GROUP BY cp.market_date, cp.vendor_id
    ORDER BY cp.market_date, cp.vendor_id
)

SELECT
    s.market_year,
    s.market_week,
    SUM(s.sales) AS weekly_sales
FROM sales_by_day_vendor AS s
GROUP BY s.market_year, s.market_week
```

A subset of results of this query is shown in Figure 10.4.

market_year	market_week	weekly_sales
2019	14	743.00
2019	15	630.50
2019	16	708.00
2019	17	593.50
2019	18	742.00
2019	19	642.50
2019	20	585.50
2019	21	725.50
2019	22	621.60
2019	23	765.00
2019	24	846.20
2019	25	648.70
2019	26	679.20

Figure 10.4

Notice how the SELECT statement at the bottom references the sales_by_day_vendor Common Table Expression using its alias, treating it just like a table, and even giving it an even shorter alias, s. You can filter it, perform calculations, and do anything with its fields that you would do with a normal database table. By using a WITH statement instead of a subquery, it keeps this query at the bottom cleaner and easier to understand.

In most SQL editors, you can highlight the query within each set of parentheses to run just that code inside the WITH statement and view its results, so you know what data is available as you develop your SELECT query below the WITH statement. You can't highlight only the SELECT statement at the bottom to run it alone, however, because it references sales_by_day_vendor, which is dynamically created by running the WITH statement above it along with it.

Another approach allows you to develop SELECT statements that depend on a custom dataset in their own SQL editor window, or inside other code such as a Python script, without first including the entire CTE. This involves storing the query as a database *view*. A view is treated just like a table in SQL, the only difference being that it has run when it's referenced to dynamically generate a result set (where a table stores the data instead of storing the query), so queries that reference views can take longer to run than queries that reference tables. However, the view is retrieving the latest data from the underlying tables each time it is run, so you are working with the freshest data available when you query from a view.

If you want to store your dataset as a view (assuming you have been granted database permissions to create a view in a schema), you simply precede your SELECT statement with "CREATE VIEW [schema_name].[view_name] AS", replacing the bracketed statements with the actual schema name, and the name you are giving the view.

This is one query in this book that you will not be able to test using an online SQL editor and the sample database, because you won't have permissions to create a new database object there. The vw_ prefix in the following view name serves as an indicator when writing a query that the object you're referencing is a view (stored query) and not a table (stored data):

```
CREATE VIEW farmers_market.vw_sales_by_day_vendor AS
SELECT
    cp.market_date,
    md.market_day,
    md.market_week,
    md.market_year,
    cp.vendor_id,
    v.vendor_name,
    v.vendor_type,
    ROUND(SUM(cp.quantity * cp.cost_to_customer_per_qty),2) AS sales
```

Continues

(continued)

```
FROM farmers_market.customer_purchases AS cp
    LEFT JOIN farmers_market.market_date_info AS md
        ON cp.market_date = md.market_date
    LEFT JOIN farmers_market.vendor AS v
        ON cp.vendor_id = v.vendor_id
GROUP BY cp.market_date, cp.vendor_id
ORDER BY cp.market_date, cp.vendor_id
```

No results will be displayed when you run this query, other than a confirmation message indicating that the view was created. But if you were to select the data from this view, it would be identical to the data in Figure 10.3.

Since this dataset we created has one row per market date per vendor, we can filter this view by `vendor_id` and a range of `market_date` values, just like we could if it were a table. Our stored view query is then run to retrieve and summarize data from the underlying tables, then those results are modified by the `SELECT` statement, as shown in Figure 10.5.

```
SELECT *
FROM farmers_market.vw_sales_by_day_vendor AS s
WHERE s.market_date BETWEEN '2020-04-01' AND '2020-04-30'
    AND s.vendor_id = 7
ORDER BY market_date
```

market_date	market_day	market_week	market_year	vendor_id	vendor_name	vendor_type	sales
2020-04-01	Wednesday	14	2020	7	Marco's Peppers	Fresh Focused	120.00
2020-04-04	Saturday	14	2020	7	Marco's Peppers	Fresh Focused	68.00
2020-04-08	Wednesday	15	2020	7	Marco's Peppers	Fresh Focused	100.00
2020-04-11	Saturday	15	2020	7	Marco's Peppers	Fresh Focused	160.00
2020-04-15	Wednesday	16	2020	7	Marco's Peppers	Fresh Focused	108.00
2020-04-18	Saturday	16	2020	7	Marco's Peppers	Fresh Focused	144.00
2020-04-22	Wednesday	17	2020	7	Marco's Peppers	Fresh Focused	140.00
2020-04-25	Saturday	17	2020	7	Marco's Peppers	Fresh Focused	140.00
2020-04-29	Wednesday	18	2020	7	Marco's Peppers	Fresh Focused	112.00

Figure 10.5

Because the results of CTEs and views are not stored, they pull the data dynamically each time they are referenced. So, if you use the preceding SQL to report on weekly sales using the `vw_sales_by_day_vendor` view, each time you run the query, it will include the latest week for which data exists in the `customer_purchases` table, which the view code references.

We can also paste the SQL that generates this dataset into Business Intelligence software such as Tableau, effectively pulling our summary dataset into a visual drag-and-drop reporting and dashboarding interface.

The Tableau reports in Figures 10.6 and 10.7 were built using the same dataset query we developed earlier, and are data visualizations that filter and summarize data using the same fields and values displayed in Figures 10.4 and 10.5.

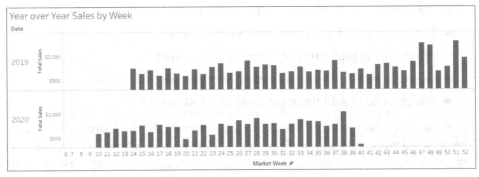

Figure 10.6

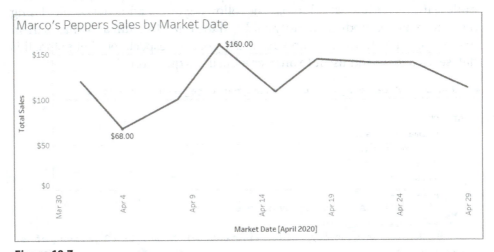

Figure 10.7

Taking SQL Reporting Further

Now that you have seen one example of the development of a reusable analytical dataset for reporting, let's walk through another example, starting with the dataset we built at the end of Chapter 9, "Exploratory Data Analysis with SQL." The last query in that chapter creates a dataset that has one row per market_date, vendor_id, and product_id, and includes information about the vendor and product, including the total inventory brought to market and the total sales for that day. This is an example of an analytical dataset that can be reused for many report variations.

Some examples of questions that could be answered with that dataset include:

- What quantity of each product did each vendor sell per market/week/month/year?
- When are certain products in season (most available for sale)?

- What percentage of each vendor's inventory is selling per time period?
- Did the prices of any products change over time?
- What are the total sales per vendor for the season?
- How frequently do vendors discount their product prices?
- Which vendor sold the most tomatoes last week?

We can't answer questions about any time periods shorter than a day, because the timestamp of the sale isn't included. We also don't have any detailed information about customers, but because we have date, vendor, and product dimensions, we can slice and dice different metrics by those values.

We can add some calculated fields to the query for reporting purposes without pulling in any additional columns. The following query adds fields calculating the percentage of product quantity sold and the total discount and aliases them `percent_of_available_sold` and `discount_amount`, respectively. Let's store this dataset as a view and use it to answer a business question:

```
CREATE VIEW farmers_market.vw_sales_per_date_vendor_product AS

SELECT
    vi.market_date,
    vi.vendor_id,
    v.vendor_name,
    vi.product_id,
    p.product_name,
    vi.quantity AS quantity_available,
    sales.quantity_sold,
    ROUND((sales.quantity_sold / vi.quantity) * 100, 2) AS percent_of_
available_sold,
    vi.original_price,
    (vi.original_price * sales.quantity_sold) - sales.total_sales AS
discount_amount,
    sales.total_sales
FROM farmers_market.vendor_inventory AS vi
    LEFT JOIN
        (
        SELECT market_date,
            vendor_id,
            product_id,
            SUM(quantity) quantity_sold,
            SUM(quantity * cost_to_customer_per_qty) AS total_sales
        FROM farmers_market.customer_purchases
        GROUP BY market_date, vendor_id, product_id
        ) AS sales
    ON vi.market_date = sales.market_date
        AND vi.vendor_id = sales.vendor_id
        AND vi.product_id = sales.product_id
    LEFT JOIN farmers_market.vendor v
        ON vi.vendor_id = v.vendor_id
```

```
LEFT JOIN farmers_market.product p
    ON vi.product_id = p.product_id
ORDER BY vi.vendor_id, vi.product_id, vi.market_date
```

To clarify what's happening in the calculation for discount_amount:

```
(vi.original_price * sales.quantity_sold) - sales.total_sales
```

we're taking the original_price of a product and multiplying it by the quantity of that product that was sold, to get the total value of the products sold, and subtracting from it the actual sales for the day, so we get a total for how much potential profit the vendor gave away in the form of discounts for that product on that day.

If a vendor asked, "What percent of my sales at each market came from each product I brought?" you could use this dataset to build a report to answer the question, because you have a summary of sales per product per vendor per market date. You will need to use a window function to get the answer, because the total you are dividing is the sum of all of a vendor's sales per date, which means adding up the total_sales values across multiple rows of the dataset. Once you have the total_sales for a vendor on a market date, then you can divide each row's total sales (remember there is one row per product per vendor per market date) into the vendor's total sales of all products for the day.

The query needed to generate this report is pictured in Figure 10.8, because the window functions make the calculations quite long, and the syntax highlighting provided by the IDE helps make the various sections of the SQL statement clearer.

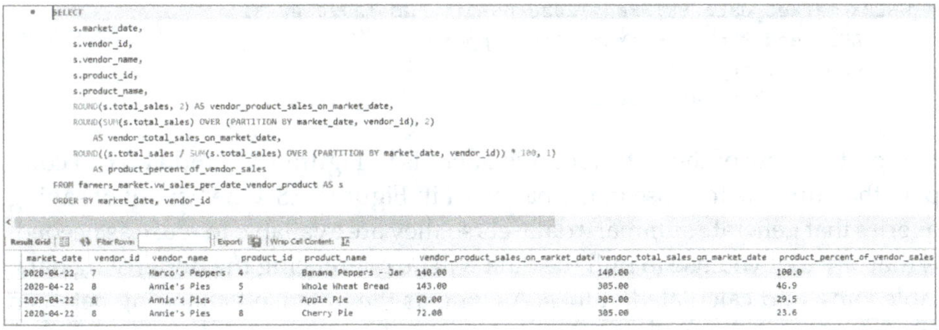

Figure 10.8

Let's walk through these calculations step by step. First, note that we're querying from the view created by the previous query, vw_sales_per_date_vendor_prod-uct. We give the total sales, which is summarized per market date, vendor, and product in the view, an alias of vendor_product_sales_on_market_date, and round it to have two digits after the decimal point, since this is a report and we want to format everything nicely.

In the next line of the SQL statement in Figure 10.8, we are summing up each vendor's sales (of all of their products) on each market date, using a window function that partitions sales by `market_date` and `vendor_id`. (See Chapter 7 for more information about window functions.) Then we give that sum an alias of `vendor_total_sales_on_market_date` and round it to two decimal places.

We now have the total sales for the vendor for the day on each row, and we already had the total sales of each product the vendor sold that day. The calculation in the next line is that first dollar amount divided by the second dollar amount, which calculates the percentage of the vendor's sales on that market date represented by each product.

In the pictured rows of output at the bottom of Figure 10.8, you can see that Marco's Peppers is only selling one product on 4/22/2020, so the sales on that row represent 100% of Marco's sales for the day. Annie's Pies is selling three different products, and you can see in the final column what portion of Annie's total sales was contributed by each product.

We can write additional queries against this reusable dataset to build other reports in SQL, too. To use SQL to get the same data summary that is shown in Figure 9.18, which was grouped and visualized in Tableau, we can query the view as follows:

```
SELECT
    market_date,
    vendor_name,
    product_name,
    quantity_available,
    quantity_sold
FROM farmers_market.vw_sales_per_date_vendor_product AS s
WHERE market_date BETWEEN '2020-06-01' AND '2020-07-31'
    AND vendor_name = 'Marco''s Peppers'
    AND product_id IN (2, 4)
ORDER BY market_date, product_id
```

A partial view of the output of this query is in Figure 10.9, and you can compare the numbers to those in the bar chart in Figure 9.18. One benefit of saving queries that generate summary datasets so they are available to reuse as needed, is that any tool you use to pull the data will be referencing the underlying data, table joins, and calculated values. As long as the data isn't changing between the report generation times, everyone using the defined dataset can get the same results.

market_date	vendor_name	product_name	quantity_available	quantity_sold
2020-07-01	Marco's Peppers	Jalapeno Peppers - Organic	24.17	21.24
2020-07-01	Marco's Peppers	Banana Peppers - Jar	40.00	10.00
2020-07-04	Marco's Peppers	Jalapeno Peppers - Organic	31.82	30.00
2020-07-04	Marco's Peppers	Banana Peppers - Jar	40.00	15.00
2020-07-08	Marco's Peppers	Jalapeno Peppers - Organic	28.19	13.79
2020-07-08	Marco's Peppers	Banana Peppers - Jar	30.00	17.00
2020-07-11	Marco's Peppers	Jalapeno Peppers - Organic	28.49	13.76
2020-07-11	Marco's Peppers	Banana Peppers - Jar	40.00	11.00
2020-07-15	Marco's Peppers	Jalapeno Peppers - Organic	29.75	21.31
2020-07-15	Marco's Peppers	Banana Peppers - Jar	40.00	17.00
2020-07-18	Marco's Peppers	Jalapeno Peppers - Organic	36.98	11.33
2020-07-18	Marco's Peppers	Banana Peppers - Jar	30.00	7.00
2020-07-22	Marco's Peppers	Jalapeno Peppers - Organic	31.27	23.82

Figure 10.9

Exercises

1. Using the view created in this chapter called `farmers_market.vw_ sales_by_day_vendor`, referring to Figure 10.3 for a preview of the data in the dataset, write a query to build a report that summarizes the sales per vendor per market week.

2. Rewrite the query associated with Figure 7.11 using a CTE (WITH clause).

3. If you were asked to build a report of total and average market sales by vendor booth type, how might you modify the query associated with Figure 10.3 to include the information needed for your report?

More Advanced Query Structures

Most of this book is targeted at beginners, but because beginners can quickly become more advanced in developing SQL, I wanted to give you some ideas of what is possible when you think a little more creatively and go beyond the simplest SELECT statements. SQL is a powerful way to shape and summarize data into a wide variety forms that can be used for many types of analyses. This chapter includes a few examples of more complex query structures.

UNIONs

One query structure that I haven't yet covered in this book, but which certainly deserves a mention, is the UNION query. Using a UNION, you can combine any two queries that result in the same number of columns with the same data types. The columns must be in the same order in both queries. There are many possible use cases for UNION queries, but the syntax is simple: write two queries with the same number and type of fields, and put a UNION keyword between them:

```
SELECT market_year, MIN(market_date) AS first_market_date
FROM farmers_market.market_date_info
WHERE market_year = '2019'

UNION
```

Continues

(continued)

```
SELECT market_year, MIN(market_date) AS first_market_date
FROM farmers_market.market_date_info
WHERE market_year = '2020'
```

Of course, this isn't a sensible use case, because you could just write one query, `GROUP BY market_year`, and filter to `WHERE market_year IN ('2019','2020')` and get the same output. There are always multiple ways to write queries, but sometimes combining two queries with identical columns selected but different criteria or different aggregation is the quickest way to get the results you want.

For a more complex example combining CTEs and `UNION`s, we'll build a report that shows the products with the largest quantities available at each market: the bulk product with the largest weight available, and the unit product with the highest count available:

```
WITH
product_quantity_by_date AS
(
    SELECT
        vi.market_date,
        vi.product_id,
        p.product_name,
        SUM(vi.quantity) AS total_quantity_available,
        p.product_qty_type
    FROM farmers_market.vendor_inventory vi
        LEFT JOIN farmers_market.product p
            ON vi.product_id = p.product_id
    GROUP BY market_date, product_id
)

SELECT * FROM
(
    SELECT
        market_date,
        product_id,
        product_name,
        total_quantity_available,
        product_qty_type,
        RANK() OVER (PARTITION BY market_date ORDER BY total_quantity_
available DESC) AS quantity_rank
    FROM product_quantity_by_date
    WHERE product_qty_type = 'unit'

    UNION

    SELECT
        market_date,
        product_id,
        product_name,
        total_quantity_available,
        product_qty_type,
```

```
        RANK() OVER (PARTITION BY market_date ORDER BY total_quantity_
available DESC) AS quantity_rank
    FROM product_quantity_by_date
    WHERE product_qty_type = 'lbs'
) x

WHERE x.quantity_rank = 1
ORDER BY market_date
```

The WITH statement (CTE) at the top of this query totals up the quantity of each product that is available at each market from the vendor_inventory table, and joins in helpful information from the product table such as product name and the type of quantity, which has product_qty_type values of "lbs" or "unit."

The inner part of the bottom query contains two different queries of the same view created in the CTE, product_quantity_by_date, UNIONed together. Each ranks the information available in the CTE by total_quantity_available (the sum of the quantity field, aggregated in the WITH clause), as well as returning all of the available fields. Note that both queries return the fields in the exact same order. The only difference between the two queries is their WHERE clauses, which separate the results by product_qty_type. In this case, we can't simply GROUP BY the product_qty_type and remove the UNION as was possible for the initial example query in this section, because the RANK() window function is ranking by quantity available in each query, and we want to see the top item per product_qty_type, so want to return the top ranked item from each set separately.

The outer part of the bottom query selects the results of the union, and filters to only the top-ranked quantities, so we get one row per market date with the highest number of lbs, and one row per market date with the highest number of units. Some results of this query are shown in Figure 11.1. You can see that for the month of August 2019, the bulk product with the highest weight each week was organic jalapeno peppers, and the product sold by unit with the highest count each week was sweet corn.

market_date	product_id	product_name	total_quantity_available	product_qty_type	quantity_rank
2019-08-03	16	Sweet Corn	300.00	unit	1
2019-08-03	2	Jalapeno Peppers - Organic	32.23	lbs	1
2019-08-07	16	Sweet Corn	300.00	unit	1
2019-08-07	2	Jalapeno Peppers - Organic	29.28	lbs	1
2019-08-10	16	Sweet Corn	250.00	unit	1
2019-08-10	2	Jalapeno Peppers - Organic	27.18	lbs	1
2019-08-14	16	Sweet Corn	200.00	unit	1
2019-08-14	2	Jalapeno Peppers - Organic	33.35	lbs	1
2019-08-17	16	Sweet Corn	300.00	unit	1
2019-08-17	2	Jalapeno Peppers - Organic	25.58	lbs	1
2019-08-21	16	Sweet Corn	250.00	unit	1
2019-08-21	2	Jalapeno Peppers - Organic	32.02	lbs	1
2019-08-24	16	Sweet Corn	250.00	unit	1
2019-08-24	2	Jalapeno Peppers - Organic	17.29	lbs	1
2019-08-28	16	Sweet Corn	250.00	unit	1
2019-08-28	2	Jalapeno Peppers - Organic	26.20	lbs	1
2019-08-31	16	Sweet Corn	300.00	unit	1
2019-08-31	2	Jalapeno Peppers - Organic	27.87	lbs	1

Figure 11.1

For the sake of instruction, and because I frequently say that there are multiple ways to construct queries in SQL that result in identical outputs, there is at least one other way to get the preceding output that doesn't require a UNION. In the following query, the second query in the WITH clause queries from the first query in the WITH clause, and the final SELECT statement simply filters the result of the second query:

```
WITH
product_quantity_by_date AS
(
    SELECT
        vi.market_date,
        vi.product_id,
        p.product_name,
        SUM(vi.quantity) AS total_quantity_available,
        p.product_qty_type
    FROM farmers_market.vendor_inventory vi
        LEFT JOIN farmers_market.product p
            ON vi.product_id = p.product_id
    GROUP BY market_date, product_id
),
rank_by_qty_type AS
(
    SELECT
        market_date,
        product_id,
        product_name,
        total_quantity_available,
        product_qty_type,
        RANK() OVER (PARTITION BY market_date, product_qty_type ORDER BY
total_quantity_available DESC) AS quantity_rank
    FROM product_quantity_by_date
)

SELECT * FROM rank_by_qty_type
WHERE quantity_rank = 1
ORDER BY market_date
```

We were able to accomplish the same result without the UNION by partitioning by both the market_date and product_qty_type in the RANK() function, resulting in a ranking for each date and quantity type.

Because I have shown two examples of UNION queries that don't actually require UNIONS, I wanted to mention one case when a UNION is definitely required: when you have separate tables with the same columns, representing different time periods. This could happen, for example, when you have event logs (such as website traffic logs) that are stored across multiple files, and each file is loaded into its own table in the database. Or, the tables could be static snapshots of the same dynamic dataset from different points in time. Or, maybe the data was migrated from one system into another, and you need to pull data from tables in two different systems and combine them together into one view to see the entire history of records.

Self-Join to Determine To-Date Maximum

A *self-join* in SQL is when a table is joined to itself (you can think of it like two copies of the table joined together) in order to compare rows to one another.

You write the SQL for a self-join just like any other join, but reference the same table name twice. To differentiate the two "copies" of the table, give each one its own alias:

SELECT t1.id1, t1.field2, t2.field2, t2.field3

FROM mytable AS t1

  LEFT JOIN mytable AS t2

    ON t1.id1 = t2.id1

This particular example is meant to demonstrate the syntax and not highlight a typical use case, because you would not normally be joining on a primary key and comparing a row to itself. One more realistic use case is using a comparison operator other than an equal sign to accomplish something such as joining every row to every previous row, as shown in the queries associated with Figures 11.3 through 11.5 below.

Let's say we wanted to show an aggregate metric changing over time, comparing each value to all previous values. One reason you might want to compare a value to all previous values is to create a "record high to-date" indicator.

One possible use case might be the need to automatically determine when the count of positive COVID-19 tests for a region on a particular day set a record as the highest count to-date. One way you could use this data point is to create a visual indicator on a COVID-19 tracking dashboard that appears when the count of new cases hits a new record high. Building this indicator into your dataset allows you to look back at the reported positive case counts at any past point in time and know if the number that day had set a new record high at the time.

We can demonstrate an example of that type of query using the Farmer's Market database by creating a report showing whether the total sales on each market date were the highest for any market to-date. If we were always looking at data filtered to dates before a selected date, we could simply use the SUM() and MAX() functions to determine the highest total sales for the given date range. But, if we're looking back at a log of sales on all dates, and want to do the calculation using data from dates prior to each past date without filtering out the later dates from view, we need a different approach.

In this case, we want to determine whether there is any previous date that has a higher sales total than the "current" row we're looking at, and we can use a self-join to do that comparison. First, we'll need to summarize the sales by `market_date`, which we have done previously. We'll put this query into a CTE (`WITH` clause), and alias it `sales_per_market_date`. If we select the first 10 rows of this query, we get the output shown in Figure 11.2:

market_date	sales
2019-04-03	439.00
2019-04-06	557.50
2019-04-10	483.43
2019-04-13	384.62
2019-04-17	507.50
2019-04-20	433.73
2019-04-24	346.42
2019-04-27	433.58
2019-05-01	488.92
2019-05-04	496.74

Figure 11.2

```
WITH
sales_per_market_date AS
(
    SELECT
        market_date,
        ROUND(SUM(quantity * cost_to_customer_per_qty),2) AS sales
    FROM farmers_market.customer_purchases
    GROUP BY market_date
    ORDER BY market_date
)

SELECT *
FROM sales_per_market_date
LIMIT 10
```

We can select data from this "table" twice. The trick here is to join the table to itself using the `market_date` field—but we won't be using an equal sign in the join. In this case, we want to join every row to all other rows that have a date that occurred prior to the "current" row's date, so we'll use a less-than sign (`<`) in the join. I'll use an alias of cm to represent the "current market date" row (the left side of the join), and an alias of pm to represent a "previous market date" row.

> **NOTE** It's easy to make an error when building this kind of join, so be sure to check your results carefully to ensure you created the intended output, especially if other tables are also joined in.

So we're joining every row to every other row in the database that has a lower `market_date` value than it does. We'll filter this to view the row from April 13, 2019, and you can see it is joined to the rows representing earlier market dates in the output in Figure 11.3:

market_date	sales	market_date	sales
2019-04-13	384.62	2019-04-03	439.00
2019-04-13	384.62	2019-04-06	557.50
2019-04-13	384.62	2019-04-10	483.43

Figure 11.3

```
WITH
sales_per_market_date AS
(
    SELECT
        market_date,
        ROUND(SUM(quantity * cost_to_customer_per_qty),2) AS sales
    FROM farmers_market.customer_purchases
    GROUP BY market_date
    ORDER BY market_date
)

SELECT *
FROM sales_per_market_date AS cm
    LEFT JOIN sales_per_market_date AS pm
        ON pm.market_date < cm.market_date
WHERE cm.market_date = '2019-04-13'
```

Now we'll use a `MAX()` function on the `pm.sales` field and `GROUP BY` `cm.market_date` to get the previous highest sales value. The output of this version of the query is shown in Figure 11.4. If you compare this to Figure 11.3, you'll recognize the sales total from April 6, 2019, which had the highest sales of any date prior to April 13, 2019:

```
WITH
sales_per_market_date AS
(
    SELECT
        market_date,
        ROUND(SUM(quantity * cost_to_customer_per_qty),2) AS sales
    FROM farmers_market.customer_purchases
    GROUP BY market_date
    ORDER BY market_date
)

SELECT
    cm.market_date,
```

Continues

(continued)

```
        cm.sales,
        MAX(pm.sales) AS previous_max_sales
    FROM sales_per_market_date AS cm
        LEFT JOIN sales_per_market_date AS pm
            ON pm.market_date < cm.market_date
    WHERE cm.market_date = '2019-04-13'
    GROUP BY cm.market_date, cm.sales
```

market_date	sales	previous_max_sales
2019-04-13	384.62	557.50

Figure 11.4

We can now remove the date filter in the WHERE clause to get the previous_max_sales for each date. Additionally, we can use a CASE statement to create a flag field that indicates whether the current sales are higher than the previous maximum sales, indicating whether each row's market_date set a sales record as of that date. This query's output is displayed in Figure 11.5. Note that now that we can see the row for April 6, 2019, we can see that it is labeled as being a record sales day at the time, and its sales record is the value we saw displayed as the previous_max_sales in Figure 11.4. You can see that after a new record is set on May 29, 2019, the value in the previous_max_sales field updates to the new record value:

```
WITH
sales_per_market_date AS
(
    SELECT
        market_date,
        ROUND(SUM(quantity * cost_to_customer_per_qty),2) AS sales
    FROM farmers_market.customer_purchases
    GROUP BY market_date
    ORDER BY market_date
)

SELECT
    cm.market_date,
    cm.sales,
    MAX(pm.sales) AS previous_max_sales,
    CASE WHEN cm.sales > MAX(pm.sales)
        THEN "YES"
        ELSE "NO"
    END sales_record_set
FROM sales_per_market_date AS cm
    LEFT JOIN sales_per_market_date AS pm
        ON pm.market_date < cm.market_date
GROUP BY cm.market_date, cm.sales
```

market_date	sales	previous_max_sales	sales_record_set
2019-04-06	557.50	439.00	YES
2019-04-10	483.43	557.50	NO
2019-04-13	384.62	557.50	NO
2019-04-17	507.50	557.50	NO
2019-04-20	433.73	557.50	NO
2019-04-24	346.42	557.50	NO
2019-04-27	433.58	557.50	NO
2019-05-01	488.92	557.50	NO
2019-05-04	496.74	557.50	NO
2019-05-08	490.86	557.50	NO
2019-05-11	446.50	557.50	NO
2019-05-15	426.00	557.50	NO
2019-05-18	465.93	557.50	NO
2019-05-22	531.40	557.50	NO
2019-05-25	376.31	557.50	NO
2019-05-29	576.30	557.50	YES
2019-06-01	472.02	576.30	NO
2019-06-05	377.54	576.30	NO
2019-06-08	470.85	576.30	NO

Figure 11.5

Counting New vs. Returning Customers by Week

Another common report has to do with summarizing customers by time period. The manager of the farmer's market might want to monitor how many customers are visiting the market per week, and how many of those are new, making a purchase for the first time.

Remember that in this case, a customer is only counted if they make a purchase. So, if the farmer's market manager asks what percentage of visitors to the market end up making a purchase, we can't give them that information using the data in this database. We can only report on customers who purchased items, and they are identified using their loyalty card with each purchase (we assume for the sake of simplicity that 100% of customers are identifiable at purchase).

We have built queries and used functions to summarize customers per week before, but how do we determine whether a customer is new? One way is to compare each purchase date to the minimum purchase date per customer. If a customer's minimum purchase date is today, then the customer made their first purchase today, and therefore is new. Let's get a summary of every market date attended by every customer, and determine their first purchase dates. This query finds the customer's first purchase date by using MIN() as a window function, partitioned by customer_id:

```
SELECT DISTINCT
    customer_id,
```

Continues

(continued)

```
    market_date,
    MIN(market_date) OVER(PARTITION BY cp.customer_id) AS first_purchase_
date
FROM farmers_market.customer_purchases cp
```

The DISTINCT has been added because there is a row in the customer_
purchases table for each item purchased, and we only need one row per market_
date per customer_id. You might have noticed that we didn't need a GROUP
BY here. Because the window function does its own partitioning, and the DIS-
TINCT ensures we don't return duplicate rows, no further grouping is needed.
A portion of the results from the preceding query is shown in Figure 11.6. You
can see that each row depicts a date that customer shopped at the farmer's
market alongside the customer's first purchase date.

customer_id	market_date	first_purchase_date
2	2020-08-15	2019-04-06
2	2020-09-19	2019-04-06
2	2020-10-07	2019-04-06
2	2019-06-05	2019-04-06
2	2019-07-27	2019-04-06
3	2019-07-10	2019-04-03
3	2019-07-31	2019-04-03
3	2019-09-25	2019-04-03
3	2019-09-28	2019-04-03
3	2020-09-16	2019-04-03
3	2020-09-26	2019-04-03
3	2019-07-06	2019-04-03
3	2019-07-20	2019-04-03

Figure 11.6

Now we can put that query inside a WITH clause and query its results with
some calculations added. We also need to join it to the market_date_info table
to get the year and week of each market_date. We're going to group by week,
so if a customer made purchases at both markets within that week, they will
have two rows to be grouped into each year-week combination. So let's do two
types of counts. The field we alias, customer_visit_count, will count each of
those rows, so a customer shopping at both markets in a week would be counted
twice in that summary. We'll create a second calculation that counts unique
customer_id values using DISTINCT and alias that distinct_customer_count,
which will only count unique customers per week without double-counting
anyone. The results of the following counts are shown in Figure 11.7:

```
WITH
customer_markets_attended AS
  (
```

```
SELECT DISTINCT
    customer_id,
    market_date,
    MIN(market_date) OVER(PARTITION BY cp.customer_id) AS first_purchase_
date
FROM farmers_market.customer_purchases cp
)

SELECT
    md.market_year,
    md.market_week,
    COUNT(customer_id) AS customer_visit_count,
    COUNT(DISTINCT customer_id) AS distinct_customer_count
FROM customer_markets_attended AS cma
    LEFT JOIN farmers_market.market_date_info AS md
        ON cma.market_date = md.market_date
GROUP BY md.market_year, md.market_week
ORDER BY md.market_year, md.market_week
```

market_year	market_week	customer_visit_count	distinct_customer_count
2019	14	25	19
2019	15	23	16
2019	16	27	18
2019	17	29	20
2019	18	27	21
2019	19	25	18
2019	20	23	19
2019	21	24	18
2019	22	27	19
2019	23	28	20
2019	24	30	22

Figure 11.7

The results are something we could've achieved with a much simpler query, so what was the point of the query we turned into a CTE? The data is now in a form that facilitates performing further calculations, and we also have access to each customer's first purchase date, which we haven't made use of yet. We also want to get a count of new customers per week, so let's add a column displaying what percent of each week's customers are new. This requires adding two more fields to the query. The first looks like this:

```
COUNT(
    DISTINCT
    CASE WHEN cma.market_date = cma.first_purchase_date
        THEN customer_id
        ELSE NULL
    END
    ) AS new_customer_count
```

Inside the COUNT() function is a CASE statement. Can you tell what it does? It is looking for rows in the results of the customer_markets_attended CTE where the market_date (the date when the customer made the purchase) is equal to the customer's first purchase date. If those values match, the CASE statement returns a customer_id to count. If not, the CASE statement returns NULL. So, the result is a distinct count of customers that made their first purchase that week.

The second field, which is the last listed in the following full query, then divides that same value by the total distinct count of customer IDs, giving us a percentage. The result of this query is shown in Figure 11.8.

```
WITH
customer_markets_attended AS
(
    SELECT DISTINCT
        customer_id,
        market_date,
        MIN(market_date) OVER(PARTITION BY cp.customer_id) AS first_purchase_
date
    FROM farmers_market.customer_purchases cp
)

SELECT
    md.market_year,
    md.market_week,
    COUNT(customer_id) AS customer_visit_count,
    COUNT(DISTINCT customer_id) AS distinct_customer_count,
    COUNT(DISTINCT
        CASE WHEN cma.market_date = cma.first_purchase_date
            THEN customer_id
            ELSE NULL
        END) AS new_customer_count,
    COUNT(DISTINCT
        CASE WHEN cma.market_date = cma.first_purchase_date
            THEN customer_id
            ELSE NULL
        END)
        / COUNT(DISTINCT customer_id)
        AS new_customer_percent
FROM customer_markets_attended AS cma
    LEFT JOIN farmers_market.market_date_info AS md
        ON cma.market_date = md.market_date
GROUP BY md.market_year, md.market_week
ORDER BY md.market_year, md.market_week
```

market_year	market_week	customer_visit_count	distinct_customer_count	new_customer_count	new_customer_percent
2019	14	25	19	19	1.0000
2019	15	23	16	2	0.1250
2019	16	27	18	3	0.1667
2019	17	29	20	1	0.0500
2019	18	27	21	1	0.0476
2019	19	25	18	0	0.0000
2019	20	23	19	0	0.0000
2019	21	24	18	0	0.0000
2019	22	27	19	0	0.0000
2019	23	28	20	0	0.0000
2019	24	30	22	0	0.0000

Figure 11.8

It makes sense that on the first market date, 100% of the customers are new. With the data that's currently entered into the Farmer's Market database as of the time of this writing, there are no new customers added after week 18 of 2019.

Summary

These are just a few examples of more complicated query structures that can be created with SQL. I hope by demonstrating these approaches that it gives you a sense of the wide variety of analyses and datasets you can create with different combinations of the SQL you have learned in this book. In the next chapter, we'll reuse some of these concepts to generate datasets designed specifically to be used as inputs into machine learning and forecasting algorithms.

Exercises

1. Starting with the query associated with Figure 11.5, put the larger SELECT statement in a second CTE, and write a query that queries from its results to display the current record sales and associated market date. Can you think of another way to generate the same results?

2. Modify the "New vs. Returning Customers Per Week" report (associated with Figure 11.8) to summarize the counts by vendor by week.

3. Using a UNION, write a query that displays the market dates with the highest and lowest total sales.

Creating Machine Learning Datasets Using SQL

In previous chapters, we introduced SQL concepts and walked through some analytical reporting examples, but we have not yet focused on the specifics of dataset design for predictive modeling applications. In this chapter, we'll discuss the development of datasets for two types of algorithms: classification and time series models.

A *binary classification model* predicts whether a record belongs to one category or another. For example, a heart disease classification model might analyze data from a patient's medical history to determine whether they're likely to develop heart disease, or not. A weather model could use past and current temperature, precipitation, pressure, and wind measurements, as well as those from surrounding geographic areas, to predict whether or not it will rain in the next 24 hours. In a retail scenario like a farmer's market, the seller may want to predict whether a customer will return to make another purchase within a certain time frame, or not.

In order to make predictions, the model needs to be trained. Binary classifiers are a type of *supervised learning* model, which means they are trained by passing example rows of data (also called instances, observations, or feature vectors) labeled with each of the possible outcomes into the algorithm, so it can detect patterns and identify characteristics that are more strongly associated with one result or the other. Some example instances are set aside to test the trained model, feeding them into the algorithm to generate predictions we can compare to the known actual outcomes in order to check the model's performance and determine in what ways the model is incorrect, so we can make adjustments to it.

A *time series model* performs statistical operations on a series of measurements over time to forecast what the measurement might be at some point in time in the future. The training data for a time series model is a running log of data measurements from past points in time. Someone could use an hourly history of a stock's prices to attempt to predict the value of an investment at the end of the day. A college might use historical counts of applications, admission offers, enrolled students, and deposits paid per week to generate a weekly forecast of incoming freshman class enrollment. A farmer's market may use purchases over time to detect seasonal product sales trends and growth in the customer base, or try to predict how many ears of corn will sell per week next month.

Each type of model requires a different type of dataset, and we'll review some approaches for preparing datasets for these two common types of models using SQL.

Datasets for Time Series Models

The simplest type of time series forecasting uses a single variable measured over specified time intervals to predict the value of that same variable at a future point in time. A dataset for training a simple time series model can consist of just two columns: a column with dates or datetime values that indicate the time of measurement, and a column with the value being measured.

For example, a model to predict the high temperature in a location tomorrow could have a dataset with years' worth of daily high temperatures measured at that location. The dataset would have one row per day, with one column for the date, and another for the daily high temperature measured. A time series algorithm could detect seasonal temperature patterns, long-term trends, and the most recent daily high temperatures to predict what the high temperature might be tomorrow.

Let's create a dataset that allows us to plot a time series of farmer's market sales per week. Note that this will be a simplistic view of sales, because it will not take into consideration changes in vendors over time, available inventory at different times of year, or external economic factors.

In Chapter 10, "Building SQL Datasets for Analytical Reporting," we created a dataset that summarized sales per market date. Here, we'll further summarize that data to a weekly level. Because we have joined the `customer_purchases` table to the `market_date_info` table and there is a `market_week` field available, you may assume that we want to group by that field. However, remember that `market_week` is a number that represents the week of the year, and every year has week numbers 1 through 52. So, if you group by `market_week` only, you will be adding sales from the same calendar weeks from different years together! Therefore, we will need to GROUP BY both `market_year` and `market_week`. However, we want only a single field indicating the time period in our dataset, so we don't want to output the `market_year` and `market_week` fields in the results.

Because so many time series algorithms are designed to use calendar dates to indicate when an event occurred or a measurement was taken, we're going to use the first market date of each week to label the weekly intervals. So, we'll find the minimum market date per week and output that, with the column alias `first_market_date_of_week`:

```
SELECT
    MIN(cp.market_date) AS first_market_date_of_week,
    ROUND(SUM(cp.quantity * cp.cost_to_customer_per_qty),2) AS weekly_sales
FROM farmers_market.customer_purchases AS cp
    LEFT JOIN farmers_market.market_date_info AS md
        ON cp.market_date = md.market_date
GROUP BY md.market_year, md.market_week
ORDER BY md.market_year, md.market_week
```

Figure 12.1 shows the last 13 rows of data generated by this query.

first_market_date_of_week	weekly_sales
2020-07-15	903.09
2020-07-22	829.79
2020-07-29	724.19
2020-08-05	983.64
2020-08-12	1055.41
2020-08-19	992.47
2020-08-26	954.71
2020-09-02	893.38
2020-09-09	969.53
2020-09-16	1091.76
2020-09-23	846.83
2020-09-30	1011.90
2020-10-07	1135.33

Figure 12.1

Tableau has some built-in time series forecasting functions, including one that uses a method called exponential smoothing. We'll import the results of our query into Tableau and have it use the weekly sales data to generate a sales forecast for the eight weeks beyond the last date in our dataset.

The line chart in Figure 12.2 shows a visualization of the numbers generated by the preceding query, in the lighter gray color labeled "Actual" in the legend. These are the actual sales per week from our query. The forecasted sales for the next eight weeks are plotted in a darker gray color. These "Estimate" values are surrounded by a shaded area that represents a 90% confidence interval for each forecasted value.

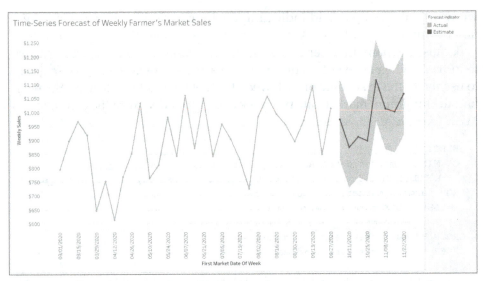

Figure 12.2

By summarizing past sales into a dataset that has one row per week, with a date column and a weekly sales total column, we enabled Tableau's forecast to identify patterns in past weekly sales and use those to forecast future weekly sales. However, we didn't provide it with enough granularity to forecast daily sales. There is no information in our dataset indicating that each week in our dataset actually represents sales from two market dates (as opposed to, say, seven different days of sales summarized by week). And if we asked Tableau to forecast monthly sales using this dataset, it only has the date of the first market per week, so if a new month started between two market dates we grouped into a single week, the second market's sales will be categorized into the wrong month, creating erroneous training data for the forecasting algorithm.

It's important to know the intended use of a dataset in order to make the correct choices when designing it. It's also important to provide documentation to accompany a dataset, so others who might use it later are aware of its original purpose, and any caveats that might be important to know when using it for analysis.

Datasets for Binary Classification

Classification algorithms detect patterns in training datasets, which contain example records from the past that fall into known categories, and use those detected patterns to then categorize new data. Binary classification algorithms categorize inputs into one of two outcomes, which are determined according to the purpose of the model and the available data. For example: Given the medical history of a patient, is it likely that they have heart disease, or not? Given the current and summarized past weather data, is it likely to rain within the next 24 hours, or not? Many of these algorithms can also output a probability or likelihood score, so you can also determine how "sure" the algorithm is that the instance should be classified into one category or the other (how well it matches the patterns detected for training examples in either class).

These algorithms need training data that is in the same form as the data to be classified. For example, if you want the algorithm to take a patient's medical history, including current vital measurements, as input, then the training data has to be at the same granularity and level of summary. Based on the dataset it was trained on, your classification model may expect one row of data per patient, with input fields such as a patient's age, sex, cholesterol as of five years ago, cholesterol as of one year ago, cholesterol measured today (the day of diagnosis), number of years that the patient has smoked cigarettes (as of the day of diagnosis), resting blood pressure as of five years ago, resting blood pressure as of one year ago, resting blood pressure measured today, resting ECG results, chest pain level indicator, and other summary metrics. In this case, each training "instance" (row of data, or vector) should have the data as of the diagnosis date, as well as the measurements or cholesterol and blood pressure from one and five years prior to the diagnosis date, so the duration between those two data points in the training data is as similar as possible to the duration between those two data points in the data you are passing through the trained model to be classified. The conditions under which the model will be applied need to be considered when designing the dataset.

Say you trained your model on data from a study that was structured that way, collecting data over a five-year period, but it's unlikely that you will have a five-year history of those measurements for current patients you want this algorithm to make a prediction for. You might not want to include the data from five years ago in the training dataset, since the model might not be good at classifying records with NULL values in the "resting blood pressure as of five years ago" field and other fields requiring past data, if all of the training instances included those values. Alternatively, training a model on data collected five years ago with outcomes as of the current year would be ideal if the thing you're trying to predict is whether a patient will develop heart disease five years from now.

Every classification model requires a *target variable*, which is the thing you're trying to predict. In binary classifiers, you can usually input the target as a binary value of 1 or 0, with each number representing each outcome. The target variable in the preceding example is a binary flag indicating a diagnosis of heart disease (or no heart disease) as of the date of the latest cholesterol and blood pressure measurements.

We won't get into the details of how much past data with known outcomes is required for training and testing a model here, as it depends on the type of model, the number of columns, the variation in the data values, and many other factors beyond the scope of this book. We also won't be training classification models in this book. However, we will discuss how to structure the datasets needed for binary classification model training and prediction, and how to use SQL to pull the data you need to train and run a classifier.

When thinking about how to structure a dataset for binary classification, the first thing you'll need to determine is the target variable, meaning the categories you're building a model to classify records into. Often, the target variable needs a time bounding, so instead of predicting "Will this patient develop heart disease?" the outcome being predicted could be "Will this patient be diagnosed with heart disease in the next five years?" The time bounding will affect choices you make when designing the training dataset.

Creating the Dataset

To have a concrete example to discuss, we'll build a dataset that could be used to train a model that can predict an answer to the question "Will this customer who just made a purchase return to make another purchase within the next month?" The binary target variable is "makes another purchase within 30 days," with the values 1 for "yes" and 0 for "no." With this time-limited target variable, we can create a training dataset that summarizes information about each customer as of the date of each purchase, and flag that row with a 1 if that customer made another purchase within a month, and 0 if they did not. Now, instead of having one training example per customer, we have one training example per customer per purchase date.

The benefit of having multiple records per customer is that a lot more training instances are available for the model to use to detect patterns in the data. Additionally, a person's behavior can change over time, so having a snapshot record of their summary activity every time they make a purchase, and a record of whether they came back within a month of making that purchase, can help the algorithm determine what impact certain activities may have on behavior. One effect of this approach to be aware of is that frequent customers will be over-represented in the dataset, which could have different impacts depending on the model, and could lead to overfitting the model to that type of customer. (Because a one-time customer will only be in the training dataset one time, while a frequent customer will be in the training dataset many times.)

Setting up your query to produce a dataset that is at the correct granularity with a target variable that is time-bound can be the most complicated step of the query design process, and it's worth taking the time to make sure it is calculated correctly before pulling in any other data fields. When I first designed this example and the dataset to pair with it, I set it up to determine whether each customer makes a purchase in the next calendar month (for example: if the purchase record is from April, will the customer make a purchase in May?). That is one way to approach this model that would be perfectly valid, if that's the type of prediction you wanted to make. However, I quickly realized that the time duration for the target variable wouldn't be consistent. Depending on when in April the customer made a purchase, the target variable could be 1 (yes) if the next purchase date was one day after the initial purchase, up to almost two months later if the initial purchase was on April 1 and the second purchase was on May 30. So, I decided to instead put a dynamic one-month time limit after each purchase for determining the returning customer flag value. So in the following queries, the target variable `purchased_again_within_30_days` represents whether the customer returned within 30 days of making a purchase, without considering the calendar month.

With this approach, we can start by creating a CTE that has a row for every purchase, like the query we developed in Chapter 11, "More Advanced Query Structures," that was associated with Figure 11.5. We can reuse the `customer_markets_attended` CTE in the following query to look up whether a customer made another purchase within 30 days after the date of each purchase.

Before we look at the calculated columns in the following query, let's look at its FROM, WHERE, and GROUP BY clauses, which determine which table(s) we're selecting from, how they're filtered, and the granularity of the final result. You can see that we're selecting from the `customer_purchases` table, which has one row per customer per product purchased. There is no WHERE clause, so we're returning all rows. The GROUP BY clause includes the `customer_id` and `market_date` from the `customer_purchases` table, so we'll end up with one row per customer per market date at which they made a purchase:

```
WITH
customer_markets_attended AS
(
    SELECT DISTINCT
        customer_id,
        market_date
    FROM farmers_market.customer_purchases
    ORDER BY customer_id, market_date
)

SELECT
    cp.market_date,
    cp.customer_id,
    SUM(cp.quantity * cp.cost_to_customer_per_qty) AS purchase_total,
    COUNT(DISTINCT cp.vendor_id) AS vendors_patronized,
    COUNT(DISTINCT cp.product_id) AS different_products_purchased,
    (SELECT MIN(cma.market_date)
    FROM customer_markets_attended AS cma
```

Continues

(continued)

```
    WHERE cma.customer_id = cp.customer_id
        AND cma.market_date > cp.market_date
    GROUP BY cma.customer_id) AS customer_next_market_date,
    DATEDIFF(
        (SELECT MIN(cma2.market_date)
        FROM customer_markets_attended AS cma2
        WHERE cma2.customer_id = cp.customer_id
            AND cma2.market_date > cp.market_date
        GROUP BY cma2.customer_id),
    cp.market_date) AS days_until_customer_next_market_date,
    CASE WHEN
        DATEDIFF(
            (SELECT MIN(cma3.market_date)
            FROM customer_markets_attended AS cma3
            WHERE cma3.customer_id = cp.customer_id
                AND cma3.market_date > cp.market_date
            GROUP BY cma3.customer_id),
        cp.market_date) <=30
    THEN 1
    ELSE 0 END AS purchased_again_within_30_days
FROM farmers_market.customer_purchases AS cp
GROUP BY cp.customer_id, cp.market_date
ORDER BY cp.customer_id, cp.market_date
```

The `purchase_total` column should be familiar by now, multiplying the quantity and cost of each item purchased and summing that up to get the total spent by each customer at each market date. The `vendors_patronized` column is a distinct count of how many different vendors the customer made purchases from that day, and the `different_products_purchased` column is a distinct count of how many different kinds of products the customer purchased. These calculated columns are also called *engineered features* when you're talking about datasets for machine learning, and we're including them so we can explore the relationship between these values and the target variable. Maybe the more vendors the customer makes purchases from, the more likely they are to purchase an item they like so much that they'll return within 30 days to buy more. Including this column in the dataset enables the exploration of the relationship between this feature and the target variable.

The next column, `customer_next_market_date`, is generated by a subquery that references our CTE. Look at all of the code inside parentheses after `different_products_purchased`, and before `customer_next_market_date`. This subquery selects the minimum market date a customer attended, which occurs after the current row's `market_date` value. In other words, we're finding the date of this customer's next purchase. In the WHERE clause of this subquery, we're matching up the subquery's `customer_id` with the main query's `customer_id` (to ensure we're looking at a single customer's trips to the market). We're also limiting the subquery rows to those where the market date occurs after the main query's market date, with the `cma.market_date > cp.market_date` filter. In effect, we're pulling a list of all of this customer's future market dates, and then only returning the minimum date from that list, and aliasing it `customer_next_market_date`.

The next column, aliased `days_until_customer_next_market_date`, uses the same subquery, but this time calculates the difference between the current row's date and that calculated next market date. Then the last column, aliased `purchased_again_within_30_days`, uses the same calculation and wraps it inside a `CASE` statement that returns a binary flag (1 or 0) value indicating whether that next purchase was made within 30 days. If you review these three calculated columns, you will see that the subqueries are all the same, and we're just performing different calculations on the result. Some example rows generated by this query are shown in Figure 12.3.

market_date	customer_id	purchase_total	vendors_patronized	different_products	customer_next_market_date	days_until_customer_next_	purchased_again_within_30_days
2020-06-27	25	1.5000	1	1	2020-07-01	4	1
2020-07-01	25	13.0171	2	2	2020-07-22	21	1
2020-07-22	25	21.9735	2	2	2020-08-22	31	0
2020-08-22	25	7.3124	2	2	2020-08-26	4	1
2020-08-26	25	45.5000	1	1	2020-09-05	10	1
2020-09-05	25	31.4735	2	3	2020-09-19	14	1

Figure 12.3

I aliased the `customer_markets_attended` CTE reference differently in each of the subqueries, as `cma`, `cma2`, and `cma3` for clarity, though that isn't actually necessary. The table alias only applies within the subquery. Also note that each of these subqueries are aggregates that return only one value to be inserted into each row of the dataset.

The `customer_next_market_date` and `days_until_customer_next_market` are useful for validating the output of the preceding query, but once we have checked that the target variable `purchased_again_within_30_days` looks correct in context, we can remove those two columns from our machine learning dataset. All of the columns other than the target variable will be available as inputs to our algorithm, so we don't want to encode that value indicating whether or not they returned within 30 days in any other field, to avoid *data leakage*. Data leakage occurs when data that would not have been known as of the snapshot in time that the row represents is fed into the algorithm, artificially improving the predictions.

Expanding the Feature Set

What other features might we include that might contain "signal (detectable patterns)" for the model to detect? Maybe particular vendors have more loyal customers, or sell items that need to be replenished more frequently, so shopping at a particular vendor is an indicator that a shopper might return sooner. Or, the number of days since a customer's last purchase could be an indicator that they are a frequent shopper and have a higher likelihood to come back again soon. Let's add some columns that indicate which vendors each customer shopped at on each market day and flip the `days_until_customer_next_market_date` calculation to instead indicate how long it's been since the customer last shopped before the visit represented by the row:

```sql
WITH
customer_markets_attended AS
(
    SELECT DISTINCT
        customer_id,
        market_date
    FROM farmers_market.customer_purchases
    ORDER BY customer_id, market_date
)

SELECT cp.market_date,
    cp.customer_id,
    SUM(cp.quantity * cp.cost_to_customer_per_qty) AS purchase_total,
    COUNT(DISTINCT cp.vendor_id) AS vendors_patronized,
    MAX(CASE WHEN cp.vendor_id = 7 THEN 1 ELSE 0 END) AS
purchased_from_vendor_7,
    MAX(CASE WHEN cp.vendor_id = 8 THEN 1 ELSE 0 END) AS
purchased_from_vendor_8,
    COUNT(DISTINCT cp.product_id) AS different_products_purchased,
    DATEDIFF(cp.market_date,
        (SELECT MAX(cma.market_date)
        FROM customer_markets_attended AS cma
        WHERE cma.customer_id = cp.customer_id
            AND cma.market_date < cp.market_date
        GROUP BY cma.customer_id)) AS days_since_last_customer_market_date,
    CASE WHEN
    DATEDIFF(
        (SELECT MIN(cma.market_date)
        FROM customer_markets_attended AS cma
        WHERE cma.customer_id = cp.customer_id
            AND cma.market_date > cp.market_date
        GROUP BY cma.customer_id),
        cp.market_date) <=30 THEN 1 ELSE 0 END AS
purchased_again_within_30_days
FROM farmers_market.customer_purchases AS cp
GROUP BY cp.customer_id, cp.market_date
ORDER BY cp.customer_id, cp.market_date
```

You can see in the preceding query that we added a couple demonstration columns indicating whether each customer purchased from vendors 7 or 8. This technique could be repeated to create a column for every vendor. We also flipped the greater-than sign in the date comparison to a less-than sign, to find how many days it had been since the customer last made a purchase, in the feature aliased `days_since_last_customer_market_date`.

Another type of aggregate value that might be useful to input into a predictive model is some type of representation of the customer's entire history of farmer's market shopping, up to the date the row represents. For example, how many times has the customer shopped at the farmer's market before? A long-time shopper might be more likely to return than a brand-new shopper.

The `ROW_NUMBER` window function is one way to calculate this value, counting how many prior rows exist for each customer, but you have to be careful where you put it in the query, because `ROW_NUMBER` only counts the rows returned by the query. So, if we wanted to count how many times the customer has shopped at the market before as of the market date in the current row, but our main query is filtered to only return data from the year 2019, then our `ROW_NUMBER` window function will only be able to count previous purchases in 2019 and not the customer's entire shopping history.

One solution for our use case is to put the `ROW_NUMBER` function in the `customer_markets_attended` CTE, which doesn't need to be filtered by date, even if you wanted to filter the final output, so we can calculate the number of past markets attended using a similar approach we used to determine the previous purchase date, referencing that CTE. This time, instead of returning the maximum market date that's less than the `market_date` in the row, we'll return the row number that's associated with the current `market_date` from that same query. In the following query, this value has the alias `market_count` in the CTE and is summarized as `customer_markets_attended_count` in the main query.

One important note is that when we add the `ROW_NUMBER` to the `customer_markets_attended` query in the `WITH` clause, we have to modify it to use a `GROUP BY` instead of a `COUNT DISTINCT` to summarize per `customer_id` and `market_date`. The first eight rows of the output of the `COUNT DISTINCT` approach are shown in Figure 12.4, and the first eight rows of the output of the `GROUP BY` approach are shown in Figure 12.5. The reason the `ROW_NUMBER` returns much higher counts when the query is summarized using `COUNT DISTINCT` is that the window function is calculated on the dataset before the `DISTINCT`, so since the results aren't grouped, it's returning one row per customer per product purchased, not one row per customer per `market_date`, then numbering every row in the `customer_purchases` table for that customer. Grouping by `market_date` solves that issue because the window function is calculated after the data is aggregated by the `GROUP BY`. Sometimes it takes trial and error to get the order of operations correct, and this is why it's important to view the details of the underlying data prior to aggregating, so you know whether the resulting summary data is correct.

customer_id	market_date	market_count
1	2019-04-06	1
1	2019-04-13	2
1	2019-04-17	3
1	2019-04-17	4
1	2019-04-20	5
1	2019-04-20	6
1	2019-04-24	7
1	2019-04-24	8

Figure 12.4

customer_id	market_date	market_count
1	2019-04-06	1
1	2019-04-13	2
1	2019-04-17	3
1	2019-04-20	4
1	2019-04-24	5
1	2019-04-27	6
1	2019-05-01	7
1	2019-05-04	8

Figure 12.5

Like with most SQL queries, there are actually several ways to accomplish the same result. The following approach, which moves the ROW_NUMBER() into the WHERE clause, will return the same count for customer_markets_attended_count as a version that has it in the main query, even if the main query is filtered to a date range that doesn't include a customer's entire purchase history:

```
WITH
customer_markets_attended AS
(
    SELECT
        customer_id,
        market_date,
        ROW_NUMBER() OVER (PARTITION BY customer_id ORDER BY market_date)
AS market_count
    FROM farmers_market.customer_purchases
    GROUP BY customer_id, market_date
    ORDER BY customer_id, market_date
)
select cp.customer_id, cp.market_date,
    (SELECT MAX(market_count)
        FROM customer_markets_attended AS cma
        WHERE cma.customer_id = cp.customer_id
        AND cma.market_date <= cp.market_date) AS customer_markets_
attended_count
```

```
FROM farmers_market.customer_purchases AS cp
GROUP BY cp.customer_id, cp.market_date
ORDER BY cp.customer_id, cp.market_date
```

One feature we could add that is likely predictive of whether a customer returns in the next 30 days is how many times they shopped in the previous 30 days. So, we can create another column that puts a time range on the calculation for past markets attended and counts the market dates in the last 30 days. This is demonstrated in the following query by the calculation aliased `customer_markets_attended_30days_count`. You might extrapolate from this calculation one of the aforementioned alternative ways of determining the total count of markets attended:

```
WITH
customer_markets_attended AS
(
    SELECT
        customer_id,
        market_date,
        ROW_NUMBER() OVER (PARTITION BY customer_id ORDER BY market_date)
AS market_count
    FROM farmers_market.customer_purchases
    GROUP BY customer_id, market_date
    ORDER BY customer_id, market_date
)
select cp.customer_id, cp.market_date,
    (SELECT COUNT(market_date)
        FROM customer_markets_attended AS cma
        WHERE cma.customer_id = cp.customer_id
            AND cma.market_date < cp.market_date
            AND DATEDIFF(cp.market_date, cma.market_date) <= 30) AS
customer_markets_attended_30days_count
FROM farmers_market.customer_purchases AS cp
GROUP BY cp.customer_id, cp.market_date
ORDER BY cp.customer_id, cp.market_date
```

Feature Engineering

This process of creating different input values that might be helpful to the prediction algorithm is called *feature engineering*. Most binary classification algorithms require numeric inputs, so sometimes features are engineered to convert another data type into a numeric representation. Other types of features you might create include sets of one-hot encoded flag columns (as mentioned in Chapter 4, "CASE Statements"), converting categorical text columns to numeric values, aggregate high or low metrics (such as the maximum ever spent by the customer at a market to-date), other incrementing totals (such as the length of time the person has been a customer of the market), and other summaries for different time periods.

One important factor when engineering features is that each of these feature values is only what would be knowable as of the date represented by the row—the `market_date` in this case. We want to train the model on examples of customers with a variety of traits as of specific points in time that can be correlated with a specific outcome or target variable relative to that time. In fact, I've been outputting the `market_date` in each of the previous queries for verification purposes, but I wouldn't input the full date into a predictive model, because then the training data would all be tied to past dates, when only the relative dates for the events of interest (the time between purchases) are important. If we ran a current customer's record through the model to try to make a prediction based on data collected this week, but the model had been trained on full date values from the past, the model wouldn't know what to do with the `market_date`, because there will have been no training examples with similar dates. So, when I train my classification model using this dataset, I will not input the `customer_id` or `market_date` into the algorithm. I will only use them as unique identifiers, or index values, so the predictions the model outputs can be tied back to their respective rows.

However, the month of the market date is likely predictive, because the market closes for the months of January and February. So, customers shopping in December would have a lower likelihood of returning in the next 30 days than customers in other months. The final version of this example classification dataset query will include a column representing the month, which can be seen in Figures 12.6 and 12.7. The number of columns is too wide to fit into one figure, so the output is split into two figures, with the `customer_id` and `market_date` index visible in both sections so you can find the continuation of each row in the second block:

```
WITH
customer_markets_attended AS
(
    SELECT
        customer_id,
        market_date,
        ROW_NUMBER() OVER (PARTITION BY customer_id ORDER BY market_date)
AS market_count
    FROM farmers_market.customer_purchases
    GROUP BY customer_id, market_date
    ORDER BY customer_id, market_date
)
```

```
SELECT
    cp.customer_id,
    cp.market_date,
    EXTRACT(MONTH FROM cp.market_date) as market_month,
    SUM(cp.quantity * cp.cost_to_customer_per_qty) AS purchase_total,
    COUNT(DISTINCT cp.vendor_id) AS vendors_patronized,
    MAX(CASE WHEN cp.vendor_id = 7 THEN 1 ELSE 0 END) purchased_from_
vendor_7,
    MAX(CASE WHEN cp.vendor_id = 8 THEN 1 ELSE 0 END) purchased_from_
vendor_8,
    COUNT(DISTINCT cp.product_id) AS different_products_purchased,
    DATEDIFF(cp.market_date,
        (SELECT MAX(cma.market_date)
            FROM customer_markets_attended AS cma
            WHERE cma.customer_id = cp.customer_id
                AND cma.market_date < cp.market_date
            GROUP BY cma.customer_id)
        ) days_since_last_customer_market_date,
    (SELECT MAX(market_count)
        FROM customer_markets_attended AS cma
        WHERE cma.customer_id = cp.customer_id
        AND cma.market_date <= cp.market_date) AS customer_markets_
attended_count,
    (SELECT COUNT(market_date)
        FROM customer_markets_attended AS cma
        WHERE cma.customer_id = cp.customer_id
            AND cma.market_date < cp.market_date
            AND DATEDIFF(cp.market_date, cma.market_date) <= 30) AS
customer_markets_attended_30days_count,
    CASE WHEN
        DATEDIFF(
            (SELECT MIN(cma.market_date)
                FROM customer_markets_attended AS cma
                WHERE cma.customer_id = cp.customer_id
                    AND cma.market_date > cp.market_date
                GROUP BY cma.customer_id),
        cp.market_date) <=30
    THEN 1
    ELSE 0
    END AS purchased_again_within_30_days
FROM farmers_market.customer_purchases AS cp
GROUP BY cp.customer_id, cp.market_date
ORDER BY cp.customer_id, cp.market_date
```

customer_id	market_date	market_month	purchase_total	vendors_patronized	purchased_from_vendor_7	purchased_from_vendor_8	different_products_purchased
25	2019-12-04	12	179.5000	1	1	1	2
25	2019-12-14	12	36.0000	1	0	1	1
25	2019-12-18	12	6.5000	1	0	1	1
25	2020-05-06	5	36.0000	1	0	1	1
25	2020-05-16	5	58.5000	1	0	1	1
25	2020-05-23	5	49.0000	1	0	1	2
25	2020-06-13	6	92.0000	2	0	1	2
25	2020-06-27	6	1.5000	1	0	0	1
25	2020-07-01	7	12.0171	2	1	0	2
25	2020-07-22	7	21.9735	2	1	0	2
25	2020-08-22	8	7.3124	2	1	0	2
25	2020-08-26	8	45.5000	1	0	1	1
25	2020-09-05	9	31.4735	2	1	0	3
25	2020-09-19	9	10.4151	1	1	0	1
25	2020-10-03	10	39.0000	1	0	1	1

Figure 12.6

customer_id	market_date	days_since_last_customer_market_date	customer_markets_attended_count	customer_markets_attended_30days_count	purchased_again_within_30_days
25	2019-12-04	4	30	3	1
25	2019-12-14	10	31	3	1
25	2019-12-18	4	32	4	0
25	2020-05-06	140	33	0	1
25	2020-05-16	10	34	1	1
25	2020-05-23	7	35	2	1
25	2020-06-13	21	36	2	1
25	2020-06-27	14	37	1	1
25	2020-07-01	4	38	2	1
25	2020-07-22	21	39	2	0
25	2020-08-22	31	40	0	1
25	2020-08-26	4	41	1	1
25	2020-09-05	10	42	2	1
25	2020-09-19	14	43	3	1
25	2020-10-03	14	44	2	0

Figure 12.7

Taking Things to the Next Level

In this chapter, we have built datasets that could be used as inputs to train time series models and binary classification models. Sometimes you will be joining in data from additional tables to add columns to your dataset, and you'll have to be careful not to change the granularity as you do so. In this case, we engineered features using only data in the customer_purchases table in the Farmer's Market database, aggregating data from the same table in many ways. You can use the SQL you have learned in this book to engineer a wide variety of features, improving your model by providing it with many different signals to correlate with the target variable.

Some people do feature engineering in their model-building script or other software. Tools like the pandas package in Python do make certain types of feature engineering straightforward to include in your machine learning script. Benefits of conducting some feature engineering in the SQL code as a separate step in your data pipeline include the ability to easily store your results in a database table to use repeatedly during training (without having to regenerate the calculated columns each time your script is run) or to share with others. Additionally, some types of summarization are more efficient to do in SQL at the point of data extraction from the database than in other coding environments. If you need it to run more quickly, you could ask an experienced data engineer to help make your SQL more computationally efficient, once you have it returning the results you want. Now that you know how to build your own dataset, you can provide them with a query that generates the results you need instead of having to explain the granularity and define every column. And you don't have to rely on a data engineer to simply add a column to an existing dataset, since you can now read SQL that someone else has developed and modify it yourself.

The next step after building the dataset will be conducting Exploratory Data Analysis (EDA) on it to better understand the relationship between your input features and the target variable. Then you will go through a training and testing process with the portion of the dataset that contains known outcomes from the past. Once your model is trained, you can feed in current data summarized using the same query, but without values in the target variable column, and have it predict what those values will be. Then, after evaluating your model's performance, you'll likely be right back here engineering more features or joining in more data in order to improve your model's predictions!

Exercises

1. Add a column to the final query in the chapter that counts how many markets were attended by each customer in the past 14 days.

2. Add a column to the final query in the chapter that contains a 1 if the customer purchased an item that cost over $10, and a 0 if not. HINT: The calculation will follow the same form as the `purchased_from_vendor_x` flags.

3. Let's say that the farmer's market started a customer reward program that gave customers a market goods gift basket and branded reusable market bag when they had spent at least $200 total. Create a flag field (with a 1 or 0) that indicates whether the customer has reached this loyal customer status. HINT: One way to accomplish this involves modifying the CTE (`WITH` clause) to include purchase totals, and adding a column to the main query with a similar structure to the one that calculates `customer_markets_attended_count`, to calculate a running total spent.

CHAPTER 13

Analytical Dataset Development Examples

In this chapter, I will walk through the development of datasets for answering different types of analytical questions. This involves combining multiple concepts from previous chapters into more complex queries and therefore is more advanced. Note that the example database doesn't currently contain enough data with correlations for actually doing the analyses that would follow the dataset development, so we won't be looking for trends in the output screenshots. The focus here is on how I would go about designing and building a dataset from our Farmer's Market database using SQL to answer each of the following analytical questions:

- What factors correlate with fresh produce sales?
- How do sales vary by customer zip code, market distance, and demographic data?
- How does product price distribution affect market sales?

What Factors Correlate with Fresh Produce Sales?

Let's say we're asked the analytical question "What factors are correlated with sales of fresh produce at the farmer's market?" So what we're being asked is to determine the relationships between a selection of different variables and a subset of market product sales. That means from a data perspective that we'll need to summarize different variables over periods of time and explore how sales during those same time periods change as each variable changes.

For example, "As the number of different available products at the market increases, do sales of fresh produce go up or down?" is a question exploring the relationship between two variables: product variety and sales. If sales go up when the product variety goes up, then the two variables are positively correlated. If sales go down when product variety goes up, then the two variables are negatively correlated.

I could choose to summarize each value per week and then create a scatterplot of the weekly pairs of numbers to visualize the relationship between them, for example. To do that for a variety of variables, I'll need to write a query that generates a dataset with one row per market week containing weekly summaries of each value to be explored.

I'll first need to determine what products are considered "fresh produce," then calculate sales of those products per week, and pull in other variables (factors) summarized per week to explore in relation to those sales. Some ideas for values to compare to sales include: product availability (number of vendors carrying the products, volume of inventory available for purchase, or special high-demand product seasonal availability, to give a few examples), product cost, time of year/season, sales trends over time, and things that affect all sales at the market such as weather and the number of customers shopping at the market.

First, I will look at all of the different product categories to determine which make the most sense to use to answer this question. The result of the following query is shown in Figure 13.1:

```
SELECT * FROM farmers_market.product_category
```

product_category_id	product_category_name
1	Fresh Fruits & Vegetables
2	Packaged Pantry Goods
3	Packaged Prepared Food
4	Freshly Prepared Food
5	Plants & Flowers
6	Eggs & Meat (Fresh or Frozen)
7	Non-Edible Products

Figure 13.1

From the list in Figure 13.1, I can see that product category 1 is "Fresh Fruits & Vegetables," which sounds like "fresh produce" to me. The "Plants & Flowers" and "Eggs & Meat" categories may contain products that the requester considers fresh produce, so I can generate a list of all products in categories 1, 5, and 6 and take this list to the requester to double-check that category 1 contains the types of products they would like me to analyze sales for. If they request analysis of a list of products instead of an entire category, I might mention that if this analysis is meant to be repeated over time, we will need to check for product additions and changes to assess the included product list every time we run the report (where if we simply filter to a category, any product added to that category in the future will be automatically included).

The output from this query is shown in Figure 13.2:

```
SELECT * FROM farmers_market.product
WHERE product_category_id IN (1, 5, 6)
ORDER BY product_category_id
```

product_id	product_name	product_size	product_category_id	product_qty_type
1	Habanero Peppers - Organic	medium	1	lbs
2	Jalapeno Peppers - Organic	small	1	lbs
3	Poblano Peppers - Organic	large	1	unit
9	Sweet Potatoes	medium	1	lbs
12	Baby Salad Lettuce Mix ...	1/2 lb	1	unit
13	Baby Salad Lettuce Mix	1 lb	1	lbs
14	Red Potatoes	NULL	1	NULL
15	Red Potatoes - Small		1	NULL
16	Sweet Corn	Ear	1	unit
17	Carrots	sold by weight	1	lbs
18	Carrots - Organic	bunch	1	unit
21	Organic Cherry Tomatoes	pint	1	unit
22	Roma Tomatoes	medium	1	lbs
6	Cut Zinnias Bouquet	medium	5	unit
10	Eggs	1 dozen	6	unit
11	Pork Chops	1 lb	6	lbs

Figure 13.2

We'll assume that going with product category 1 was the correct guess. Now that I have the basic filter requirements, I can design the structure of my query. I know that I want some summary information about sales, which will need to come from the customer_purchases table. I'll need data about the availability, which will come from the vendor_inventory table. And I'll want some time-related information. Both the customer_purchases and vendor_inventory tables have market dates in them. Even though neither is directly related to the market_date_info table in the E-R diagram, I can join it to them by market_date to pull in additional information about that date.

Because this is a question about something related to sales over time, I'm going to start with the product sales part of the question, then join other information to the results of that query.

I need to select the details needed to summarize sales per week for products in the "Fresh Fruits & Vegetables" category 1 by inner joining sales (customer_purchases) and products (product) by product_id. If we were looking at products in multiple categories, it might also be worth joining in the product_category table to get the category names, but for now, I'll simplify and leave that out. Let's look at the details, shown in Figure 13.3, first:

```
SELECT *
FROM customer_purchases cp
    INNER JOIN product p
        ON cp.product_id = p.product_id
WHERE p.product_category_id = 1
```

I used an INNER JOIN instead of a LEFT JOIN, because for this sales calculation, I'm not interested in products that don't have purchases. At this stage, it's good to check the count of rows returned, to ensure it makes sense given your join selection. I also look at the details, to make sure I'm pulling the right data from the tables I meant to pull from, that I'm joining on the correct fields, and that my results are filtered the way I expect.

Since I'll be summarizing by week, I don't need the transaction_time field, and I don't currently have a need to know about the size of each product. We might eventually need the product quantity type and vendor information for when we start adding up how much product is available for purchase. However, do we need those fields from these tables? Total sales is the dependent variable—the value we're trying to correlate different values with. If we wanted to get a count of vendors who had the product for sale, we don't want to get that from the customer_purchases table, because there could be products available for sale that no one purchased, which means their existence wouldn't be recorded in the customer_purchases table. So, we'll want to get those pieces of data from the vendor_inventory table at a later step, and not from the customer_purchases table.

I can join in the market_date_info table to get the week number, to make summarization easier, as well as other date-related information such as the season and the weather. I decided to RIGHT JOIN it to the other tables, because I want to know whether there are market dates with no fresh produce sales at all, and the RIGHT JOIN will still pull in market dates with no corresponding records in the customer_purchases table, as shown in Figure 13.4:

```
SELECT
    cp.market_date,
    cp.customer_id,
    cp.quantity,
    cp.cost_to_customer_per_qty,
    p.product_category_id,
    mdi.market_date,
    mdi.market_week,
    mdi.market_year,
    mdi.market_rain_flag,
    mdi.market_snow_flag
FROM customer_purchases cp
    INNER JOIN product p
        ON cp.product_id = p.product_id
    RIGHT JOIN market_date_info mdi
        ON mdi.market_date = cp.market_date
WHERE p.product_category_id = 1
```

product_id	vendor_id	market_date	customer_id	quantity	cost_to_customer_per_	transaction_time	product_id	product_name	product_siz	product_categor	product_qty_typ
16	4	2019-07-13	13	2.00	0.50	12:25:00	16	Sweet Corn	Ear	1	unit
16	4	2019-07-13	23	2.00	0.50	10:40:00	16	Sweet Corn	Ear	1	unit
16	4	2019-07-13	26	5.00	0.50	12:23:00	16	Sweet Corn	Ear	1	unit
1	7	2019-07-17	4	3.03	6.99	18:44:00	1	Habanero Peppers - Organic	medium	1	lbs
1	7	2019-07-17	5	4.11	6.99	16:30:00	1	Habanero Peppers - Organic	medium	1	lbs
2	7	2019-07-17	1	4.88	3.49	18:26:00	2	Jalapeno Peppers - Organic	small	1	lbs
2	7	2019-07-17	4	1.55	3.49	17:45:00	2	Jalapeno Peppers - Organic	small	1	lbs
2	7	2019-07-17	7	4.13	3.49	18:51:00	2	Jalapeno Peppers - Organic	small	1	lbs
2	7	2019-07-17	9	0.11	3.49	16:44:00	2	Jalapeno Peppers - Organic	small	1	lbs
2	7	2019-07-17	13	3.09	3.49	17:29:00	2	Jalapeno Peppers - Organic	small	1	lbs
2	7	2019-07-17	22	2.56	3.49	18:31:00	2	Jalapeno Peppers - Organic	small	1	lbs
3	7	2019-07-17	2	3.00	0.50	18:45:00	3	Poblano Peppers - Organic	large	1	unit
3	7	2019-07-17	5	1.00	0.50	18:56:00	3	Poblano Peppers - Organic	large	1	unit
3	7	2019-07-17	8	4.00	0.50	18:45:00	3	Poblano Peppers - Organic	large	1	unit
3	7	2019-07-17	14	5.00	0.50	17:47:00	3	Poblano Peppers - Organic	large	1	unit

Figure 13.3

market_date	customer_id	quantity	cost_to_customer_per_	product_categor	market_date	market_week	market_year	market_rain_flag	market_snow_flag
2019-06-29	2	4.00	0.50	1	2019-06-29	26	2019	0	0
2019-06-29	4	10.00	0.45	1	2019-06-29	26	2019	0	0
2019-06-29	4	8.00	0.45	1	2019-06-29	26	2019	0	0
2019-06-29	5	5.00	0.50	1	2019-06-29	26	2019	0	0
2019-06-29	6	5.00	0.50	1	2019-06-29	26	2019	0	0
2019-06-29	19	5.00	0.50	1	2019-06-29	26	2019	0	0
2019-06-29	25	2.00	0.50	1	2019-06-29	26	2019	0	0
2019-07-03	14	0.99	6.99	1	2019-07-03	27	2019	0	0
2019-07-03	14	2.18	6.99	1	2019-07-03	27	2019	0	0
2019-07-03	15	1.53	6.99	1	2019-07-03	27	2019	0	0
2019-07-03	16	2.02	6.99	1	2019-07-03	27	2019	0	0
2019-07-03	22	0.66	6.99	1	2019-07-03	27	2019	0	0
2019-07-03	4	3.73	3.49	1	2019-07-03	27	2019	0	0
2019-07-03	9	4.85	3.49	1	2019-07-03	27	2019	0	0
2019-07-03	12	0.12	3.49	1	2019-07-03	27	2019	0	0
2019-07-03	16	3.46	3.49	1	2019-07-03	27	2019	0	0
2019-07-03	17	1.76	3.49	1	2019-07-03	27	2019	0	0

Figure 13.4

But look what happened. Even though I'm right joining the `market_date_info` table to the `customer_purchases` table, I'm not seeing any market dates that don't have sales in this category, even though I know they exist in the data! This is a common SQL design error. You might think that the solution is to rearrange all of the joins, but if that's the only change you make, you will still have the same issue. What's happening is that our WHERE clause is filtering the results to only rows with a customer purchase from product category 1. So if there are no sales on a market date, there are no product categories associated with that date, so we are filtering it out, defeating the purpose of the RIGHT JOIN. (This is also a good reason to look at the data in each table before joining and write some quality control queries such as distinct counts of market dates, so you are aware if some expected values are missing after you join the tables together.)

The solution to this filter issue is to put the product category filter in the JOIN ON clause instead of in the WHERE clause, which is something we haven't covered previously. I can join to the `product` table on the `product_id` and `product_category_id` fields, and filter the `product_category_id` in the ON clause. This makes the filter only apply to the data from the product table (and now the `customer_purchases` table, since they're inner joined), and not to the results set, the way the WHERE clause does. So now all of our market dates will be returned. I moved the `market_date_info` fields to appear first, and modified the join to include the filter. You can now see that we're joining on the `product_id` and filtering the `product_category_id` in the ON section of the JOIN. Note that now there is no WHERE clause, but we are still filtering the results of one of the tables being joined into the dataset! The output of this query is displayed in Figure 13.5:

```
SELECT
    mdi.market_date,
    mdi.market_week,
    mdi.market_year,
    mdi.market_rain_flag,
    mdi.market_snow_flag,
    cp.market_date,
    cp.customer_id,
    cp.quantity,
    cp.cost_to_customer_per_qty,
    p.product_category_id
FROM customer_purchases cp
    INNER JOIN product p
        ON cp.product_id = p.product_id
            AND p.product_category_id = 1
    RIGHT JOIN market_date_info mdi
        ON mdi.market_date = cp.market_date
```

market_date	market_week	market_year	market_rain_flag	market_snow_flag	market_date	customer_id	quantity	cost_to_customer_per_qty	product_category_id
2019-09-28	39	2019	0	0	2019-09-28	7	3.00	0.50	1
2019-09-28	39	2019	0	0	2019-09-28	8	3.00	0.50	1
2019-09-28	39	2019	0	0	2019-09-28	9	5.00	0.50	1
2019-09-28	39	2019	0	0	2019-09-28	12	3.00	0.50	1
2019-09-28	39	2019	0	0	2019-09-28	18	5.00	0.50	1
2019-09-28	39	2019	0	0	2019-09-28	19	8.00	0.50	1
2019-09-28	39	2019	0	0	2019-09-28	21	3.00	0.50	1
2019-09-28	39	2019	0	0	2019-09-28	4	10.00	0.45	1
2019-09-28	39	2019	0	0	2019-09-28	14	5.00	0.50	1
2019-09-28	39	2019	0	0	2019-09-28	14	4.00	0.50	1
2019-09-28	39	2019	0	0	2019-09-28	15	1.00	0.50	1
2019-09-28	39	2019	0	0	2019-09-28	20	4.00	0.50	1
2019-10-02	40	2019	0	0	NULL	NULL	NULL	NULL	NULL
2019-10-05	40	2019	0	0	NULL	NULL	NULL	NULL	NULL
2019-10-09	41	2019	0	0	NULL	NULL	NULL	NULL	NULL
2019-10-12	41	2019	0	0	NULL	NULL	NULL	NULL	NULL
2019-10-16	42	2019	0	0					

Figure 13.5

Now we can see rows for market dates with no fresh produce purchases.

I can summarize the customer purchases to one row per week to get sales per week by grouping on `market_year` and `market_week`, and we don't need most of the other columns with additional details about the purchases, so we can remove them from our query. The sales calculation is the same one we used in Chapter 12, "Creating Machine Learning Datasets Using SQL," with a slight addition. `COALESCE` is a function that returns the first non-NULL value in a list of values. In this case, when the query returns a market date with no sales in product category 1, the `weekly_category1_sales` value would be NULL. If we want it to be 0 instead, we can use the syntax

```
COALESCE([value 1], 0)
```

which will return a 0 if "value 1" is NULL, and will otherwise return the calculated value. We wrap our `SUM` function in this `COALESCE` function, then `ROUND` the result of the `COALESCE` function to two digits after the decimal point. To summarize, in that final line before the `FROM` clause, we're adding up the sales, converting the result to 0 if there are no sales, then rounding the numeric result to two digits.

I'm also returning the `MAX` of the snow and rain flags, because if there was precipitation at either of the markets during the week, I want to return a 1 in this field. And I returned the minimum `market_season` value, so only one value is returned if a week happens to be split across two seasons. The updated result using the following query is displayed in Figure 13.6:

```
SELECT
    mdi.market_year,
    mdi.market_week,
    MAX(mdi.market_rain_flag) AS market_week_rain_flag,
    MAX(mdi.market_snow_flag) AS market_week_snow_flag,
    MIN(mdi.market_min_temp) AS minimum_temperature,
    MAX(mdi.market_max_temp) AS maximum_temperature,
    MIN(mdi.market_season) AS market_season,
    ROUND(COALESCE(SUM(cp.quantity * cp.cost_to_customer_per_qty), 0), 2) AS
weekly_category1_sales
FROM customer_purchases cp
    INNER JOIN product p
        ON cp.product_id = p.product_id
            AND p.product_category_id = 1
    RIGHT JOIN market_date_info mdi
        ON mdi.market_date = cp.market_date
GROUP BY
    mdi.market_year,
    mdi.market_week
```

market_year	market_week	market_week_rain_flag	market_week_snow_flag	minimum_temperature	maximum_temperature	market_season	weekly_category1_sales
2019	22	0	0	49	69	Spring	8.60
2019	23	0	0	57	82	Summer/Early Fall	42.50
2019	24	0	0	56	82	Summer/Early Fall	47.20
2019	25	0	0	65	80	Summer/Early Fall	41.20
2019	26	0	0	72	85	Summer/Early Fall	55.70
2019	27	0	0	67	89	Summer/Early Fall	287.38
2019	28	0	0	65	90	Summer/Early Fall	266.09

Figure 13.6

So now we have total sales by week.

Some of the other aggregate values that could be added to this dataset include the number of vendors carrying products in the category, the volume of inventory available for purchase, and special high-demand product seasonal availability. These are values that come from the vendor_inventory table, because I want to know what the vendors brought to market, regardless of whether people purchased the items.

We can set up the query for vendor_inventory just like we did for customer_purchases, joining it to the product and market_date_info tables the same way, and filtering to product_category_id = 1 in the JOIN statement as we did previously. The results of this query are shown in Figure 13.7:

```
SELECT
    mdi.market_date,
    mdi.market_year,
    mdi.market_week,
    vi.*,
    p.*
FROM vendor_inventory vi
    INNER JOIN product p
        ON vi.product_id = p.product_id
            AND p.product_category_id = 1
    RIGHT JOIN market_date_info mdi
        ON mdi.market_date = vi.market_date
```

Removing the fields we don't need for our weekly summary, we can narrow down the vendor_inventory table to keep the features we need for calculating the number of vendors (vendor_id), the number of products (product_id), and volume of products (quantity). We can also use the product_id to flag the existence of certain products. Let's say that we suspect that when the sweet corn vendors are at the market, some customers come that don't come at any other time of year, just to get the locally famous corn on the cob. We want to know if overall fresh produce sales go up during the weeks when corn is available, so we'll create a product availability flag for product 16, sweet corn, called corn_available_flag, as shown in the following query and in Figure 13.8:

```
SELECT
    mdi.market_year,
    mdi.market_week,
    COUNT(DISTINCT vi.vendor_id) AS vendor_count,
    COUNT(DISTINCT vi.product_id) AS unique_product_count,
    SUM(CASE WHEN p.product_qty_type = 'unit' THEN vi.quantity ELSE 0 END)
AS unit_products_qty,
    SUM(CASE WHEN p.product_qty_type = 'lbs' THEN vi.quantity ELSE 0 END) AS
bulk_products_lbs,
    ROUND(COALESCE(SUM(vi.quantity * vi.original_price), 0), 2) AS
total_product_value,
```

Continues

(continued)

```
        MAX(CASE WHEN p.product_id = 16 THEN 1 ELSE 0 END) AS corn_available_flag
  FROM vendor_inventory vi
        INNER JOIN product p
            ON vi.product_id = p.product_id
        RIGHT JOIN market_date_info mdi
            ON mdi.market_date = vi.market_date
    GROUP BY
        mdi.market_year,
        mdi.market_week
```

Now that I see these results, I realize that I would like to have a count of vendors selling and products available at the entire market, in addition to the product availability for product category 1. To avoid developing another query that will need to be joined in, I will remove the `product_category_id` filter and use `CASE` statements to create a set of fields that provides the same metrics, but only for products in the category. Then, the existing fields will turn into a count for all vendors and products at the market:

```
SELECT
    mdi.market_year,
    mdi.market_week,
    COUNT(DISTINCT vi.vendor_id) AS vendor_count,
    COUNT(DISTINCT CASE WHEN p.product_category_id = 1 THEN vi.vendor_id
ELSE NULL END) AS vendor_count_product_category1,
    COUNT(DISTINCT vi.product_id) AS unique_product_count,
    COUNT(DISTINCT CASE WHEN p.product_category_id = 1 THEN vi.product_id
ELSE NULL END) AS unique_product_count_product_category1,
    SUM(CASE WHEN p.product_qty_type = 'unit' THEN vi.quantity ELSE 0 END)
AS unit_products_qty,
    SUM(CASE WHEN p.product_category_id = 1 AND p.product_qty_type = 'unit'
THEN vi.quantity ELSE 0 END) AS unit_products_qty_product_category1,
    SUM(CASE WHEN p.product_qty_type   = 'lbs' THEN vi.quantity ELSE 0 END)
AS bulk_products_lbs,
    SUM(CASE WHEN p.product_category_id = 1 AND p.product_qty_type   = 'lbs'
THEN vi.quantity ELSE 0 END) AS bulk_products_lbs_product_category1,
    ROUND(COALESCE(SUM(vi.quantity * vi.original_price), 0), 2) AS total_
product_value,
    ROUND(COALESCE(SUM(CASE WHEN p.product_category_id = 1 THEN vi.quantity
* vi.original_price ELSE 0 END), 0), 2) AS total_product_value_product_
category1,
    MAX(CASE WHEN p.product_id = 16 THEN 1 ELSE 0 END) AS corn_available_
flag
FROM vendor_inventory vi
    INNER JOIN product p
        ON vi.product_id = p.product_id
    RIGHT JOIN market_date_info mdi
        ON mdi.market_date = vi.market_date
GROUP BY
    mdi.market_year,
    mdi.market_week
```

market_date	market_year	market_week	market_date	quantity	vendor_id	product_id	original_price	product_id	product_name	product_size	product_category	product_qty_type
2019-06-08	2019	23	2019-06-08	100.00	4	16	0.50	16	Sweet Corn	Ear	1	unit
2019-06-12	2019	24	2019-06-12	120.00	4	16	0.50	16	Sweet Corn	Ear	1	unit
2019-06-15	2019	24	2019-06-15	140.00	4	16	0.50	16	Sweet Corn	Ear	1	unit
2019-06-19	2019	25	2019-06-19	120.00	4	16	0.50	16	Sweet Corn	Ear	1	unit
2019-06-22	2019	25	2019-06-22	120.00	4	16	0.50	16	Sweet Corn	Ear	1	unit
2019-06-26	2019	26	2019-06-26	140.00	4	16	0.50	16	Sweet Corn	Ear	1	unit
2019-06-29	2019	26	2019-06-29	100.00	4	16	0.50	16	Sweet Corn	Ear	1	unit
2019-07-03	2019	27	2019-07-03	7.38	7	1	6.99	1	Habanero Peppers...	medium	1	lbs
2019-07-03	2019	27	2019-07-03	33.63	7	2	3.49	2	Jalapeno Peppers...	small	1	lbs
2019-07-03	2019	27	2019-07-03	70.00	7	3	0.50	3	Poblano Peppers ...	large	1	unit
2019-07-03	2019	27	2019-07-03	300.00	4	16	0.50	16	Sweet Corn	Ear	1	unit
2019-07-06	2019	27	2019-07-06	10.96	7	1	6.99	1	Habanero Peppers...	medium	1	lbs
2019-07-06	2019	27	2019-07-06	24.56	7	2	3.49	2	Jalapeno Peppers...	small	1	lbs
2019-07-06	2019	27	2019-07-06	70.00	7	3	0.50	3	Poblano Peppers ...	large	1	unit
2019-07-06	2019	27	2019-07-06	200.00	4	16	0.50	16	Sweet Corn	Ear	1	unit
2019-07-10	2019	28	2019-07-10	13.08	7	1	6.99	1	Habanero Peppers...	medium	1	lbs
2019-07-10	2019	28	2019-07-10	28.83	7	2	3.49	2	Jalapeno Peppers...	small	1	lbs
2019-07-10	2019	28	2019-07-10	60.00	7	3	0.50	3	Poblano Peppers ...	large	1	unit
2019-07-10	2019	28	2019-07-10	300.00	4	16	0.50	16	Sweet Corn	Ear	1	unit
2019-07-13	2019	28	2019-07-13	10.22	7	1	6.99	1	Habanero Peppers...	medium	1	lbs
2019-07-13	2019	28	2019-07-13	29.17	7	2	3.49	2	Jalapeno Peppers...	small	1	lbs

Figure 13.7

market_year	market_week	vel	uni	unit_p	bulk_p	total_product_value	corn_available_flag
2019	25	3	5	386.00	0.00	1202.50	1
2019	26	3	5	380.00	0.00	1165.50	1
2019	27	3	8	778.00	76.53	1660.78	1
2019	28	3	8	821.00	81.30	1708.79	1
2019	29	3	8	882.00	77.83	1849.83	1
2019	30	3	8	785.00	74.55	1742.15	1
2019	31	3	8	811.00	84.05	1651.16	1
2019	32	3	8	836.00	74.17	1702.34	1
2019	33	3	8	764.00	77.44	1645.05	1
2019	34	3	8	754.00	67.73	1663.85	1
2019	35	3	8	856.00	70.81	1802.72	1
2019	36	3	8	524.00	88.54	1692.50	1
2019	37	3	8	522.00	67.76	1540.54	1
2019	38	3	8	514.00	79.10	1616.82	1
2019	39	3	8	538.00	78.46	1702.23	1
2019	40	2	4	139.00	0.00	1062.00	0
2019	41	2	4	150.00	0.00	1097.00	0
2019	42	2	4	138.00	0.00	1092.00	0
2019	43	2	4	149.00	0.00	1067.50	0
2019	44	2	4	143.00	0.00	1040.00	0
2019	45	2	4	145.00	0.00	1076.00	0

Figure 13.8

Figures 13.9, 13.10, and 13.11 display the columns resulting from this query, with each figure compressing the width of the previously displayed columns so examples of all columns in the output can be shown.

One easy quality check to do on the output here is to make sure that every field with the _category1 suffix has an equal or lower value than the corresponding field without the suffix, since the totals include product category 1, so the category value should never come out to be higher than the overall total.

Now I can combine the results of these two queries. I'll alias each of them in the WITH clause (CTE), then join the views:

```
WITH
my_customer_purchases AS
(
        SELECT
                mdi.market_year,
                mdi.market_week,
                MAX(mdi.market_rain_flag) AS market_week_rain_flag,
                MAX(mdi.market_snow_flag) AS market_week_snow_flag,
                MIN(mdi.market_min_temp) AS minimum_temperature,
                MAX(mdi.market_max_temp) AS maximum_temperature,
                MIN(mdi.market_season) AS market_season,
                ROUND(COALESCE(SUM(cp.quantity * cp.cost_to_customer_per_qty), 0), 2)
AS weekly_category1_sales
        FROM customer_purchases cp
            INNER JOIN product p
```

```
                    ON cp.product_id = p.product_id
                        AND p.product_category_id = 1
                RIGHT JOIN market_date_info mdi
                    ON mdi.market_date = cp.market_date
            GROUP BY
                mdi.market_year,
                mdi.market_week
),
my_vendor_inventory AS
(
    SELECT
        mdi.market_year,
        mdi.market_week,
        COUNT(DISTINCT vi.vendor_id) AS vendor_count,
        COUNT(DISTINCT CASE WHEN p.product_category_id = 1 THEN vi.vendor_id ELSE NULL
END) AS vendor_count_product_category1,
        COUNT(DISTINCT vi.product_id) unique_product_count,
        COUNT(DISTINCT CASE WHEN p.product_category_id = 1 THEN vi.product_id ELSE
NULL END) AS unique_product_count_product_category1,
        SUM(CASE WHEN p.product_qty_type = 'unit' THEN vi.quantity ELSE 0 END) AS
unit_products_qty,
        SUM(CASE WHEN p.product_category_id = 1 AND p.product_qty_type = 'unit' THEN
vi.quantity ELSE 0 END) AS unit_products_qty_product_category1,
        SUM(CASE WHEN p.product_qty_type <> 'unit' THEN vi.quantity ELSE 0 END) AS
bulk_products_qty,
        SUM(CASE WHEN p.product_category_id = 1 AND p.product_qty_type <> 'unit' THEN
vi.quantity ELSE 0 END) AS bulk_products_qty_product_category1,
        ROUND(COALESCE(SUM(vi.quantity * vi.original_price), 0), 2) AS
total_product_value,
        ROUND(COALESCE(SUM(CASE WHEN p.product_category_id = 1 THEN vi.quantity *
vi.original_price ELSE 0 END), 0), 2) AS total_product_value_product_category1,
        MAX(CASE WHEN p.product_id = 16 THEN 1 ELSE 0 END) AS corn_available_flag
    FROM vendor_inventory vi
        INNER JOIN product p
            ON vi.product_id = p.product_id
        RIGHT JOIN market_date_info mdi
            ON mdi.market_date = vi.market_date
    GROUP BY
        mdi.market_year,
        mdi.market_week
)


SELECT *
FROM my_vendor_inventory
    LEFT JOIN my_customer_purchases
        ON my_vendor_inventory.market_year = my_customer_purchases.market_year
            AND my_vendor_inventory.market_week = my_customer_purchases.market_week
ORDER BY my_vendor_inventory.market_year, my_vendor_inventory.market_week
```

market_year	market_week	vendor_count	vendor_count_product_category1	unique_product_count	unique_product_count_product_category1
2019	25	3	1	5	1
2019	26	3	1	5	1
2019	27	3	2	8	4
2019	28	3	2	8	4
2019	29	3	2	8	4
2019	30	3	2	8	4
2019	31	3	2	8	4
2019	32	3	2	8	4
2019	33	3	2	8	4
2019	34	3	2	8	4
2019	35	3	2	8	4
2019	36	3	2	8	4
2019	37	3	2	8	4
2019	38	3	2	8	4
2019	39	3	2	8	4
2019	40	2	0	4	0
2019	41	2	0	4	0
2019	42	2	0	4	0
2019	43	2	0	4	0
2019	44	2	0	4	0

Figure 13.9

market_year	market_week	ver	ver	uni	un	unit_products_qty	unit_products_qty	product_category1	bulk_products_lbs	bulk_products_lbs	product_category1
2019	25	3	1	5	1	386.00	240.00		0.00	0.00	
2019	26	3	1	5	1	380.00	240.00		0.00	0.00	
2019	27	3	2	8	4	778.00	640.00		76.53	76.53	
2019	28	3	2	8	4	821.00	690.00		81.30	81.30	
2019	29	3	2	8	4	882.00	730.00		77.83	77.83	
2019	30	3	2	8	4	785.00	640.00		74.55	74.55	
2019	31	3	2	8	4	811.00	680.00		84.05	84.05	
2019	32	3	2	8	4	836.00	690.00		74.17	74.17	
2019	33	3	2	8	4	764.00	630.00		77.44	77.44	
2019	34	3	2	8	4	754.00	610.00		67.73	67.73	
2019	35	3	2	8	4	856.00	710.00		70.81	70.81	
2019	36	3	2	8	4	524.00	370.00		88.54	88.54	
2019	37	3	2	8	4	522.00	380.00		67.76	67.76	
2019	38	3	2	8	4	514.00	370.00		79.10	79.10	
2019	39	3	2	8	4	538.00	390.00		78.46	78.46	
2019	40	2	0	4	0	139.00	0.00		0.00	0.00	
2019	41	2	0	4	0	150.00	0.00		0.00	0.00	
2019	42	2	0	4	0	138.00	0.00		0.00	0.00	
2019	43	2	0	4	0	149.00	0.00		0.00	0.00	
2019	44	2	0	4	0	143.00	0.00		0.00	0.00	

Figure 13.10

market_year	market_week	ver	ver	uni	un	unit_p	unit_p	bulk_p	bulk_p	total_product_value	total_product_value_product_category1	corn_available_flag
2019	25	3	1	5	1	386.00	240.00	0.00	0.00	1202.50	120.00	1
2019	26	3	1	5	1	380.00	240.00	0.00	0.00	1165.50	120.00	1
2019	27	3	2	8	4	778.00	640.00	76.53	76.53	1660.78	651.28	1
2019	28	3	2	8	4	821.00	690.00	81.30	81.30	1708.79	710.29	1
2019	29	3	2	8	4	882.00	730.00	77.83	77.83	1849.83	705.33	1
2019	30	3	2	8	4	785.00	640.00	74.55	74.55	1742.15	641.15	1
2019	31	3	2	8	4	811.00	680.00	84.05	84.05	1651.16	710.16	1
2019	32	3	2	8	4	836.00	690.00	74.17	74.17	1702.34	665.84	1
2019	33	3	2	8	4	764.00	630.00	77.44	77.44	1645.05	650.05	1
2019	34	3	2	8	4	754.00	610.00	67.73	67.73	1663.85	605.85	1
2019	35	3	2	8	4	856.00	710.00	70.81	70.81	1802.72	660.72	1
2019	36	3	2	8	4	524.00	370.00	88.54	88.54	1692.50	569.50	1
2019	37	3	2	8	4	522.00	380.00	67.76	67.76	1540.54	493.54	1
2019	38	3	2	8	4	514.00	370.00	79.10	79.10	1616.82	535.82	1
2019	39	3	2	8	4	538.00	390.00	78.46	78.46	1702.23	524.23	1
2019	40	2	0	4	0	139.00	0.00	0.00	0.00	1062.00	0.00	0
2019	41	2	0	4	0	150.00	0.00	0.00	0.00	1097.00	0.00	0
2019	42	2	0	4	0	138.00	0.00	0.00	0.00	1092.00	0.00	0
2019	43	2	0	4	0	149.00	0.00	0.00	0.00	1067.50	0.00	0
2019	44	2	0	4	0	143.00	0.00	0.00	0.00	1040.00	0.00	0
2019	45	2	0	4	0	145.00	0.00	0.00	0.00	1076.00	0.00	0

Figure 13.11

I can alter the final SELECT statement to include the prior week's product category 1 sales, too, because the prior week's sales might be a good indicator of what to expect this week. I can use the LAG window function that was introduced in Chapter 7, "Window Functions and Subqueries." And I'll go ahead and list all of the column names to avoid showing the duplicate market_year and market_week columns that are in both CTEs which therefore show in the output twice when we use *. (This query should be preceded by the same CTE/WITH clause as the previous query, but removed here to save space.)

```
SELECT
    mvi.market_year,
    mvi.market_week,
    mcp.market_week_rain_flag,
    mcp.market_week_snow_flag,
    mcp.minimum_temperature,
    mcp.maximum_temperature,
    mcp.market_season,
    mvi.vendor_count,
    mvi.vendor_count_product_category1,
    mvi.unique_product_count,
    mvi.unique_product_count_product_category1,
    mvi.unit_products_qty,
    mvi.unit_products_qty_product_category1,
    mvi.bulk_products_qty,
    mvi.bulk_products_qty_product_category1,
    mvi.total_product_value,
    mvi.total_product_value_product_category1,
    LAG(mcp.weekly_category1_sales, 1) OVER (ORDER BY mvi.market_year,
mvi.market_week) AS previous_week_category1_sales,
    mcp.weekly_category1_sales
FROM my_vendor_inventory mvi
    LEFT JOIN my_customer_purchases mcp
        ON mvi.market_year = mcp.market_year
            AND mvi.market_week = mcp.market_week
ORDER BY mvi.market_year, mvi.market_week
```

Now we have a detailed dataset summarized to one row per week that we could use to explore the relationships between the market weather, product availability, and fresh produce sales. Some of the columns in Figure 13.12 that were shown in previous figures have been condensed so the newly added LAG column is visible.

Before you read this book, a query like this might have looked large and indecipherable, but now you know that it's made by using various combinations of straightforward SQL statements you learned in other chapters, which are then combined into datasets with a progressively larger number of columns to use in analysis.

market_	market mar	minim	maxim	market_season	vendor	venc	uniqu	unic	unit_pr	unit_proc	bulk_pr	bulk_p	total_p	total_prc	previous_week_category1_sales	weekly_category1_sales
2019	22	0	49	69	Spring	3	1	5	1	262.00	120.00	0.00	0.00	1233.50	60.00	0.00	8.60
2019	23	0	57	82	Summer/Early Fall	3	1	5	1	376.00	240.00	0.00	0.00	1151.00	120.00	8.60	42.50
2019	24	0	56	82	Summer/Early Fall	3	1	5	1	401.00	260.00	0.00	0.00	1274.00	130.00	42.50	47.20
2019	25	0	65	80	Summer/Early Fall	3	1	5	1	386.00	240.00	0.00	0.00	1202.50	120.00	47.20	41.20
2019	26	0	72	85	Summer/Early Fall	3	1	5	1	380.00	240.00	0.00	0.00	1165.50	120.00	41.20	55.70
2019	27	0	67	89	Summer/Early Fall	3	2	8	4	778.00	640.00	76.53	76.53	1660.78	651.28	55.70	287.38
2019	28	0	65	90	Summer/Early Fall	3	2	8	4	821.00	690.00	81.30	81.30	1708.79	710.29	287.38	266.09

Figure 13.12

How Do Sales Vary by Customer Zip Code, Market Distance, and Demographic Data?

We have a couple of core questions here. How do sales vary by customer zip code and distance from the market? Can we integrate demographic data into this analysis? We will need to pull together several pieces of information to answer these questions. We could group all sales by zip code, but we might get more meaningful answers if we group sales by customer, then look at the summary statistics and distributions of per-customer sales totals by zip code.

We have the 5-digit zip (postal) code of each customer in the `customer` table, but we don't have their full address or 9-digit zip code, so the closest we can get to a "distance from the market" calculation is by calculating the distances between the market location and some location associated with each zip code, such as a centrally located latitude and longitude (keeping in mind that zip codes can be any kind of shape, so the "center" of the area isn't a great representation of the location of most residences in the postal code). One source of latitudes and longitudes by zip is `https://public.opendatasoft.com/explore/dataset/us-zip-code-latitude-and-longitude/table/?q=22821`. If we import this data into our database, we can join it to our queries to add a latitude and longitude per zip code to our dataset.

There is also plenty of demographic data online related to zip codes, such as census data summarized by ZCTAs (Zip Code Tabulation Areas), so we can pull in age distributions, wealth statistics, and other demographics summarized by zip.

For this example, I decided to summarize the sales per customer first, then join in the demographic data to every customer's record, even though it's not customer-specific. Then, if I were to train a model based on the behavior of customers, I could use the zip code data as an input into the customer-level model, or as a dimension to summarize the other per-customer fields by for reporting purposes.

So I'll first summarize sales per customer, including for how long they've been a customer, the count of market dates at which they've made a purchase, and the total each customer has spent to date. I'll also join the purchase summary to the customer table, in order to include each customer's zip code. The output of the following query is shown in Figure 13.13:

```
SELECT
    c.customer_id,
    c.customer_zip,
    DATEDIFF(MAX(market_date), MIN(market_date)) customer_duration_days,
    COUNT(DISTINCT market_date) number_of_markets,
    ROUND(SUM(quantity * cost_to_customer_per_qty), 2) total_spent,
```

Continues

(continued)

```
        ROUND(SUM(quantity * cost_to_customer_per_qty) / COUNT(DISTINCT
    market_date), 2) average_spent_per_market
    FROM farmers_market.customer c
    LEFT JOIN farmers_market.customer_purchases cp
        ON cp.customer_id = c.customer_id
    GROUP BY c.customer_id
```

Note that because of the nature of the sample data, the customers in this case have pretty similar values in this output, which isn't typical when you look at data collected from real-world scenarios.

I have loaded some example demographic data into a new table in the database I called `zip_data`, which is shown in Figure 13.14:

```
SELECT * FROM zip_data
```

I will join this table to my existing query by the zip code fields, so every customer in a zip code will have the same demographic data added to their record, as shown in Figure 13.15. I condensed the columns that were already shown in Figure 13.13 in order to fit the newly added columns in view:

```
SELECT
    c.customer_id,
    DATEDIFF(MAX(market_date), MIN(market_date)) AS customer_duration_days,
    COUNT(DISTINCT market_date) AS number_of_markets,
    ROUND(SUM(quantity * cost_to_customer_per_qty), 2) AS total_spent,
    ROUND(SUM(quantity * cost_to_customer_per_qty) / COUNT(DISTINCT
market_date), 2) AS average_spent_per_market,
    c.customer_zip,
    z.median_household_income AS zip_median_household_income,
    z.percent_high_income AS zip_percent_high_income,
    z.percent_under_18 AS zip_percent_under_18,
    z.percent_over_65 AS zip_percent_over_65,
    z.people_per_sq_mile AS zip_people_per_sq_mile,
    z.latitude,
    z.longitude
FROM farmers_market.customer c
    LEFT JOIN farmers_market.customer_purchases cp
        ON cp.customer_id = c.customer_id
    LEFT JOIN zip_data z
        ON c.customer_zip = z.zip_code_5
GROUP BY c.customer_id
```

customer_id	customer_zip	customer_duration_days	number_of_markets	total_spent	average_spent_per_market
1	22801	553	107	3530.92	33.00
2	22821	553	117	4179.45	35.72
3	22821	553	112	3832.16	34.22
4	22801	549	115	3561.63	30.97
5	22801	556	113	3932.83	34.80
6	22801	556	95	3016.47	31.75
7	22821	556	100	2921.17	29.21
8	22821	553	101	3403.68	33.70
9	22801	556	92	3015.73	32.78
10	22801	556	96	2495.41	25.99

Figure 13.13

zip_code_5	median_household_income	percent_high_income	percent_under_18	percent_over_65	people_per_sq_mile	latitude	longitude
22821	65417	0.053	0.25	0.17	66.3	38.437	-78.99
22802	48746	0.028	0.23	0.14	321.2	38.478	-78.863
22801	53042	0.05	0.16	0.11	1279.6	38.427	-78.882

Figure 13.14

One part of the analysis question was about distance from the market, which the data we have doesn't exactly tell us. There is a calculation for distance between two latitudes and longitudes that I found on Dayne Batten's blog at `https://daynebatten.com/2015/09/latitude-longitude-distance-sql/`. If the Farmer's Market is at the coordinates 38.4463, –78.8712, the calculation for distance between the latitude and longitude fields of a record in the dataset and the Farmer's Market location is:

```
ROUND(2 * 3961 * ASIN(SQRT(POWER(SIN(RADIANS((latitude - 38.4463) / 2)),2) +
COS(RADIANS(38.4463)) * COS(RADIANS(latitude)) * POWER((SIN(RADIANS((longitude - -
78.8712) / 2))), 2))))
```

Don't worry about understanding how that calculation works, just know that it returns the distance between two pairs of latitude and longitude rounded to the nearest mile. Replacing the latitude and longitude fields in our query with this calculation, we now have the query:

```
SELECT
    c.customer_id,
    DATEDIFF(MAX(market_date), MIN(market_date)) AS customer_duration_days,
    COUNT(DISTINCT market_date) AS number_of_markets,
    ROUND(SUM(quantity * cost_to_customer_per_qty), 2) AS total_spent,
    ROUND(SUM(quantity * cost_to_customer_per_qty) / COUNT(DISTINCT
market_date), 2) AS average_spent_per_market,
    c.customer_zip,
    z.median_household_income AS zip_median_household_income,
    z.percent_high_income AS zip_percent_high_income,
    z.percent_under_18 AS zip_percent_under_18,
    z.percent_over_65 AS zip_percent_over_65,
    z.people_per_sq_mile AS zip_people_per_sq_mile,
    ROUND(2 * 3961 * ASIN(SQRT(POWER(SIN(RADIANS((z.latitude - 38.4463) / 2)),2) +
COS(RADIANS(38.4463)) * COS(RADIANS(z.latitude)) * POWER((SIN(RADIANS((z.longitude - -
78.8712) / 2))), 2)))) AS zip_miles_from_market
FROM farmers_market.customer AS c
    LEFT JOIN farmers_market.customer_purchases AS cp
        ON cp.customer_id = c.customer_id
    LEFT JOIN zip_data AS z
        ON c.customer_zip = z.zip_code_5
GROUP BY c.customer_id
```

Again, I have condensed the fields shown in Figures 13.13 and 13.15 in order to display the new fields fully in Figure 13.16.

This will allow me to analyze customer metrics like total amount spent and number of markets attended by customer zip code or by calculated distance from the market. I could now build a scatterplot of `zip_miles_from_market`

custom	custr number	total_spi	average_	customer_zip	zip_median_household_income	zip_percent_high_income	zip_percent_under_18	zip_percent_over_65	zip_people_per_sq_mile	latitude	longitude
6	556	95	3016.47	31.75	22801	53042	0.05	0.16	0.11	1279.6	38.427	-78.882
7	556	100	2921.17	29.21	22821	65417	0.053	0.25	0.17	66.3	38.437	-78.99
8	553	101	3403.68	33.70	22821	65417	0.053	0.25	0.17	66.3	38.437	-78.99
9	556	92	3015.73	32.78	22801	53042	0.05	0.16	0.11	1279.6	38.427	-78.882
10	556	96	2495.41	25.99	22801	53042	0.05	0.16	0.11	1279.6	38.427	-78.882
11	556	100	3499.99	35.00	22801	53042	0.05	0.16	0.11	1279.6	38.427	-78.882
12	549	103	3290.08	31.94	22821	65417	0.053	0.25	0.17	66.3	38.437	-78.99
13	546	71	1582.98	22.30	22821	65417	0.053	0.25	0.17	66.3	38.437	-78.99
14	543	68	2322.54	34.16	22801	53042	0.05	0.16	0.11	1279.6	38.427	-78.882
15	536	55	1506.35	27.39	22801	53042	0.05	0.16	0.11	1279.6	38.427	-78.882
16	553	73	2015.00	27.60	22801	53042	0.05	0.16	0.11	1279.6	38.427	-78.882
17	543	78	1882.61	24.14	22802	48746	0.028	0.23	0.14	321.2	38.478	-78.863
18	550	66	1964.08	29.76	22802	48746	0.028	0.23	0.14	321.2	38.478	-78.863
19	535	44	1772.93	40.29	22802	48746	0.028	0.23	0.14	321.2	38.478	-78.863

Figure 13.15

custom	custr number	total_spi	average_	customer_zip	zip_median_household_income	zip_percent_high_income	zip_percent_under_18	zip_percent_over_65	zip_people_per_sq_mile	zip_miles_from_market
4	549	115	3561.63	30.97	22801	53042	0.05	0.16	0.11	1279.6	1
5	556	113	3932.83	34.80	22801	53042	0.05	0.16	0.11	1279.6	1
6	556	95	3016.47	31.75	22821	65417	0.053	0.25	0.17	1279.6	1
7	556	100	2921.17	29.21	22821	65417	0.053	0.25	0.17	66.3	6
8	553	101	3403.68	33.70	22821	65417	0.053	0.25	0.17	66.3	6
9	556	92	3015.73	32.78	22801	53042	0.05	0.16	0.11	1279.6	1
10	556	96	2495.41	25.99	22801	53042	0.05	0.16	0.11	1279.6	1
11	556	100	3499.99	35.00	22821	65417	0.053	0.25	0.17	1279.6	1
12	549	103	3290.08	31.94	22821	65417	0.053	0.25	0.17	66.3	6
13	546	71	1582.98	22.30	22821	65417	0.053	0.25	0.17	66.3	6
14	543	68	2322.54	34.16	22801	53042	0.05	0.16	0.11	1279.6	1
15	536	55	1506.35	27.39	22801	53042	0.05	0.16	0.11	1279.6	1
16	553	73	2015.00	27.60	22801	53042	0.05	0.16	0.11	1279.6	1
17	543	78	1882.61	24.14	22802	48746	0.028	0.23	0.14	321.2	2
18	550	66	1964.08	29.76	22802	48746	0.028	0.23	0.14	321.2	2
19	535	44	1772.93	40.29	22802	48746	0.028	0.23	0.14	321.2	2

Figure 13.16

versus `total_spent` (though all of the customer data points in each zip code would overlap on the distance axis, so I would have to add some jitter or size the dots in order to indicate how many people were represented by that point).

With the newly added information per zip, I could create a rural versus urban flag based on the population density of the zip code and look at customer behavior based on that value. I could assess customer longevity by zip code, or look at the distributions of amount spent or customer durations by zip code. I could correlate the percent of high-income residents per zip code with the customers' total amount spent at the market. There are a wide variety of analyses I could do with just this dataset.

Some other ideas of additional customer summary fields that could be added to this dataset if we also joined in details about the products include total purchases by product category, top vendor purchased from, number of different vendors purchased from, number of different products purchased, most frequent time of day of purchase, etc.

Here is one example usage of this dataset where I put the preceding query into a CTE and select from it to get the count of customers and the average total spent per customer for each zip code. Note that in this case, the `zip_miles_from_market` is the same per row, so I could take the min, max, or average and would get the same value returned because all of the values are identical per zip, which we're grouping by. I could also add `zip_miles_from_market` to the GROUP BY statement, or even change the structure of my query so I'm only joining in the zip code data at this point, when I'm summarizing the customers by zip, instead of joining the zip code data to the query inside the CTE. For the purposes of summary, either approach is fine. The output of the following approach is shown in Figure 13.17:

```
WITH customer_and_zip_data AS
(
    SELECT
        c.customer_id,
        DATEDIFF(MAX(market_date), MIN(market_date)) AS customer_duration_days,
        COUNT(DISTINCT market_date) AS number_of_markets,
        ROUND(SUM(quantity * cost_to_customer_per_qty), 2) AS total_spent,
        ROUND(SUM(quantity * cost_to_customer_per_qty) / COUNT(DISTINCT market_date),
2) AS average_spent_per_market,
        c.customer_zip,
        z.median_household_income AS zip_median_household_income,
        z.percent_high_income AS zip_percent_high_income,
        z.percent_under_18 AS zip_percent_under_18,
        z.percent_over_65 AS zip_percent_over_65,
        z.people_per_sq_mile AS zip_people_per_sq_mile,
```

```
        ROUND(2 * 3961 * ASIN(SQRT(POWER(SIN(RADIANS((z.latitude - 38.4463) / 2)),2) +
COS(RADIANS(38.4463)) * COS(RADIANS(z.latitude)) * POWER((SIN(RADIANS((z.longitude - -
78.8712) / 2))), 2)))) AS zip_miles_from_market
    FROM farmers_market.customer AS c
        LEFT JOIN farmers_market.customer_purchases AS cp
            ON cp.customer_id = c.customer_id
        LEFT JOIN zip_data AS z
            ON c.customer_zip = z.zip_code_5
    GROUP BY c.customer_id
)

SELECT
    cz.customer_zip,
    COUNT(cz.customer_id) AS customer_count,
    ROUND(AVG(cz.total_spent)) AS average_total_spent,
    MIN(cz.zip_miles_from_market) AS zip_miles_from_market
FROM customer_and_zip_data AS cz
GROUP BY cz.customer_zip
```

customer_zip	customer_count	average_total_spent	zip_miles_from_market
22801	15	2681	1
22821	7	3084	6
22802	4	1857	2

Figure 13.17

One caveat to this analysis that we would want to inform the recipient about is that we only store the customer's current zip code in this database, so if a customer used to live in a different zip code, that past connection is lost, and all of their purchase history is now associated with the current zip code on their customer record. To maintain the changes in zip code over time, we would need to add another table to the database in which to store the customer zip code history.

How Does Product Price Distribution Affect Market Sales?

What if a manager of the market asks, "What does our distribution of product prices look like at the market? Are our low-priced items or high-priced items generating more sales for the market?" You might have guessed that in order to answer these questions, I'm going to be using window functions.

One clarifying question I would have for the requester in this case before trying to answer these questions is related to time, because I know that the distribution of prices can change over time, and the answer to the second question might have changed at some point as well. So, should we answer these questions only for the most recent market season? Compare year over year? Or just look at all sales for the entire history we have tracked, ignoring any possible changes over time?

Let's say that the requester replied to clarify that they want to look at product price distributions for each market season over time (because the types of products sold can be very different in the heat of summer versus at the winter holidays, for example, as well as changing over the years).

So first, I want to get the product pricing details prior to completing the level of summarization required to answer the questions.

The first step in this analysis is to get raw data on the price per product per market date. But that seemingly simple task then raises another question: What do we mean by "product"? Is each `product_id` in the database a product? Like "Carrots" sold by weight? Or do the products differ enough by vendor that I should consider each `product_id` sold by each vendor as a separate "product"? We were asked to look at the distribution of product prices over time, and different vendors do charge different amounts for the same products if we go by `product_id`, so I will choose to look at the average price per product per vendor per season. I will start with the `original_price` per product specified by the vendor in the `vendor_inventory` table, and won't consider special discounts given to customers, which would appear in the `customer_purchases` table. This query's results are shown in Figure 13.18:

```
SELECT
    p.product_id,
    p.product_name,
    p.product_category_id,
    p.product_qty_type,
    vi.vendor_id,
    vi.market_date,
    SUM(vi.quantity),
    AVG(vi.original_price)
FROM product AS p
    LEFT JOIN vendor_inventory AS vi
        ON vi.product_id = p.product_id
GROUP BY
    p.product_id,
    p.product_name,
    p.product_category_id,
    p.product_qty_type,
    vi.vendor_id,
    vi.market_date
```

product_id	product_name	product_category_id	product_qty_type	vendor_id	market_date	SUM(vi.quantity)	AVG(vi.original_price)
1	Habanero Peppers - Organic	1	lbs	7	2020-08-29	9.38	6.990000
1	Habanero Peppers - Organic	1	lbs	7	2020-09-02	14.23	6.990000
1	Habanero Peppers - Organic	1	lbs	7	2020-09-05	9.38	6.990000
1	Habanero Peppers - Organic	1	lbs	7	2020-09-09	10.75	6.990000
1	Habanero Peppers - Organic	1	lbs	7	2020-09-12	10.84	6.990000
1	Habanero Peppers - Organic	1	lbs	7	2020-09-16	10.11	6.990000
1	Habanero Peppers - Organic	1	lbs	7	2020-09-19	10.04	6.990000
1	Habanero Peppers - Organic	1	lbs	7	2020-09-23	10.19	6.990000
1	Habanero Peppers - Organic	1	lbs	7	2020-09-26	9.88	6.990000
1	Habanero Peppers - Organic	1	lbs	7	2020-09-30	13.76	6.990000
2	Jalapeno Peppers - Organic	1	lbs	7	2019-07-03	33.63	3.490000
2	Jalapeno Peppers - Organic	1	lbs	7	2019-07-06	24.56	3.490000
2	Jalapeno Peppers - Organic	1	lbs	7	2019-07-10	28.83	3.490000
2	Jalapeno Peppers - Organic	1	lbs	7	2019-07-13	29.17	3.490000
2	Jalapeno Peppers - Organic	1	lbs	7	2019-07-17	29.89	3.490000

Figure 13.18

Next, since it was determined that we're looking at prices per season over time, I need to pull in the `market_season` from the `market_date_info` table. I can also use the year so we're talking about seasons over time. And here's another challenge I can anticipate might arise later when I'm building the reports: The seasons are strings, so how do I know what order they should go in when sorting by season and year? I will keep the minimum month value in the dataset so it can later be used to sort the seasons in the correct order. See Figure 13.19 for the output of this query:

```
SELECT
    p.product_id,
    p.product_name,
    p.product_category_id,
    p.product_qty_type,
    vi.vendor_id,
    MIN(MONTH(vi.market_date)) AS month_market_season_sort,
    mdi.market_season,
    mdi.market_year,
    SUM(vi.quantity) AS quantity_available,
    AVG(vi.original_price) AS avg_original_price
FROM product AS p
    LEFT JOIN vendor_inventory AS vi
        ON vi.product_id = p.product_id
    LEFT JOIN market_date_info AS mdi
        ON vi.market_date = mdi.market_date
GROUP BY
    p.product_id,
    p.product_name,
    p.product_category_id,
    p.product_qty_type,
    vi.vendor_id,
    mdi.market_year,
    mdi.market_season
```

One thing you might have noticed is that my attempt to pull in a sortable value to order the market seasons has resulted in multiple `month_market_season_sort` values per season, because we are getting the minimum month per season per product, and some products aren't offered in the earliest month of each season. These differing values could have detrimental effects to our results later on, depending on how we use the sorting field, so we'll have to be careful how items group and sort with this value involved. We could also use a window function to get the minimum month per `market_season` across all rows for that season, ignoring the `product_id` values, which we'll switch to in the next version of the query.

product_id	product_name	product_category_id	product_qty_type	vendor_id	month	market_season_sort	market_season	market_year	quantity_available	avg_original_price
1	Habanero Peppers - Organic	1	lbs	7	7		Summer/Early Fall	2019	249.94	6.990000
1	Habanero Peppers - Organic	1	lbs	7	7		Summer/Early Fall	2020	288.01	6.990000
2	Jalapeno Peppers - Organic	1	lbs	7	7		Summer/Early Fall	2019	748.33	3.490000
2	Jalapeno Peppers - Organic	1	lbs	7	7		Summer/Early Fall	2020	807.90	3.490000
3	Poblano Peppers - Organic	1	unit	7	7		Summer/Early Fall	2019	1750.00	0.500000
3	Poblano Peppers - Organic	1	unit	7	7		Summer/Early Fall	2020	1730.00	0.500000
4	Banana Peppers - Jar	3	unit	7	4		Spring	2019	610.00	4.000000
4	Banana Peppers - Jar	3	unit	7	6		Summer/Early Fall	2019	1610.00	4.000000
4	Banana Peppers - Jar	3	unit	7	11		Late Fall/Holiday	2019	630.00	4.000000
4	Banana Peppers - Jar	3	unit	7	3		Spring	2020	970.00	4.000000
4	Banana Peppers - Jar	3	unit	7	6		Summer/Early Fall	2020	1410.00	4.000000
5	Whole Wheat Bread	3	unit	8	4		Spring	2019	349.00	6.500000
5	Whole Wheat Bread	3	unit	8	6		Summer/Early Fall	2019	892.00	6.500000
5	Whole Wheat Bread	3	unit	8	11		Late Fall/Holiday	2019	322.00	6.500000

Figure 13.19

At this point, I also realized that I do need to pull in the `customer_purchases` data, because the second question is about sales, and the `vendor_inventory` table only contains available items, not items sold or the total amount generated by sales of each item. So I'll join that table in and use it to calculate the aggregate sales data for the second question. Note that we need to join on all three matching keys: `product_id`, `vendor_id`, and `market_date`, as shown here, and reflected in the results in Figure 13.20:

```
SELECT
    p.product_id,
    p.product_name,
    p.product_category_id,
    p.product_qty_type,
    vi.vendor_id,
    MIN(MONTH(vi.market_date)) OVER (PARTITION BY market_season) AS
month_market_season_sort,
    mdi.market_season,
    mdi.market_year,
    AVG(vi.original_price) AS avg_original_price,
    SUM(cp.quantity) AS quantity_sold,
    SUM(cp.quantity * cp.cost_to_customer_per_qty) AS total_sales
FROM product AS p
    LEFT JOIN vendor_inventory AS vi
        ON vi.product_id = p.product_id
    LEFT JOIN market_date_info AS mdi
        ON vi.market_date = mdi.market_date
    LEFT JOIN customer_purchases AS cp
        ON vi.product_id = cp.product_id
        AND vi.vendor_id = cp.vendor_id
        AND vi.market_date = cp.market_date
GROUP BY
    p.product_id,
    p.product_name,
    p.product_category_id,
    p.product_qty_type,
    vi.vendor_id,
    mdi.market_year,
    mdi.market_season
```

It would be good at this point to pick a few products and look through the detailed availability and purchase data, to quality check these summarized results before continuing.

product_id	product_name	product_category_id	product_qty_type	vendor_id	month	market_season_sort	market_season	market_year	avg_original_price	quantity_sold	total_sales
4	Banana Peppers - Jar	3	unit	7	11		Late Fall/Holiday	2019	4.000000	412.00	1648.0000
5	Whole Wheat Bread	3	unit	8	11		Late Fall/Holiday	2019	6.500000	267.00	1735.5000
7	Apple Pie	3	unit	8	11		Late Fall/Holiday	2019	18.000000	190.00	3420.0000
8	Cherry Pie	3	unit	8	11		Late Fall/Holiday	2019	18.000000	232.00	4176.0000
4	Banana Peppers - Jar	3	unit	7	3		Spring	2019	4.000000	411.00	1612.0000
4	Banana Peppers - Jar	3	unit	7	3		Spring	2020	4.000000	661.00	2577.0000
5	Whole Wheat Bread	3	unit	8	3		Spring	2019	6.500000	280.00	1820.0000
5	Whole Wheat Bread	3	unit	8	3		Spring	2020	6.500000	365.00	2372.5000
7	Apple Pie	3	unit	8	3		Spring	2019	18.000000	123.00	2214.0000
7	Apple Pie	3	unit	8	3		Spring	2020	18.000000	158.00	2844.0000
8	Cherry Pie	3	unit	8	3		Spring	2019	18.000000	136.00	2448.0000
8	Cherry Pie	3	unit	8	3		Spring	2020	18.000000	172.00	3096.0000
4	Banana Peppers - Jar	3	unit	7	6		Summer/Early Fall	2019	4.000000	829.00	3307.5000
4	Banana Peppers - Jar	3	unit	7	6		Summer/Early Fall	2020	4.000000	697.00	2710.5000
5	Whole Wheat Bread	3	unit	8	6		Summer/Early Fall	2019	6.500000	671.00	4361.5000
5	Whole Wheat Bread	3	unit	8	6		Summer/Early Fall	2020	6.500000	489.00	3178.5000

Figure 13.20

Now that I have a sale price of each item (the average price each vendor offered each product for each season), I could start exploring the distribution of prices. When developing these queries, I actually tried several different approaches at this point and landed on this one, partly because the small number of products in the database can expose an issue with using NTILES: two different items of the same price can end up in different NTILES if the number of NTILES you choose splits the set at that point. After attempting multiple NTILE number options, I realized that if I wanted to end up with high and low price points in order to answer the second question, I probably shouldn't be ranking the products anyway. I should be ranking the prices.

In that case, I decided to modify my approach to group the records by market_year, market_season, and original_price. I used an NTILE value of 3, which then gives me groupings of the top, middle, and bottom 1/3 of prices. I can then summarize the sales of products that fall into each of these price points.

Here's the query that creates three price groupings per season:

```
SELECT
    mdi.market_season,
    mdi.market_year,
    MIN(MONTH(vi.market_date)) OVER (PARTITION BY market_season) AS
month_market_season_sort,
    vi.original_price,
    NTILE(3) OVER (PARTITION BY market_year, market_season ORDER BY original_price) AS
price_ntile,
    NTILE(3) OVER (PARTITION BY market_year, market_season ORDER BY original_price
DESC) AS price_ntile_desc,
    COUNT(DISTINCT CONCAT(vi.product_id, vi.vendor_id)) product_count,
    SUM(cp.quantity) AS quantity_sold,
    SUM(cp.quantity * cp.cost_to_customer_per_qty) AS total_sales
FROM product AS p
    LEFT JOIN vendor_inventory AS vi
        ON vi.product_id = p.product_id
    LEFT JOIN market_date_info AS mdi
        ON vi.market_date = mdi.market_date
    LEFT JOIN customer_purchases AS cp
        ON vi.product_id = cp.product_id
        AND vi.vendor_id = cp.vendor_id
        AND vi.market_date = cp.market_date
WHERE market_year IS NOT NULL
GROUP BY
    mdi.market_year,
    mdi.market_season,
    vi.original_price
```

The results of this query are shown in Figure 13.21.

market_season	market_year	month	market_season_sort	original_price	price_ntile	price_ntile_desc	product_count	quantity_sold	total_sales
Late Fall/Holiday	2019	11		18.00	3	1	2	422.00	7596.0000
Late Fall/Holiday	2019	11		6.50	2	2	1	267.00	1735.5000
Late Fall/Holiday	2019	11		4.00	1	3	1	412.00	1648.0000
Spring	2019	3		18.00	3	1	2	259.00	4662.0000
Spring	2019	3		6.50	2	2	1	280.00	1820.0000
Spring	2019	3		4.00	1	3	1	411.00	1612.0000
Summer/Early Fall	2019	6		18.00	3	1	2	559.00	10062.0000
Summer/Early Fall	2019	6		6.99	3	1	1	175.18	1224.5082
Summer/Early Fall	2019	6		6.50	2	2	1	671.00	4361.5000
Summer/Early Fall	2019	6		4.00	2	2	2	829.00	3307.5000
Summer/Early Fall	2019	6		3.49	1	3	1	397.91	1382.3506
Summer/Early Fall	2019	6		0.50	1	3	2	1718.00	825.6000

Figure 13.21

Note that the `price_ntile` break points vary by season. In Summer 2019 and Summer 2020, a $4.00 item is in the second of the three NTILE groups, so it's in the middle price grouping. In Spring, the distribution of product prices changes, so a $4.00 item is in `price_ntile` 1, or the low price grouping.

Also note that I created a column using the NTILE window function with the same number of groups as `price_ntile`, but sorting the price descending. This way, if you are using the output and don't know how many groups there are, you can filter to `price_ntile` = 1 to get the lowest price group, and `price_ntile_desc` = 1 to get the highest price group.

Another thing I want to point out in the previous query is that I didn't COUNT(DISTINCT `product_id`) values, but first concatenated `product_id` and `vendor_id` and did a distinct count of the combined values. The reason is because of how we're defining "product," where the same `product_id` sold by different vendors, possibly for different prices, is considered a different product for our purposes.

One caveat with these results is that we're summing up different types of quantities, so we're counting an ounce, pound, or unit product as "an item sold." So our quantity isn't exactly apples-to-apples across seasons, but gives us a quick sales volume measure for rough comparison.

The output in Figure 13.21 also illustrates why I wanted to create a `month_market_season_sort`, because alphabetically, the seasons sort out of order as "Late Fall," "Spring," and "Summer." We will make use of the sort values in the next query.

Now we'll use the previous query as a CTE and summarize it:

```
WITH product_prices AS
(
    SELECT
        mdi.market_season,
        mdi.market_year,
        MIN(MONTH(vi.market_date)) OVER (PARTITION BY market_season) AS
month_market_season_sort,
        vi.original_price,
        NTILE(3) OVER (PARTITION BY market_year, market_season ORDER BY
original_price) AS price_ntile,
        NTILE(3) OVER (PARTITION BY market_year, market_season ORDER BY
original_price DESC) AS price_ntile_desc,
        COUNT(DISTINCT CONCAT(vi.product_id, vi.vendor_id)) AS product_count,
        SUM(cp.quantity) AS quantity_sold,
        SUM(cp.quantity * cp.cost_to_customer_per_qty) AS total_sales
    FROM product AS p
        LEFT JOIN vendor_inventory AS vi
            ON vi.product_id = p.product_id
        LEFT JOIN market_date_info AS mdi
            ON vi.market_date = mdi.market_date
```

```
            LEFT JOIN customer_purchases AS cp
                ON vi.product_id = cp.product_id
                AND vi.vendor_id = cp.vendor_id
                AND vi.market_date = cp.market_date
        WHERE market_year IS NOT NULL
        GROUP BY
            mdi.market_year,
            mdi.market_season,
            vi.original_price
)

SELECT
    market_year,
    market_season,
    price_ntile,
    SUM(product_count) AS product_count,
    SUM(quantity_sold) AS quantity_sold,
    MIN(original_price) AS min_price,
    MAX(original_price) AS max_price,
    SUM(total_sales) AS total_sales
FROM product_prices
GROUP BY
    market_year,
    market_season,
    price_ntile
ORDER BY
    market_year,
    month_market_season_sort,
    price_ntile
```

In Figure 13.22, you'll see that we're now sorting the seasons in the correct order (even though we're not outputting the sort value), and we're displaying the minimum and maximum price per grouping, as well as the total_sales. This gives us the data to answer the second question, and we can see that with this sample data, the total_sales is highest for price_ntile 3 in every season, so the higher-priced items are generating the most sales for the market.

market_	market_season	price_ntile	product_count	quantity_sold	min_price	max_price	total_sales
2019	Spring	1	1	411.00	4.00	4.00	1612.0000
2019	Spring	2	1	280.00	6.50	6.50	1820.0000
2019	Spring	3	2	259.00	18.00	18.00	4662.0000
2019	Summer/Early Fall	1	3	2115.91	0.50	3.49	2207.9506
2019	Summer/Early Fall	2	2	1500.00	4.00	6.50	7669.0000
2019	Summer/Early Fall	3	3	734.18	6.99	18.00	11286.5082
2019	Late Fall/Holiday	1	1	412.00	4.00	4.00	1648.0000
2019	Late Fall/Holiday	2	1	267.00	6.50	6.50	1735.5000
2019	Late Fall/Holiday	3	2	422.00	18.00	18.00	7596.0000

Figure 13.22

Hopefully these dataset creation walkthroughs have given you a sense of the variety of ways you can combine and summarize data to create a dataset to answer analytical questions, and the kinds of clarifying questions an experienced analyst might ask while going through this process. Keep in mind that each dataset can now be refreshed to pull in the latest data by rerunning the queries, and the results can be reused to answer many questions, not just the ones initially asked!

Storing and Modifying Data

We have covered many aspects of developing datasets for machine learning that involve selecting data from a database and preparing it for machine learning models, but what do you do once you have designed your query and are ready to start analyzing the results? Your SQL editor will often allow you to write the results of your query to a CSV file to be imported into Business Intelligence (BI) software such as Tableau or machine learning scripts in a language like Python. However, sometimes for data governance, data security, teamwork, or file size and processing speed purposes, it is preferable to store the dataset within the database.

In this chapter, we'll cover some types of SQL queries beyond SELECT statements, such as INSERT statements, which allow you to store the results of your query in a new table in the database.

Storing SQL Datasets as Tables and Views

In most databases, you can store the results of a query as either a table or a view. Storing results as a *table* takes a snapshot of whatever the results are at the time the query is run and saves the data returned as a new table object, or as new rows appended to an existing table, depending on how you write your SQL statement. A database *view* instead stores the SQL itself and runs it on-demand when you write a query that references the name of the view, to dynamically generate a new dataset based on the state of the referenced database objects at the time you run the query. (You may have also heard of the term *materialized view*, which is more like a stored snapshot and is not what I'm referring to here.)

If you have database storage space available, permissions to create tables or insert records into tables in your database, and it is not cost-prohibitive to do so, it can be good practice to store snapshots of the datasets you are using in your machine learning applications. You can check with your database administrator to determine whether you can and should create and modify tables, and which schema(s) you have permission to write to.

When you're iteratively testing various combinations of fields and parameters in your machine learning algorithm, you'll want to test multiple different approaches with the same static dataset, so you can be sure your input data isn't changing each time you run your script by writing the results to a table. You might also decide to store a copy of the dataset for later reference if the dataset you're querying could change over time and you want to keep a record of the exact values that were run through your model at the time you ran it.

One way to store the results of a query is to use a CREATE TABLE statement. The syntax is

```
CREATE TABLE [schema_name].[new_table_name] AS

(

    [your query here]

)
```

As with the SELECT statements, the indentation and line breaks in these queries don't matter to the database and are just used to format for readability. The table name used in a CREATE TABLE statement must be new and unique within the schema. If you try to run the same CREATE TABLE statement twice in a row, you will get an error stating that the table already exists.

Once you create the table, you can query it like any other table or view, referencing the new name you gave it. If you created a table by accident or want to re-create it with a different name or definition, you can DROP the table.

> **WARNING** Be very careful when using the DROP TABLE statement, or you might accidentally delete something that should not have been be deleted! Depending on the database settings and backup frequency, the data you delete may not be recoverable! I usually ensure that I am only granted database permissions to create and drop tables in a personal schema, which is separate from the schema used to run applications or where tables that others are using are stored, so I can't accidentally delete a table I did not create or that is used in a production application.

The syntax for dropping a table is simply:

```
DROP TABLE [schema_name].[table_name]
```

So, to create, select from, and drop a table that contains a snapshot of the data that is currently in the Farmer's Market database `product` table, filtered to products with a quantity type "unit," run the following three queries in sequence:

```
CREATE TABLE farmers_market.product_units AS
(
    SELECT *
    FROM farmers_market.product
    WHERE product_qty_type = "unit"
)
;


SELECT * FROM farmers_market.product_units
;


DROP TABLE farmers_market.product_units
;
```

The semicolons are used to separate multiple queries in the same file.

> **TIP** If you don't want to accidentally run a DROP TABLE statement that is included in a file with other SQL statements (since many SQL editors have a "run all" command), comment it out immediately after running it, and save the file with that query commented out, so you don't accidentally run it the next time you open the file and drop a table you didn't intend to! In MySQL Workbench, you can comment out code by preceding each line with two dashes and a space or by surrounding a block of code with / * and */.

Database views are created and dropped the same exact way as tables, though when you create a view, you are not actually storing the data, but storing the query to be run when you query the view. So when you drop a view, you are not actually deleting any data, since the data isn't stored; you are just dropping the named reference to the query:

```
CREATE VIEW farmers_market.product_units_vw AS
(
    SELECT *
    FROM farmers_market.product
    WHERE product_qty_type = "unit"
)
;


SELECT * FROM farmers_market.product_units_vw
;


DROP VIEW farmers_market.product_units_vw
;
```

Note that some database systems, like SQL Server, support a SELECT INTO syntax, which operates much like the CREATE TABLE statement previously demonstrated, and is often used to create backups of existing tables. Check your database's documentation online to determine which syntax to use.

Adding a Timestamp Column

When you create or modify a database table, you might want to keep a record of when each row in the table was created or last modified. You can do this by adding a timestamp column to your CREATE TABLE or UPDATE statement. The syntax for creating a timestamp varies by database system, but in MySQL, the function that returns the current date and time is called CURRENT_TIMESTAMP. You can give the timestamp column an alias like any calculated column.

Keep in mind that the timestamp is generated by the database server, so if the database is in another time zone, the timestamp returned by the function may be different than the current time at your physical location. Many databases use Coordinated Universal Time (UTC) as their default timestamp time, which is a global time standard that is synchronized using atomic clocks, aligns in hour offset with the Greenwich Mean Time time zone, and doesn't change for Daylight Savings Time. Eastern Standard Time, which is observed in the Eastern Time Zone in North America during the winter, can be signified as UTC-05:00, meaning it is five hours behind UTC. Eastern Daylight Time, observed during the summer, has an offset of UTC-04:00, because the Eastern Time Zone observes Daylight Savings Time and shifts by an hour, while UTC does not shift. You can see how time zone math can quickly get complicated, which is why many databases simplify by using a standard UTC clock time instead of a developer's local time.

We can modify the preceding CREATE TABLE example to include a timestamp column as follows:

```
CREATE TABLE farmers_market.product_units AS
(
    SELECT p.*,
        CURRENT_TIMESTAMP AS snapshot_timestamp
    FROM farmers_market.product AS p
    WHERE product_qty_type = "unit"
)
```

Example output from this query is shown in Figure 14.1.

product_id	product_name	product_size	product_category_id	product_qty_type	snapshot_timestamp
3	Poblano Peppers - Organic	large	1	unit	2021-04-18 00:49:24
4	Banana Peppers - Jar	8 oz	3	unit	2021-04-18 00:49:24
5	Whole Wheat Bread	1.5 lbs	3	unit	2021-04-18 00:49:24
6	Cut Zinnias Bouquet	medium	5	unit	2021-04-18 00:49:24
7	Apple Pie	10"	3	unit	2021-04-18 00:49:24
8	Cherry Pie	10"	3	unit	2021-04-18 00:49:24
10	Eggs	1 dozen	6	unit	2021-04-18 00:49:24
12	Baby Salad Lettuce Mix - Bag	1/2 lb	1	unit	2021-04-18 00:49:24
16	Sweet Corn	Ear	1	unit	2021-04-18 00:49:24
18	Carrots - Organic	bunch	1	unit	2021-04-18 00:49:24
19	Farmer's Market Resuable Shopping Bag	medium	7	unit	2021-04-18 00:49:24

Figure 14.1

Inserting Rows and Updating Values in Database Tables

If you want to modify data in an existing database table, you can use an INSERT statement to add a new row or an UPDATE statement to modify an existing row of data in a table.

In this chapter, we're specifically inserting results of a query into another table, which is a specific kind of INSERT statement called INSERT INTO SELECT. The syntax is

INSERT INTO [schema_name].[table_name] ([comma-separated list of column names])

[your SELECT query here]

So if we wanted to add rows to our product_units table created earlier, we would write:

```
INSERT INTO farmers_market.product_units (product_id, product_name,
product_size, product_category_id, product_qty_type, snapshot_timestamp)
    SELECT
        product_id,
        product_name,
        product_size,
        product_category_id,
        product_qty_type,
        CURRENT_TIMESTAMP
    FROM farmers_market.product AS p
    WHERE product_id = 23
```

It is important that the columns in both queries are in the same order. The corresponding fields may not have identical names, but the system will attempt to insert the returned values from the SELECT statement in the column order listed in parentheses.

Now when we query the product_units table, we'll have a snapshot of the same product row at two different times, as shown in Figure 14.2.

product_id	product_name	product_size	product_category_id	product_qty_type	snapshot_timestamp
23	Maple Syrup - Jar	8 oz	2	unit	2021-04-11 23:41:41
23	Maple Syrup - Jar	8 oz	2	unit	2021-04-18 00:49:24

Figure 14.2

If you make a mistake when inserting a row and want to delete it, the syntax is simply

DELETE FROM [schema_name].[table_name]

WHERE [set of conditions that uniquely identifies the row]

You may want to start with SELECT * instead of DELETE so you can see what rows will be deleted before running the DELETE statement!

The product_id and snapshot_timestamp uniquely identify rows in the product_units table, so we can run the following statement to delete the row added by our previous INSERT INTO:

```
DELETE FROM farmers_market.product_units
WHERE product_id = 23
    AND snapshot_timestamp = '2021-04-18 00:49:24'
```

Sometimes you want to update a value in an existing row instead of inserting a totally new row. The syntax for an UPDATE statement is as follows:

UPDATE [schema_name].[table_name]

SET [column_name] = [new value]

WHERE [set of conditions that uniquely identifies the rows you want to change]

Let's say that you've already entered all of the farmer's market vendor booth assignments for the next several months, but vendor 4 informs you that they can't make it on October 10, so you decide to upgrade vendor 8 to vendor 4's booth, which is larger and closer to the entrance, for the day.

Before making any changes, let's snapshot the existing vendor booth assignments, along with the vendor name and booth type, into a new table using the following SQL:

```
CREATE TABLE farmers_market.vendor_booth_log AS
(
    SELECT vba.*,
        b.booth_type,
        v.vendor_name,
        CURRENT_TIMESTAMP AS snapshot_timestamp
    FROM farmers_market.vendor_booth_assignments vba
        INNER JOIN farmers_market.vendor v
            ON vba.vendor_id = v.vendor_id
        INNER JOIN farmers_market.booth b
            ON vba.booth_number = b.booth_number
    WHERE market_date >= '2020-10-01'
)
```

Selecting all records from this new log table produces the results shown in Figure 14.3.

vendor_id	booth_number	market_date	booth_type	vendor_name	snapshot_timestamp
1	2	2020-10-07	Standard	Chris's Sustainable Eggs & Meats	2021-04-18 01:23:24
3	1	2020-10-07	Standard	Mountain View Vegetables	2021-04-18 01:23:24
4	7	2020-10-07	Standard	Fields of Corn	2021-04-18 01:23:24
7	11	2020-10-07	Large	Marco's Peppers	2021-04-18 01:23:24
8	6	2020-10-07	Small	Annie's Pies	2021-04-18 01:23:24
9	8	2020-10-07	Small	Mediterranean Bakery	2021-04-18 01:23:24
1	2	2020-10-10	Standard	Chris's Sustainable Eggs & Meats	2021-04-18 01:23:24
3	1	2020-10-10	Standard	Mountain View Vegetables	2021-04-18 01:23:24
4	7	2020-10-10	Standard	Fields of Corn	2021-04-18 01:23:24
7	11	2020-10-10	Large	Marco's Peppers	2021-04-18 01:23:24
8	6	2020-10-10	Small	Annie's Pies	2021-04-18 01:23:24
9	8	2020-10-10	Small	Mediterranean Bakery	2021-04-18 01:23:24

Figure 14.3

To update vendor 8's booth assignment, we can run the following SQL:

```
UPDATE farmers_market.vendor_booth_assignments
SET booth_number = 7
WHERE vendor_id = 8 and market_date = '2020-10-10'
```

And we can delete vendor 4's booth assignment with the following SQL:

```
DELETE FROM farmers_market.vendor_booth_assignments
WHERE vendor_id = 4 and market_date = '2020-10-10'
```

Now, when we query the vendor_booth_assignments table, there is no record that vendor 4 had a booth assignment on that date, or that vendor 8's booth assignment used to be different. But we do have a record of the previous assignments in the vendor_booth_log we created! Now we can insert new records into the log table to record the latest changes:

```
INSERT INTO farmers_market.vendor_booth_log (vendor_id, booth_number,
market_date, booth_type, vendor_name, snapshot_timestamp)
    SELECT
        vba.vendor_id,
        vba.booth_number,
        vba.market_date,
        b.booth_type,
        v.vendor_name,
        CURRENT_TIMESTAMP AS snapshot_timestamp
    FROM farmers_market.vendor_booth_assignments vba
        INNER JOIN farmers_market.vendor v
            ON vba.vendor_id = v.vendor_id
        INNER JOIN farmers_market.booth b
            ON vba.booth_number = b.booth_number
    WHERE market_date >= '2020-10-01'
```

So now even though the original vendor_booth_assignments table doesn't contain the original booth assignments for these two vendors on October 10, if we had run an analysis at an earlier date and wanted to see what the database values were at that time, we could query this `vendor_booth_log` table to look at the values at different points time, as shown in Figure 14.4.

vendor_id	booth_number	market_date	snapshot_timestamp
4	7	2020-10-03	2021-04-18 01:23:24
4	7	2020-10-07	2021-04-18 01:23:24
4	7	2020-10-10	2021-04-18 01:23:24
8	6	2020-10-03	2021-04-18 01:23:24
8	6	2020-10-07	2021-04-18 01:23:24
8	6	2020-10-10	2021-04-18 01:23:24
4	7	2020-10-03	2021-04-18 01:35:14
4	7	2020-10-07	2021-04-18 01:35:14
8	6	2020-10-03	2021-04-18 01:35:14
8	6	2020-10-07	2021-04-18 01:35:14
8	7	2020-10-10	2021-04-18 01:35:14

Figure 14.4

Using SQL Inside Scripts

Importing the datasets you develop into your machine learning script is beyond the scope of this book, but you can search the internet for the combination of SQL and your chosen scripting language and packages to find tutorials. For example, searching "import SQL python pandas dataframe" will lead you to tutorials for connecting to a database from within your Python script, running a SQL query, and importing the results into a pandas dataframe for analysis. You can usually either paste the SQL query into your script and store it in a string variable or reference the SQL stored in a text document.

Keep in mind that some special characters in your query will need to be "escaped." For example, if you surround your SQL query in double quotes to store it in a string variable in Python, it will interpret any double quotes within your query as ending the string and raise an error. To use quotes inside quoted strings in Python, you can precede them with a backslash.

Representing this SQL query as a string in Python

```
SELECT * FROM farmers_market.product WHERE product_qty_type = "unit"
```

requires escaping the internal double quotes, like so:

```
my_query = "SELECT * FROM farmers_market.product WHERE product_qty_type
= \"unit\""
```

This is common in programming languages where strings are surrounded by quotes, since many strings contain quotes in the enclosed text, so you can search for "string escape characters" along with your chosen machine learning script tool or language to find out how to modify your SQL for use within your script.

You can also write data from your script back to the database using SQL, but the approach varies based on the scripting language you're using and the type of database you're connecting to. In Python, for example, there are packages available to help you connect and write to a variety of databases without even needing to write dynamic SQL INSERT statements—the packages generate the SQL for you to insert values from an object in Python like a dataframe into a database table for persistent storage.

Another approach is to programmatically create a file to temporarily store your data, transfer the file to a location that is accessible from your script and your database, and load the results from the file into your table. For example, you might use Python to write data from a pandas dataframe to a CSV file, transfer the CSV file to an Amazon Web Services S3 bucket, then access the file from the database and copy the records into an existing table in a Redshift database. All of these steps can be automated from your script.

One machine learning use case for writing data from your script to the database is if you want to store your transformed dataset after you have completed feature engineering and data preprocessing steps in your script that weren't completed in the original dataset-generating SQL.

Another use case for writing values generated within your script back to the database is when you want to store the results that your predictive model generates and associate them with the original dataset. You can create a table that stores the unique identifiers for the rows in your input dataset for which you have scores, a timestamp, the name or ID of your model, and the score or classification generated by the model for each record. You can insert new rows into the table each time you refresh your model scores. Then, use a SQL query to filter this model score log table to a specific date and model identifier and join it to the table with your input dataset, joining on the unique row identifiers. This will allow you to analyze the results of the model alongside the input data used to generate the predictions at the time.

There are many ways to connect to and interact with data from a database in your other scripts that may or may not require SQL.

In Closing

Now that you know SQL basics, you should have the foundation needed to create datasets for your machine learning models, even if you need to search the internet for functions and syntax that were not covered in this book.

I have been a data scientist for five years now, and all of the queries I have written to generate my datasets for machine learning have been variations of the SQL I originally learned in school 20 years ago. I hope that this book has given you the SQL skills you need to achieve your analysis goals faster and more independently, and that you find pulling and modifying your own datasets as empowering as I do!

Exercises

1. If you include a CURRENT_TIMESTAMP column when you create a view, what would you expect the values of that column to be when you query the view?

2. Write a query to determine what the data from the vendor_booth_assignment table looked like on October 3, 2020 by querying the vendor_booth_log table created in this chapter. (Assume that records have been inserted into the log table any time changes were made to the vendor_booth_assignment table.)

Answers to Exercises

Chapter 1: Data Sources

Answers

1. If the "Author Full Name" field is updated (overwritten) in the existing Authors table record for the author, then when a query is run to retrieve a list of authors and their books, all past books associated with the author will now be associated with the author's new name in the database, even if that wasn't the name printed on the cover of the book.

   If instead a new row is added to the Authors table to record the new name (leaving the existing books associated with the prior name), then there might be no way to know that the two authors, who now have different Author IDs, are actually the same person.

   There are solutions to this problem that include designing the database tables and relationships to allow multiple names per Author ID, with start and stop dates, or adding a field to the Authors table such as "prior Author ID" that associates an Authors table record with another record in the same table, if one exists.

   Understanding these relationships and when and how data is updated in the database you're querying is important for understanding and explaining the results of your queries.

2. One example might be tracking personal exercise routines. You could have a table of workout sessions and a table of exercises, which would be a *many to many* relationship: each workout could contain multiple exercises, and each exercise could be part of multiple workouts. If you included a table of workout session locations, that could be designed as a "one to many" relationship with the workout sessions table, assuming each workout could only take place in one location (say, at home or at the gym), but each location could be the site of many workout sessions.

Chapter 2: The SELECT Statement

Answers

1. This query returns everything in the `customer` table:

```
SELECT * FROM farmers_market.customer
```

2. This query displays all of the columns and 10 rows from the `customer` table, sorted by `customer_last_name`, then `customer_first_name`:

```
SELECT *
FROM farmers_market.customer
ORDER BY customer_last_name, customer_first_name
LIMIT 10
```

3. This query lists all customer IDs and first names in the `customer` table, sorted by `first_name`:

```
SELECT
    customer_id,
    customer_first_name
FROM farmers_market.customer
ORDER BY customer_first_name
```

Chapter 3: The WHERE Clause

Answers

There are multiple answers to most SQL questions, but here are some possible solutions for the exercises in Chapter 3:

1. Remember that even though the English phrasing is "product ids 4 and 9," using AND between the conditions in the query will not return any results, because there is only one `product_id` per `customer_purchase`. Use

an OR between the conditions in the WHERE clause to return every row that has a product_id of either 4 or 9:

```
SELECT *
FROM farmers_market.customer_purchases
WHERE product_id = 4
    OR product_id = 9
```

2. Note that the first query uses >= and <= to establish the inclusive range, while the second query uses BETWEEN to achieve the same result:

```
SELECT *
FROM farmers_market.customer_purchases
WHERE vendor_id >= 8
    AND vendor_id <= 10


SELECT *
FROM farmers_market.customer_purchases
WHERE vendor_id BETWEEN 8 AND 10
```

3. One approach is to filter to market dates that are not in the "rainy dates" list, by using the NOT operator to negate the IN condition. This will return TRUE for the rows in the customer_purchases table with a market_date that is NOT IN the query in the WHERE clause:

```
SELECT
    market_date,
    customer_id,
    vendor_id,
    quantity * cost_to_customer_per_qty AS price
FROM farmers_market.customer_purchases
WHERE
    market_date NOT IN
        (
        SELECT market_date
        FROM farmers_market.market_date_info
        WHERE market_rain_flag = 1
        )
```

Another option is to keep the IN condition but change the query in the WHERE clause to return dates where it was not raining, when market_rain_flag is set to 0:

```
SELECT
    market_date,
    customer_id,
    vendor_id,
    quantity * cost_to_customer_per_qty AS price
FROM farmers_market.customer_purchases
```

Continues

(continued)

```
WHERE
    market_date IN
        (
        SELECT market_date
        FROM farmers_market.market_date_info
        WHERE market_rain_flag = 0
        )
```

Chapter 4: CASE Statements

Answers

1. Look back at Figure 2.1 for sample data and column names for the `product` table referenced in this exercise. This query outputs the `product_id` and `product_name` columns from `product`, with a column called `prod_qty_type_condensed` that displays the word "unit" if the `product_qty_type` is "unit," and otherwise displays the word "bulk":

```
SELECT
    product_id,
    product_name,
    CASE WHEN product_qty_type = "Unit"
        THEN "unit"
        ELSE "bulk"
    END AS prod_qty_type_condensed
FROM farmers_market.product
```

2. To add a column to the previous query called `pepper_flag` that outputs a 1 if the `product_name` contains the word "pepper" (regardless of capitalization), and otherwise outputs 0, do the following:

```
SELECT
    product_id,
    product_name,
    CASE WHEN product_qty_type = "Unit"
        THEN "per unit"
        ELSE "bulk"
    END AS prod_qty_type_condensed,
    CASE WHEN LOWER(product_name) LIKE '%pepper%'
        THEN 1
        ELSE 0
    END AS pepper_flag
FROM farmers_market.product
```

3. If the product name doesn't include the word "pepper," spelled exactly that way, it won't be flagged. For example, a product might only be labeled as "Jalapeno" instead of Jalapeno pepper.

Chapter 5: SQL JOINs

Answers

1. This query INNER JOINs the vendor table to the `vendor_booth_assignments` table and sorts the result by `vendor_name`, then `market_date`:

```
SELECT *
FROM vendor AS v
    INNER JOIN vendor_booth_assignments AS vba
        ON v.vendor_id = vba.vendor_id
ORDER BY v.vendor_name, vba.market_date
```

2. The following query uses a LEFT JOIN to produce output identical to the output of this exercise's query:

```
SELECT c.*, cp.*
FROM customer_purchases AS cp
    LEFT JOIN customer AS c
        ON cp.customer_id = c.customer_id
```

This could have been written with SELECT * and be considered correct. Using the table aliases in this way allows you to control which table's columns are displayed first, so in addition to returning the same data, it's also returned with the same column order as the given query.

3. One approach is to INNER JOIN the product table and the product_category table, to get the category of every product (a new category with no products in it yet wouldn't need to be included here, and there shouldn't be any products without categories), then LEFT JOIN the vendor_inventory table to the product table. I chose a LEFT JOIN instead of an INNER JOIN because we might want to know if products exist in the database that are never in season because they have never been offered by a vendor at the farmer's market. There are acceptable answers that include all types of JOINs, as long as the reason for each choice is explained.

Because we haven't learned about aggregation (summarization) yet, the dataset you can create using the information included in this chapter will have one row per product per vendor who offered it per market date it was offered, labeled with the product category. Because the vendor_inventory table includes the date the product was offered for sale, you could sort by product_category, product, and market_date, and scroll through the query results to determine when each type of item is in season.

Chapter 6: Aggregating Results for Analysis

Answers

1. This query determines how many times each vendor has rented a booth at the farmer's market:

```
SELECT
    vendor_id,
    count(*) AS count_of_booth_assignments
FROM farmers_market.vendor_booth_assignments
GROUP BY vendor_id
```

2. This query displays the product category name, product name, earliest date available, and latest date available for every product in the "Fresh Fruits & Vegetables" product category:

```
SELECT
    pc.product_category_name,
    p.product_name,
    min(market_date) AS first_date_available,
    max(market_date) AS last_date_available
FROM farmers_market.vendor_inventory vi
    INNER JOIN farmers_market.product p
        ON vi.product_id = p.product_id
    INNER JOIN farmers_market.product_category pc
        ON p.product_category_id = pc.product_category_id
WHERE product_category_name = 'Fresh Fruits & Vegetables'
```

3. This query joins two tables, uses an aggregate function, and uses the HAVING keyword to generate a list of customers who have spent more than $50, sorted by last name, then first name:

```
SELECT
    cp.customer_id,
    c.customer_first_name,
    c.customer_last_name,
    SUM(quantity * cost_to_customer_per_qty) AS total_spent
FROM farmers_market.customer c
    LEFT JOIN farmers_market.customer_purchases cp
        ON c.customer_id = cp.customer_id
GROUP BY
    cp.customer_id,
    c.customer_first_name,
    c.customer_last_name
HAVING total_spent > 50
ORDER BY c.customer_last_name, c.customer_first_name
```

Chapter 7: Window Functions and Subqueries

Answers

1. Here are the answers to the two parts of this exercise:

   a. These queries use DENSE_RANK() or ROW_NUMBER() to select from the customer_purchases table and numbers each customer's visits to the Farmer's Market using DENSE_RANK():

```
select cp.*,
    DENSE_RANK() OVER (PARTITION BY customer_id ORDER BY market_date)
AS visit_number
FROM farmers_market.customer_purchases AS cp
ORDER BY customer_id, market_date
```

   or

```
select customer_id, market_date,
    ROW_NUMBER() OVER (PARTITION BY customer_id ORDER BY market_date)
AS visit_number
FROM farmers_market.customer_purchases
GROUP BY customer_id, market_date
ORDER BY customer_id, market_date
```

   b. This is how to reverse the numbering of the preceding query so each customer's most recent visit is labeled 1, and then use another query to filter the results to only the customer's most recent visit:

```
SELECT * FROM
(
    select customer_id, market_date,
        ROW_NUMBER() OVER (PARTITION BY customer_id ORDER BY market_
date DESC) AS visit_number
    FROM farmers_market.customer_purchases
    GROUP BY customer_id, market_date
    ORDER BY customer_id, market_date
) x
where x.visit_number = 1
```

   Or

```
SELECT * FROM
(
select cp.*,
    DENSE_RANK() OVER (PARTITION BY customer_id ORDER BY market_
date DESC) AS visit_number
FROM farmers_market.customer_purchases AS cp
ORDER BY customer_id, market_date
) x
where x.visit_number = 1
```

2. Here's how to use a COUNT() window function and include a value along with each row of the customer_purchases table that indicates how many different times that customer has purchased that product_id:

```
select cp.*,
    COUNT(product_id) OVER (PARTITION BY customer_id, product_id) AS
product_purchase_count
FROM farmers_market.customer_purchases AS cp
ORDER BY customer_id, product_id, market_date
```

3. If you swap out LEAD for LAG, you're looking at the next row instead of the previous, so to get the same output, you just have to sort market_date in descending order, so everything is reversed!

```
SELECT
    market_date,
    SUM(quantity * cost_to_customer_per_qty) AS market_date_total_sales,
    LEAD(SUM(quantity * cost_to_customer_per_qty), 1) OVER (ORDER BY
market_date DESC) AS previous_market_date_total_sales
FROM farmers_market.customer_purchases
GROUP BY market_date
ORDER BY market_date
```

Chapter 8: Date and Time Functions

Answers

1. Here is how to get the customer_id, month, and year (in separate columns) of every purchase in the farmers_market.customer_purchases table:

```
SELECT customer_id,
    EXTRACT(MONTH FROM market_date) AS purchase_month,
    EXTRACT(YEAR FROM market_date) AS purchase_year
FROM farmers_market.customer_purchases
```

2. Here is an example of filtering and summing purchases made in the past two weeks.

Using March 31, 2019 as the reference date:

```
SELECT MIN(market_date) AS sales_since_date,
    SUM(quantity * cost_to_customer_per_qty) AS total_sales
FROM farmers_market.customer_purchases
WHERE DATEDIFF('2019-03-31', market_date) <= 14
```

Using CURDATE(), which will result in NULL results on the sample database, since all dates are more than two weeks ago:

```
SELECT MIN(market_date) AS sales_since_date,
    SUM(quantity * cost_to_customer_per_qty) AS total_sales
FROM farmers_market.customer_purchases
WHERE DATEDIFF(CURDATE(), market_date) <= 14
```

3. This is an example of using a quality control query to check manually entered data for correctness:

```
SELECT
    market_date,
    market_day,
    DAYNAME(market_date) AS calculated_market_day,
    CASE WHEN market_day <> DAYNAME(market_date) then "INCORRECT"
        ELSE "CORRECT" END AS entered_correctly
FROM farmers_market.market_date_info
```

Chapter 9: Exploratory Data Analysis with SQL

Answers

1. The following query gets the earliest and latest dates in the customer_purchases table:

```
SELECT MIN(market_date), MAX(market_date)
FROM farmers_market.customer_purchases
```

2. Here is how to use the DAYNAME() and EXTRACT() functions to select and group by the weekday and hour of the day, and count the distinct number of customers during each hour of the Wednesday and Saturday markets:

```
SELECT DAYNAME(market_date),
    EXTRACT(HOUR FROM transaction_time),
    COUNT(DISTINCT customer_id)
FROM farmers_market.customer_purchases
GROUP BY DAYNAME(market_date),  EXTRACT(HOUR FROM transaction_time)
ORDER BY DAYNAME(market_date),  EXTRACT(HOUR FROM transaction_time)
```

3. A variety of answers would be acceptable. Two examples are shown here.

How many customers made purchases at each market?

```
SELECT market_date, COUNT(DISTINCT customer_id)
FROM customer_purchases
GROUP BY market_date
ORDER BY market_date
```

What is the total value of the inventory each vendor brought to each market?

```
SELECT market_date, vendor_id,
    ROUND(SUM(quantity * original_price),2) AS inventory_value
FROM vendor_inventory
GROUP BY market_date, vendor_id
ORDER BY market_date, vendor_id
```

Chapter 10: Building SQL Datasets for Analytical Reporting

Answers

1. Sales per vendor per market week:

   ```
   SELECT market_week, vendor_id, vendor_name,
       SUM(sales) AS weekly_sales
   FROM farmers_market.vw_sales_by_day_vendor AS s
   GROUP BY market_week, vendor_id, vendor_name
   ORDER BY market_date
   ```

2. Subquery rewritten using a WITH clause:

   ```
   WITH x AS
   (
   SELECT
       market_date,
       vendor_id,
       booth_number,
       LAG(booth_number,1) OVER (PARTITION BY vendor_id ORDER BY market_
   date, vendor_id) AS previous_booth_number
   FROM farmers_market.vendor_booth_assignments
   ORDER BY market_date, vendor_id, booth_number
   )

   SELECT *
   FROM x
   WHERE
       x.market_date = '2020-03-13'
       AND
       (x.booth_number <> x.previous_booth_number
       OR x.previous_booth_number IS NULL)
   ```

3. There is one vendor booth assignment per vendor per market date, so we don't need to change the granularity of our dataset in order to summarize by booth type, but we do need to pull that booth type into the dataset. We can accomplish that by LEFT JOINing in the vendor_booth_assignments

and `booth` tables, and including the `booth_number` and `booth_type` columns
in our `SELECT` statement:

```
SELECT
    cp.market_date,
    md.market_day,
    md.market_week,
    md.market_year,
    cp.vendor_id,
    v.vendor_name,
    v.vendor_type,
    vba.booth_number,
    b.booth_type,
    ROUND(SUM(cp.quantity * cp.cost_to_customer_per_qty),2) AS sales
FROM farmers_market.customer_purchases AS cp
    LEFT JOIN farmers_market.market_date_info AS md
        ON cp.market_date = md.market_date
    LEFT JOIN farmers_market.vendor AS v
        ON cp.vendor_id = v.vendor_id
    LEFT JOIN farmers_market.vendor_booth_assignments AS vba
        ON cp.vendor_id = vba.vendor_id
        AND cp.market_date = vba.market_date
    LEFT JOIN farmers_market.booth AS b
        ON vba.booth_number = b.booth_number
    GROUP BY cp.market_date, cp.vendor_id
    ORDER BY cp.market_date, cp.vendor_id
```

Chapter 11: More Advanced Query Structures

Answers

1. There are multiple possible solutions. Here is one:

```
WITH
sales_per_market_date AS
(
    SELECT
        market_date,
        ROUND(SUM(quantity * cost_to_customer_per_qty),2) AS sales
    FROM farmers_market.customer_purchases
    GROUP BY market_date
    ORDER BY market_date
),
record_sales_per_market_date AS
(
    SELECT
        cm.market_date,
        cm.sales,
```

Continues

(continued)

```
            MAX(pm.sales) AS previous_max_sales,
            CASE WHEN cm.sales > MAX(pm.sales)
                THEN "YES"
                ELSE "NO"
            END sales_record_set
        FROM sales_per_market_date AS cm
            LEFT JOIN sales_per_market_date AS pm
                ON pm.market_date < cm.market_date
        GROUP BY cm.market_date, cm.sales
    )

    SELECT
        market_date,
        sales
    FROM record_sales_per_market_date
    WHERE sales_record_set = 'YES'
    ORDER BY market_date DESC
    LIMIT 1
```

2. This may be more challenging than you initially anticipated! First, we need to add `vendor_id` to the output and the partition in the CTE, so we are ranking the first purchase date per customer per vendor. Then, we need to count the distinct customers per market per vendor, so we add the `vendor_id` to the GROUP BY in the outer query, and also modify the CASE statements to use the field we have re-aliased to `first_purchase_from_vendor_date`:

```
WITH
customer_markets_vendors AS
(
    SELECT DISTINCT
        customer_id,
        vendor_id,
        market_date,
        MIN(market_date) OVER(PARTITION BY cp.customer_id,
cp.vendor_id) AS first_purchase_from_vendor_date
    FROM farmers_market.customer_purchases cp
)

SELECT
    md.market_year,
    md.market_week,
    cmv.vendor_id,
    COUNT(customer_id) AS customer_visit_count,
    COUNT(DISTINCT customer_id) AS distinct_customer_count,
    COUNT(DISTINCT
        CASE WHEN cmv.market_date = cmv.first_purchase_from_vendor_date
            THEN customer_id
                ELSE NULL
```

```
        END) AS new_customer_count,
    COUNT(DISTINCT
        CASE WHEN cmv.market_date = cmv.first_purchase_from_vendor_date
            THEN customer_id
            ELSE NULL
        END)
        / COUNT(DISTINCT customer_id)
        AS new_customer_percent
FROM customer_markets_vendors AS cmv
    LEFT JOIN farmers_market.market_date_info AS md
        ON cmv.market_date = md.market_date
GROUP BY md.market_year, md.market_week, cmv.vendor_id
ORDER BY md.market_year, md.market_week, cmv.vendor_id
```

3. Again, there are many possible solutions, but here is one where the sales per market date are ranked ascending and descending, and then the top results from each of those rankings are selected and unioned together:

```
WITH
sales_per_market AS
(
    SELECT
        market_date,
        ROUND(SUM(quantity * cost_to_customer_per_qty),2) AS sales
    FROM farmers_market.customer_purchases
    GROUP BY market_date
),
market_dates_ranked_by_sales AS
(
    SELECT
        market_date,
        sales,
        RANK() OVER (ORDER BY sales) AS sales_rank_asc,
        RANK() OVER (ORDER BY sales DESC) AS sales_rank_desc
    FROM sales_per_market
)

SELECT market_date, sales, sales_rank_desc AS sales_rank
FROM market_dates_ranked_by_sales
WHERE sales_rank_asc = 1

UNION

SELECT market_date, sales, sales_rank_desc AS sales_rank
FROM market_dates_ranked_by_sales
WHERE sales_rank_desc = 1
```

Chapter 12: Creating Machine Learning Datasets Using SQL

Answers

1. This can be accomplished by duplicating the `customer_markets_attended_30days_count` feature and replacing each "30" with 14:

```
(SELECT COUNT(market_date)
    FROM customer_markets_attended cma
    WHERE cma.customer_id = cp.customer_id
        AND cma.market_date < cp.market_date
        AND DATEDIFF(cp.market_date, cma.market_date) <= 14) AS
customer_markets_attended_14days_count,
```

2. The query is already grouped by `customer_id` and `market_date`, so we just need to add a column that determines if any underlying row has an item with a price over $10, and if so, return a 1, then use the MAX function to get the highest number per group, which will be a 1 if any row met the criteria:

```
MAX(CASE WHEN cp.cost_to_customer_per_qty > 10 THEN 1 ELSE 0 END)
purchased_item_over_10_dollars,
```

3. This is a tricky one. One way to accomplish it is to add the `purchase_total` per market date to the CTE, then add up all `purchase_total` values for dates prior to the row's `market_date`. Both `total_spent_to_date` and `customer_has_spent_over_200` fields have been added to the following query, which also includes the fields from exercises 1 and 2:

```
WITH
customer_markets_attended AS
(
    SELECT
        customer_id,
        market_date,
        SUM(quantity * cost_to_customer_per_qty) AS purchase_total,
        ROW_NUMBER() OVER (PARTITION BY customer_id ORDER BY market_
date) AS market_count
    FROM farmers_market.customer_purchases
    GROUP BY customer_id, market_date
    ORDER BY customer_id, market_date
)

SELECT
    cp.customer_id,
    cp.market_date,
```

```
    EXTRACT(MONTH FROM cp.market_date) AS market_month,
    SUM(cp.quantity * cp.cost_to_customer_per_qty) AS purchase_total,
    COUNT(DISTINCT cp.vendor_id) AS vendors_patronized,
    MAX(CASE WHEN cp.vendor_id = 7 THEN 1 ELSE 0 END) AS purchased_
from_vendor_7,
    MAX(CASE WHEN cp.vendor_id = 8 THEN 1 ELSE 0 END) AS purchased_
from_vendor_8,
    COUNT(DISTINCT cp.product_id) AS different_products_purchased,
    DATEDIFF(cp.market_date,
        (SELECT MAX(cma.market_date)
        FROM customer_markets_attended AS cma
        WHERE cma.customer_id = cp.customer_id
            AND cma.market_date < cp.market_date
        GROUP BY cma.customer_id)) days_since_last_customer_market_date,
    (SELECT MAX(market_count)
        FROM customer_markets_attended cma
        WHERE cma.customer_id = cp.customer_id
            AND cma.market_date <= cp.market_date) AS customer_
markets_attended_count,
    (SELECT COUNT(market_date)
        FROM customer_markets_attended cma
        WHERE cma.customer_id = cp.customer_id
            AND cma.market_date < cp.market_date
            AND DATEDIFF(cp.market_date, cma.market_date) <= 30) AS
customer_markets_attended_30days_count,
    (SELECT COUNT(market_date)
        FROM customer_markets_attended cma
        WHERE cma.customer_id = cp.customer_id
            AND cma.market_date < cp.market_date
            AND DATEDIFF(cp.market_date, cma.market_date) <= 14) AS
customer_markets_attended_14days_count,
    MAX(CASE WHEN cp.cost_to_customer_per_qty > 10 THEN 1 ELSE 0 END)
AS purchased_item_over_10_dollars,
    (SELECT SUM(purchase_total)
        FROM customer_markets_attended cma
        WHERE cma.customer_id = cp.customer_id
            AND cma.market_date <= cp.market_date) AS total_spent_to_
date,
        CASE WHEN
    (SELECT SUM(purchase_total)
        FROM customer_markets_attended cma
        WHERE cma.customer_id = cp.customer_id
            AND cma.market_date <= cp.market_date) > 200
        THEN 1 ELSE 0 END AS customer_has_spent_over_200,
        CASE WHEN
        DATEDIFF(
            (SELECT MIN(cma.market_date)
            FROM customer_markets_attended AS cma
                WHERE cma.customer_id = cp.customer_id
                    AND cma.market_date > cp.market_date
```

Continues

(continued)

```
                    GROUP BY cma.customer_id),
                cp.market_date) <=30 THEN 1 ELSE 0 END AS purchased_
again_within_30_days
FROM farmers_market.customer_purchases AS cp
GROUP BY cp.customer_id, cp.market_date
ORDER BY cp.customer_id, cp.market_date
```

Chapter 14: Storing and Modifying Data

Answers

1. The timestamp returned when you query the view will be the current time (on the server), because unlike with a table, the view isn't storing any data and is generating the results of the query when it is run.

2. There are multiple correct answers, but one approach is to filter to records prior to October 4, 2020 (so if a change was made at any time on October 3, it is retrieved), and include a window function that returns the maximum timestamp per vendor and booth pair, indicating the most recent record of each booth assignment on or before the filtered date range. Then, the results of the query are embedded inside an outer query that filters to rows in the subquery where the snapshot timestamp matches the maximum timestamp calculated in the window function:

```
SELECT x.* FROM
    (
        SELECT
            vendor_id,
            booth_number,
            market_date,
            snapshot_timestamp,
            MAX(snapshot_timestamp) OVER (PARTITION BY vendor_id, booth_
number) AS max_timestamp_in_filter
        FROM farmers_market.vendor_booth_log
        WHERE DATE(snapshot_timestamp) <= '2020-10-04'
    ) AS x
WHERE x.snapshot_timestamp = x.max_timestamp_in_filter
```

Index